Elusive Balances

Prashanth Parameswaran

Elusive Balances

Shaping U.S.-Southeast Asia Strategy

Prashanth Parameswaran
The Woodrow Wilson International
Center for Scholars
Washington, D.C., USA

ISBN 978-981-16-6611-7   ISBN 978-981-16-6612-4   (eBook)
https://doi.org/10.1007/978-981-16-6612-4

Cover illustration: @pengpeng/GettyImages

This Palgrave Macmillan imprint is published by the registered company Springer Nature
Singapore Pte Ltd.
The registered company address is: 152 Beach Road, #21-01/04 Gateway East, Singapore
189721, Singapore

PREFACE

The idea that eventually became this book began with a series of conversations. When sharing some of the insights I had gleaned from a project assessing regional perceptions of U.S. strategy back in 2011 amid the U.S. pivot to Asia with several Southeast Asian experts and practitioners, it became clear there were some structural factors at play leading to disjunctures between how U.S. policymakers had intended engagement to work and how it ultimately was received in the region. When I suggested my provisional hypotheses in one of these conversations to the late former ASEAN Secretary-General Rodolfo Severino about U.S. commitment to Southeast Asia, he replied pithily: "I hope you'll be asking: what kind of commitment?"

Conversations like those eventually led me to explore the question of what accounts for the persistence of ebbs, flows and imbalances in the shaping of commitment to Southeast Asia in U.S. strategy and policy over the past half-century amid wider developments, be it the withdrawal from the Vietnam War or the region's role as the so-called "second front" following the September 11 terrorist attacks. To my mind, the real puzzle was not why these changes in commitment existed at various points, but why the ebbs, flows and imbalances kept occurring in U.S. strategic thinking and what, if anything, policymakers could do to better manage them. Though the existing literature had accounts of U.S.-Southeast Asia policy focused on a particular period or in one administration, there were few comprehensive attempts at theorizing why we see these repeated cycles and changes that went beyond either a description of events or a focus on individual variables.

I did so while pursuing a doctoral program at the Fletcher School and simultaneously gaining further insights into the U.S. policy process while conducting writing, research and teaching with various institutions, including The Wilson Center, The Diplomat magazine and several U.S. government agencies. Though these many pursuits may have slowed down the writing of this book, I have benefited tremendously from interactions with hundreds of officials and experts in Washington and Southeast Asia and also weighed in on aspects related to the shaping of U.S. regional strategy along the way.

In the meantime, the question of U.S. commitment to Southeast Asia has only grown in importance in American strategy toward the region and Asia more generally. In Washington, domestic tensions over aspects of U.S. foreign policy including trade and values have reignited debates about the relationship between what the United States does at home and abroad. Meanwhile, in Southeast Asia as in the world more generally, new inflection points such as the intensification of U.S.-China competition and a once-in-a-century pandemic have raised old questions about the sustainability of the U.S. presence amid a series of other domestic, regional and global challenges that countries have to contend with.

This book is an attempt to move beyond the headlines of the day and wrestle with the broader question of how we think about the policy challenge of commitment to Southeast Asia within U.S. strategy. I lay out a conceptual framework to answer this question and apply it to several actual cases in U.S. policy across the past half-century, using a mix of primary and secondary sources as well as over a hundred conversations with practitioners and experts in the United States and in Southeast Asia. I also make a genuine effort to sieve out lessons from the past to help shape how policymakers can act to better manage issues they face in shaping U.S. commitment to the region. It is this motivation that drove me to write this book in the first place, and I hope this will inspire a continued conversation on this important subject.

Washington, D.C.   Prashanth Parameswaran

Acknowledgments

This book is the product of nearly two decades of thinking, writing and researching about the United States and Southeast Asia, during which I've received no shortage of support. Professionally, in Washington, the Wilson Center has afforded me the opportunity to engage in and shape U.S. strategy and policy over the past few years, and The Diplomat magazine has given me an outlet to engage in some of the debates that play out in this book. I am especially thankful to Ernie Bower, Abe Denmark, Derek Mitchell, Randy Schriver, Apichai Shipper and Robert Sutter for their roles in expanding my thinking on various aspects of U.S. Asia strategy and policy over the years.

In Southeast Asia, my numerous research trips covering all eleven countries in the region would not have been possible without support from some of its institutions and the scholars within them. In particular, I would like to acknowledge the ASEAN Secretariat, the Centre for Strategic and International Studies, the Diplomatic Academy of Vietnam, the Institute of Southeast Asian Studies, the International Institute for Strategic Studies, the Rajaratnam School of International Studies and the Stratbase ADR Institute.

The book benefits from conversations with hundreds of policymakers and scholars in the United States and Southeast Asia over the years, with some insights acknowledged anonymously in the book. I have also benefited from learning from a long list of individuals along the way who were generous with their time. I would especially like to thank Cara

Abercrombie, Zachary Abuza, Amitav Acharya, John Brandon, Richard Bush, Kurt Campbell, Victor Cha, Termsak Chalermpalanupap, C. Raja Mohan, Kavi Chongkittavorn, Catharin Dalpino, Renato Cruz de Castro, Dino Patti Djalal, Donald Emmerson, Yuen Foong Khong, Lindsey Ford, Bonnie Glaser, Michael Green, Brian Harding, Pek Koon Heng, Murray Hiebert, Tim Huxley, Bilahari Kausikan, Tommy Koh, Satu Limaye, Walter Lohman, Karl Jackson, Collin Koh, Joshua Kurlantzick, Joseph Liow, Dindo Manhit, Marc Mealy, David Merrill, Ann Marie Murphy, Marty Natalegawa, Nguyen Vu Tung, Ong Keng Yong, Marvin Ott, Bronson Percival, Greg Poling, Thitinan Pongsudhirak, Ely Ratner, Stapleton Roy, Amy Searight, Dave Shear, Ian Storey, Rizal Sukma, See Seng Tan, Tin Maung Maung Than, Panitan Wattanayagorn, Meredith Weiss and William Wise. I would also like to acknowledge a few individuals who I spoke to along the way in my work but who have since passed: Stephen Bosworth, Carolina Hernandez, Surin Pitsuwan and Rodolfo Severino.

Academically, I was fortunate to be in two ideal environments for my undergraduate and graduate studies. At the University of Virginia, Melvyn Leffler, Jeff Legro, Timothy Naftali, William Quandt, Hilde Restad, Larry Sabato, Michael Smith, James Wilson and Brantly Womack in particular encouraged my interest in Asia, international relations theory, and U.S. foreign policy. At the Fletcher School of Law and Diplomacy at Tufts University, Jonathan Brookfield, Bhaskar Chakravorti, Alan Henrikson, Vali Nasr, Robert Pfaltzgraff, Kelly Sims-Gallagher and Jeff Taliaferro all provided support as I worked through this project in its earlier stages. These programs helped develop my intellectual foundation and funded several research trips to Southeast Asia and institutions across the United States.

Lastly, my thanks go to my family and friends in the United States and Southeast Asia, some of whom have read or listened to parts of this project over the years and have urged me to finish what I started. My wife Pooja, brother Nishanth, and parents Param and Indra, have been pillars of support that helped get this to the finish line. I dedicate this book to them. Any errors are my own.

Washington, D.C.   Prashanth Parameswaran
December 2021

CONTENTS

LIST OF FIGURES

Chapter 7

LIST OF TABLES

Chapter 7

Chapter 8

CHAPTER 1

Introduction: The Puzzle in U.S. Southeast Asia Strategy

I am convinced that the basic difficulty arises from the failure in responsible American policy circles to answer and define in detail two basic questions: (1) What is Southeast Asia worth to the United States? (2) What is the United States able and willing within the confines of its over-all commitments and its over-all resources to pay for Southeast Asia?…Until these questions are answered and American activities oriented in line with the answers, we can only expect that American activities will be aimless, conflicting, and self-defeating.
—Final Report of the Joint MDAP Survey Mission to Southeast Asia, December 6, 1950[1]

Southeast Asians are more accurately aware of the uncertainties of U.S. policies than other regions of the world.
—Lee Kuan Yew, 1986 Message to the Heritage Foundation[2]

---

[1] Foreign Relations of the United States, "Final Report of the Joint MDAP Survey Mission to Southeast Asia," December 6, 1950.

[2] Lee Kuan Yew, "Message from Prime Minister Lee Kuan New to the Heritage Foundation," April 22, 1986, National Archives of Singapore.

© The Author(s), under exclusive license to Springer Nature
Singapore Pte Ltd. 2022
P. Parameswaran, *Elusive Balances*,
https://doi.org/10.1007/978-981-16-6612-4_1

1

1   The Puzzle

"Southeast Asians," Singapore's late founding father Lee Kuan Yew bluntly observed in an April 1986 message to the Heritage Foundation conservative think tank in Washington, DC, "are more accurately aware of the uncertainties of U.S. policies than other regions of the world."[3] Looking at Washington's record in the subregion, it is not difficult to see why. Over the past half-century, despite recognizing Southeast Asia's importance in U.S. strategy, U.S. policymakers have struggled to calibrate and sustain the levels and distributions of American commitment to Southeast Asia over time to reflect that importance amid wider domestic, regional and global changes.

Instead, periods of heightened U.S. involvement—such as the Vietnam War or former U.S. President Barack Obama's "pivot" or "rebalance" Asia—have usually either been preceded or followed by years of U.S. retrenchment, giving rise to near-persistent doubts about the sustainability of U.S. commitment.[4] Furthermore, certain periods have also witnessed imbalances in U.S. commitment, whether it be the perceived excessive focus on ideals rather than interests during the Bill Clinton years in the 1990s or the relatively heavier emphasis placed on security issues during the George W. Bush years in the early 2000s following the September 11 attacks.[5] Indeed, it would not be a stretch to suggest that balance of commitment has been a core challenge in the management of U.S. Southeast Asia policy over the past half-century.

The real puzzle about U.S. commitment to Southeast Asia, then, is not why these changes in commitment exist at a particular time, but what accounts for the persistence of these ebbs and flows as well as

[3] Lee Kuan Yew, "Message from Prime Minister Lee Kuan New to the Heritage Foundation," April 22, 1986, National Archives of Singapore.

[4] On this point, see, for example: Prashanth Parameswaran, "Obama's Legacy in U.S.-ASEAN Relations: Promises and Perils," in Oliver Turner and Inderjeet Parmar, *The United States in the Indo-Pacific: Obama's Legacy and the Trump Transition* (Manchester: Manchester University Press, 2020).

[5] See, for instance: Sheldon W. Simon, "U.S. Strategy and Southeast Asian Security: Issues of Compatibility," *Contemporary Southeast Asia*, Vol. 14, No. 4 (March 1993), pp. 301–313; and Satu Limaye, "Minding the Gaps: The Bush Administration and U.S.-Southeast Asia Relations," *Contemporary Southeast Asia*, Vol. 26, No. 1 (2004), pp. 73–93.

imbalances over time. Put differently, *why do these balances of commitment keep proving so elusive, and what, if anything, can U.S. policymakers and regional states better manage them?* The fact that these commitment ebbs, flows and imbalances endure over time yet do not track entirely with broader domestic, regional and global shifts suggest that they transcend monocausal explanations in international relations focused exclusively on power or individuals. And while the existing literature contains accounts on U.S.-Southeast Asia policy that focus on a particular country or administration, there have been few comprehensive attempts at theorizing why we have seen these repeated cycles of changes to U.S. commitment to Southeast Asia.[6]

This book argues that changes in U.S. commitment to Southeast Asia are rooted in how U.S. policymakers balance between adjusting to power shifts, perceiving threats among Washington and its competitors and extracting the resources to respond to them. Drawing on a strain of international relations theory known as neoclassical realism, I develop a systematic conceptual framework, which I term balance of commitment, to explain changes in the various components of U.S. commitment to Southeast Asia as an interrelationship between three variables: power shifts the United States experiences between itself and its competitors; U.S. policymakers' perceptions of those shifts and threats; and the mobilization and extraction of resources necessary to respond. The principal characteristic of the balance of commitment framework is its emphasis on the balancing acts that U.S. policymakers need to strike—both in terms of the level and distribution of commitment as well as the internal and external considerations faced that extend beyond—and may in fact have little to do with—Southeast Asia.

By framing U.S. commitment to Southeast Asia in this manner, the book acknowledges the role of regional and global shifts in power and the agency of Southeast Asian states but also considers them in the context of more granular changes in individual components of U.S. commitment and factoring in equally critical variables of threat perceptions of U.S. policymakers and the domestic capabilities of the United States

---

[6] On this point, see, for example: Diane K. Mauzy and Brian L. Tob. "US Policy in Southeast Asia: Limited Re-engagement After Years of Benign Neglect," *Asian Survey*, Vol. 47, No. 4 (July/August 2007), pp. 622–641; and Alice Ba, "Systemic Neglect: A Reconsideration of US-Southeast Asia Policy," *Contemporary Southeast Asia*, Vol. 31, No. 3 (December 2009), pp. 372–373.

within American strategy. This suggests that calibrating and sustaining U.S. commitment to Southeast Asia is likely to prove challenging even for the most active U.S. administration given its interrelationship with other domestic, regional and global developments. And, following from that, overcoming commitment imbalances will require not only changes to how Washington approaches Southeast Asia, but its domestic politics and foreign policy more generally as well.

2   SIGNIFICANCE

Understanding the underlying dynamics of U.S. commitment to Southeast Asia is important for several reasons. First, the book addresses U.S. relations with Southeast Asia which has an important and growing role in U.S. foreign policy and strategy, even though there may be divergent views on how to conceptualize its significance and that importance may not always translate into sustained attention and engagement. The region is home to critical sea lanes and is the hub of regional institutions led by the Association of Southeast Asian Nations (ASEAN), and its combined market of over 600 million people represents the fifth-largest economy.[7] Additionally, U.S. policymakers and scholars alike have called for more of a granular understanding in the United States on Southeast Asia, as the subregion has not enjoyed as much of significance relative to China or Japan over the past few decades.[8] Unpacking why certain patterns are recurring over a longer time period is important to comprehending U.S. interactions with a critical region.

Second, with regard to U.S. relations with Southeast Asia, this book offers a much-needed systematic explanation of Washington's commitment to the region. The literature on U.S. commitment to Southeast Asia is dominated by accounts that describe U.S. commitment during a specific administration or time period, which, while useful in understanding *what* is going on a particular time, is less so in understanding

---

[7] For a fuller statistical snapshot, see: "ASEAN Matters for America Series," East–West Center, Washington, DC.

[8] See, for instance: Kurt Campbell, *The Pivot: The Future of American Statecraft in Asia* (New York: Twelve Books, 2016); Catharin Dalpino and Bridget Welsh, "A Policy Backwater: Southeast Asia Deserves More Attention," *International Herald Tribune*, February 1, 2002.

why certain patterns recur over a longer time horizon.[9] Additionally, there is a tendency among some to assume U.S. commitment imbalances in Southeast Asia are due to more essentialist factors—be it the immutable strategic culture of the United States or the difficulty in handling a diverse region like Southeast Asia.[10] By offering a theoretical perspective based on political variables, this book attempts a fresh look that elevates a descriptive discussion to the theoretical level refocuses the conversation on the policymaking process and away from blame on either side.

Third, the balance of commitment model of U.S.-Southeast Asia policy provides potential lessons for policymakers in Washington and in Southeast Asian capitals in managing ties in the future. Understanding how the complex interrelationship between power shifts, threat perceptions and resource extraction and mobilization affects U.S. commitment to Southeast Asia during key inflection points can raise awareness among both U.S. and Southeast Asian policymakers about how to prepare for future ebbs and flows in American commitment. Additionally, being aware of the issues brought about by recurring commitment imbalances like militarization—still the subject of discussion today—can hopefully lead to a more granular understanding of dynamics and constructive conversations about how to manage them.[11]

Fourth, in terms of theory, the development of the balance of commitment model builds out a more systematic approach to understanding U.S. foreign policy commitment more generally. The framework adds rigor to the much discussed but little defined concept of commitment, broadening it to extend beyond the security realm and deepening it to include not just aggregate commitment, but also the balance or distribution between specific components of commitment (e.g., bilateralism vs. multilateralism) to allow for better detection of subtle policy shifts.[12] The model also

[9] On this point, see: Alice Ba. "Systemic Neglect: A Reconsideration of US-Southeast Asia Policy," *Contemporary Southeast Asia*, Vol. 31, No. 3 (December 2009), pp. 372–373.

[10] At the same time, this is not to understate Southeast Asia's unique features. For a balanced discussion on this point, see: Donald K. Emmerson, "Southeast Asia: What's in a Name?" *Journal of Southeast Asian Studies*, Vol. 15, No. 1 (March 1994), pp. 1–21.

[11] For a discussion on this point, see: Prashanth Parameswaran, *ASEAN's Role in a U.S. Indo-Pacific Strategy* (Washington, DC: Wilson Center Asia Program, 2018).

[12] For an explanation of the importance of analyzing individual foreign policy components, rather than aggregate outcomes, see: *Aaron L. Friedberg, The Weary Titan: Britain*

adds more nuance to the discussion of U.S. foreign policy change at the regional level that arguably better reflects the reality of policymaking, by suggesting that it is not just the direct causal product of power shifts, as outlined by some international relations approaches such as neorealism, but a complex dynamic that takes into account the interplay between material considerations, perceptions in Washington and in Southeast Asian capitals, and U.S. domestic politics.

Fifth, the balance of commitment model of U.S.-Southeast Asia policy also provides lessons regarding the explanatory power of the neoclassical realist school of international relations. The application of the model to U.S. commitment in Southeast Asia expands neoclassical realism's potential ability to explain outcomes as they relate to regional orders, which has begun to receive greater attention over the past few years as theories that have worked at the global level have been discovered to work not as well in individual regions like the Middle East.[13] And the more precise delineation of the interrelationship between relative capabilities, threat perceptions and state capacity offers a potential alternative explanation for analyzing behavior of other major powers toward Southeast Asia beyond the United States, which has thus far been dominated by neorealism.[14]

3   APPROACH

To explain what accounts for changes in U.S. commitment to Southeast Asia over time, the book constructs an original balance of commitment model of U.S.-Southeast Asia policy, tests it with respect to four periods in U.S. Southeast Asia policy from 1975 to the present where there were adjustments in U.S. commitment to Southeast Asia and then sieves out recommendations for scholars and policymakers.

---

and the Experience of Relative Decline, 1895–1905 (Princeton, NJ: Princeton University Press, 2010), Introduction, especially p. 7.

[13] For instance, the scholar Steve Yetiv has found in his research that U.S. foreign policy in the Persian Gulf did not reflect any of the grand strategies cited by theorists. See: Steve A. Yetiv, *The Absence of Grand Strategy: The United States in the Persian Gulf (1972–2005)* (Baltimore: Johns Hopkins University Press, 2008).

[14] On neoclassical realism's applicability with respect to regional orders, see: Jeffrey W. Taliaferro, "Neoclassical Realism and the Study of Regional Order," in *International Relations Theory and Regional Transformation*, ed. T. V. Paul (Cambridge, UK: Cambridge University Press, 2012), pp. 74–104.

The book itself is divided into three parts. The first part (Chapters 2–3) surveys existing ways to look at the U.S. commitment challenge in Southeast Asia and develops an alternative argument. Chapter 2 outlines the historical legacy of the challenge of U.S. commitment to Southeast Asia and assesses current approaches, detailing both their strengths and limitations. Chapter 3 then develops the original balance of commitment model of U.S.-Southeast Asia policy. After analyzing the basic tenets of neoclassical realism, it develops definitions and metrics for terms such as commitment and deduces general propositions for increases and decreases in the key variables of relative power, threat level and state capacity and their effects on the level and distribution of U.S. commitment to Southeast Asia.

The second part of the book (Chapters 4–7) tests the balance of commitment model of U.S.-Southeast Asia policy against a popular existing explanation—neorealism or balance of power theory—with respect to four periods in U.S.-Southeast Asia policy from 1975 to the present. The four periods are: the post-Vietnam War period (Chapter 4); the post-Cold War period (Chapter 5); the post-9/11 period (Chapter 6); and the post-Global Financial Crisis period (Chapter 7). To test these two general theories as well as the various specific hypotheses that they generate, the book primarily employs a qualitative, comparative case study methodology, using techniques like the congruence procedure and careful process-tracing. The cases were selected to be representative of the recent history of U.S. commitment to Southeast Asia. While they do leave out certain periods, be it the Trump administration or Covid-19's impact on U.S. commitment, they nonetheless do capture a series of broader, significant periods that cut across individual administrations.

The third part of the book (Chapter 8) summarizes the balance of commitment argument and the findings from the four cases. It will also detail theoretical and policy implications for U.S. and Southeast Asian policymakers as well as sieve out recommendations for future research.

The empirical evidence for this book was collected from various institutions in the United States and Southeast Asia, including the Library of Congress, U.S. presidential libraries and collections in Southeast Asia including those at the Institute of Southeast Asian Studies (ISEAS) in Singapore and the ASEAN Secretariat Library in Jakarta. In addition, I conducted approximately one hundred conversations with American and

Southeast Asian officials, journalists and scholars on this subject, in addition to hundreds of other related interactions that helped inform the book and my general understanding.

The limits of the scope of this book deserve mention at the outset. First, this book is not meant to provide an exhaustive, play-by-play account of every single event in U.S.-Southeast Asia relations across the economic, diplomatic, security and people-to-people realms, but rather to survey four episodes of U.S. commitment change to the region and test competing explanations for why they ended up the way they did. Second, the book is first and foremost focused on these episodes as attempted expansions and contractions of U.S. commitment by policymakers, rather than dwelling on competing, granular metrics that can be used to make subjective assessments as to whether a specific administration succeeded or failed.

There are also some limits with respect to methods used. First, though quantitative metrics are not readily available on some scores across periods and can be uneven, I have utilized them as supporting evidence where it makes sense while integrating other forms of primary and secondary sourcing. Second, though U.S. archival documentation is available mostly for the post-Vietnam War period case study, I have compensated for the lack of this in the other three case studies in several ways by including additional secondary sources, interviews and conversations with officials in both the United States and Southeast Asia, and my own knowledge of U.S.-Southeast Asia relations having worked on aspects of policy during this period. Third and finally, though there are issues with information gathered through personal interviews and conversations, I have done my best to manage them by probing into biases and contradictory information.

CHAPTER 2

The Commitment Challenge

The choice confronting the United States is to support the French in Indochina or face the extension of Communism over the remainder of the continental area of Southeast Asia and possibly farther westward.
—Indochina Problem Paper, February 1, 1950

We in Asia cannot sit idly by and wait for doomsday to come…The relevant question [is] how Southeast Asia will fare when those who have for so long cast their shadows over the region will have gone from the scene.
—Thai Foreign Minister Thanat Khoman, 1970[1]

The evolution of U.S. strategy in Southeast Asia and Washington's commitment to the region can present a challenge to explain at first glance. Existing approaches to international relations theory would expect U.S. commitment to the region to be congruent either with external developments, like changes in U.S. capabilities relative to its competitors and adversaries, or internal characteristics of the United States such as aspects of its strategic culture or its domestic politics.

However, reality has been far more complex. While U.S. policymakers have recognized Southeast Asia's strategic significance since the end of World War II and Washington's interests in the region have grown since the post-Cold War period, U.S. commitment to the region has been

---

[1] *Far Eastern Economic Review*, March 26, 1970, pp. 25–26.

subject to a continuing series of ebbs, flows and imbalances that have endured over time and do not track entirely with broader domestic, regional and global shifts. This pattern defies the predictions of existing explanations and captures the commitment challenge in U.S. Southeast Asia policy.

1   HISTORICAL VARIATION IN U.S. COMMITMENT TO SOUTHEAST ASIA

The United States was a relative latecomer to Southeast Asia. While U.S. involvement in major Northeast Asian countries was clear by the first half of the nineteenth century—from access to the China trade to the opening of Japan—U.S. government commitment to Southeast Asia as a subregion largely came about a century later. Apart from American traders and adventurers as well as colonial administrative responsibilities in the Philippines following the end of the Philippine American War (1899–1902) and diplomatic ties with Thailand, the idea of a deeper American role in Southeast Asia only really took hold in the minds of U.S. policymakers with Communist inroads following the founding of the People's Republic of China (PRC) and the outbreak of the Korean War.[2]

U.S. direct interests in Southeast Asia also remained quite limited in the lead up to the Second World War and to a large extent immediately following it as well. Few Americans were living in or traveling to the subregion, trade and investment was still small and narrowly focused on just a couple of raw materials and U.S. diplomatic presence there was also initially limited to just a handful of Southeast Asian capitals.[3] Southeast Asia was also simply lacking in other areas of conventional strategic significance in the eyes of U.S. policymakers relatively speaking—like industrial infrastructure or technological prowess—that made Western Europe and

[2] See: Russel H. Fifield, *Americans in Southeast Asia: The Roots of Commitment* (New York: Thomas Y. Crowell Company, 1973), pp. 1–24; Gary R. Hess, *The United States' Emergence as a Southeast Asian Power, 1940–1950* (New York: Columbia University Press, 1987), pp. 1–20.

[3] See, for instance: Matthew Foley, *The Cold War and Nationalist Assertion in Southeast Asia: Britain, the United States, and Burma* (New York: Routledge, 2010).

Japan areas of greater importance to U.S. interests in terms of preserving the overall balance of power.[4]

Given Washington's late involvement and limited direct interests in Southeast Asia, it was not surprising that its commitment there initially remained quite modest. Unlike European powers such as the British, French and Dutch, which had colonial possessions in Southeast Asia they were seeking to preserve to varying degrees during and after the Second World War, the United States was largely concerned with what policymakers considered more consequential issues from their perspective, such as the Far East and the evolution of Japan and China as well as Europe and the containment of the Soviet Union with the onset of the Cold War. And though Washington was no doubt aware of trends in the subregion like the nationalist tide sweeping through, with more urgent priorities elsewhere, assuming new obligations in Southeast Asia or pressuring the European allies did not strike U.S. policymakers as a wise course to pursue.[5]

But a series of developments in the late 1940s and 1950s made clear to the United States that despite its own limited direct, actual interests in Southeast Asia, the subregion's indirect and potential value to it as well as its allies and adversaries made a more robust and broad-based commitment necessary. Amid inroads being made by the Communist bloc—particularly with the rise of the People's Republic of China (PRC), the Soviet Union's explosion of the hydrogen bomb and the outbreak of the Korean War—along with a stalling of Western European and Japanese recovery and raging conflicts plaguing European powers in mainland and maritime Southeast Asia, the subregion came to be viewed as vital to forestalling communist domination and preserving free world interests.[6]

---

[4] Robert McMahon, *The Limits of Empire: The United States and Southeast Asia Since World War II* (New York: Columbia University Press, 1999), pp. 1–13. For a broader perspective on U.S. Asia policy during the period, see: Michael J. Green, *By More Than Providence: Grand Strategy and American Power in the Asia–Pacific Since 1783* (New York: Columbia University Press, 2017).

[5] This was despite the efforts of some at the State Department, including George F. Kennan and John Paton Davies, to call for a U.S. stance more in line with nationalist movements and less with the European colonial powers. See, for example: "PPS 51: Policy Planning Staff Paper on United States Policy Toward Southeast Asia," FRUS, 1949, The Far East and Australasia, Volume VII, Part 2, March 29, 1949.

[6] See, for instance National Security Council, "United States Objectives and Courses of Action with Respect to Southeast Asia," The Pentagon Papers, Volume 1, Document

The case that U.S. policymakers built rested on perceived links—some admittedly weaker than others—between Southeast Asia and wider U.S. foreign policy objectives. The stabilization of Southeast Asia, they argued consistently, was critical to not just preventing the subregion's own fall to communism, but also powering the recoveries of Japan and Western Europe and reversing the psychological gains that the communist powers were perceived to have made in recent years. As a result, by the early 1950s, it was little surprise that nearly all senior U.S. policymakers ranked Southeast Asia as a region of vital importance to the United States.[7]

With all this in mind, the United States' commitment to Southeast Asia also increased. The administration of U.S. President Harry Truman began providing uncharacteristically high levels of economic and military aid to Southeast Asian states. And despite earlier reservations, the Eisenhower administration made a formal commitment to regional security with the formation of the rather short-lived Southeast Asia Treaty Organization (SEATO) and also authorized a full-throated effort to help establish a viable, non-communist alternative in the southern part of Vietnam. These actions would sow the seeds for Washington's involvement in the Vietnam War, which represented a peak period of U.S. commitment to the region.

Following the end of the Vietnam War, U.S. commitment to Southeast Asia declined significantly. For the majority of commentators writing about this period, which started from the beginning of the administration of U.S. President Richard Nixon which saw gradual U.S. disengagement from Vietnam, Southeast Asia occupied a marginal role in U.S. foreign policy relative to its centrality in the previous period.[8] That is not to say that the United States was involved in the region: for instance, during the Carter administration, the United States played a role in responding to the Indochina refugee crisis and started the U.S.-ASEAN Dialogue

10, January 16, 1954, pp. 434–443; and, PPS 51: Policy Planning Staff Paper on United States Policy Toward Southeast Asia, FRUS, 1949, The Far East and Australasia, Volume VII, Part 2, March 29, 1949.

[7] Robert McMahon, *The Limits of Empire: The United States and Southeast Asia Since World War II* (New York: Columbia University Press, 1999), p. 43.

[8] Diane K. Mauzy and Brian L. Job characterized the period from the end of the Vietnam War up to 2002 as "benign neglect." See: "Diane K. Mauzy and Brian L. Job, U.S. Policy in Southeast Asia: Limited Re-engagement After Years of Benign Neglect," *Asian Survey*, Vol. 47, Issue 4, pp. 622–641.

mechanism which remains a key component of U.S. relations with Southeast Asia today.[9] But more generally, the sense that the United States had overcommitted during the Vietnam War led to reluctance to get too involved except during episodic crises—which some described as the Vietnam Syndrome.[10]

This persisted through the 1980s and 1990s, even though Southeast Asia's own importance continued to grow. Indeed, Washington's perceived failure to intervene decisively in developments, including the Asian Financial Crisis in 1997–1998, continued to raise questions about its commitment. Indeed, it was not until following the September 11, 2001 terrorist attacks that Southeast Asia once again surfaced at the center of U.S. policy.[11] During the aftermath of the September 11 attacks, the administration of U.S. George W. Bush (2001–2009) labeled Southeast Asia as the "second front" in the so-called "war on terror" and also undertook a series of diplomatic and economic initiatives that were overshadowed by some of the security developments, including concluding the U.S.-Singapore free trade agreement—the first of its kind in Asia—and paving the way for the appointment of the first U.S. ambassador to the Association of Southeast Asian Nations.[12]

The so-called "pivot" or "rebalance" to Asia under the administration of U.S. President Barack Obama (2009–2017) saw an initial level of commitment to Southeast Asia not seen since the Vietnam War, with officials even referring to a deliberate attempt to heighten attention to

[9] Cyrus Vance. *Hard Choices: Critical Years in America's Foreign Policy* (New York: Simon and Schuster, 1983), p. 125; Evening Post, "ASEAN in US to consult, not to beg; to reach accord, not to ask favors – Romulo," August 4, 1978.

[10] The Vietnam Syndrome refers to skepticism about the legitimacy and efficacy of the United States using military power overseas that stemmed from the experience during the Vietnam War. The Vietnam Syndrome continued to haunt U.S. policymakers even after the Cold War and, according to some accounts, even thereafter into the George W. Bush years. See, for instance; James Mann, *Rise of the Vulcans: The History of Bush's War Cabinet* (New York: Penguin, 2004), pp. 39–40, 53.

[11] Ann Marie Murphy and Bridget Welsh, *Legacy of Engagement in Southeast Asia* (Singapore: ISEAS, 2015); Joseph Chinyong Liow, *Ambivalent Engagement: The United States and Regional Security in Southeast Asia After the Cold War* (Washington, DC: Brookings University Press, 2017). For a take on the history of U.S.-ASEAN security cooperation, see: Muthiah Alagappa, *US-ASEAN Security Cooperation: Limits and Possibilities* (Kuala Lumpur: ISIS Malaysia, 1986).

[12] Richard Cronin, "The Second Bush Administration and Southeast Asia," Stimson Center, July 17, 2007.

the subregion within U.S. Asia policy as "the rebalance within the rebalance."[13] Yet the level and distribution of U.S. commitment prove difficult to sustain in some aspects, as evidenced from concerns in part of the region about the administration's approach to China and the failure of the Trans-Pacific Partnership (TPP). The drop-off seen in U.S. commitment to Southeast Asia under the Trump administration, which U.S. President Joe Biden sought to recover upon taking office, was an important reminder despite the actions of a particular administration, periods of heightened attention by Washington in the region could just as easily be reversed subsequently as well.[14]

2   FEATURES OF U.S. COMMITMENT

The ebbs, flows and imbalances we have seen in U.S. commitment level and distribution to Southeast Asia since the post-WWII period suggest that calibrating and sustaining commitment is not merely an issue limited to certain administrations or time periods, but a more serious and systemic challenge in U.S. Southeast Asia strategy and policy. Indeed, the record of U.S. commitment to the region over the past seven decades suggests a characterization of almost persistent imbalance with three characteristics: ambivalent in nature, inconsistent in level and uneven in terms of distribution.

The first feature of the U.S. commitment challenge in Southeast Asia lies in its ambivalent nature. At some points in time, such as in the 1950s and 1960s during the height of the Vietnam War, U.S. policymakers emphasized and even exaggerated the potential and indirect value that Southeast Asia presented to the United States, leading to overcommitment around a narrow conception of how the region mattered to Washington's interests that ultimately proved unsustainable. At other times, such as in the 1970s or 1990s, Washington reverted to the sense that it had very limited directed interests there relative to other regions of

---

[13] Prashanth Parameswaran, "Obama's Legacy in U.S.-ASEAN Relations: Promises and Perils," in: Oliver Turner and Inderjeet Parmar, *The United States in the Indo-Pacific: Obama's Legacy and the Trump Transition* (Manchester: Manchester University Press, 2020).

[14] Prashanth Parameswaran, *ASEAN's Role in a U.S. Indo-Pacific Strategy* (Washington, DC: Wilson Center Asia Program, 2018); Walter Lohman, "The Trump Administration's Trade Policy and the Implications for Southeast Asia," *Contemporary Southeast Asia*, Vol. 39, No. 1 (April 2017), pp. 36–41.

the world even though Southeast Asia's own importance had continued to grow, resulting in undercommitment. Periods of perceived overcommitment such as the Vietnam War can create cautionary tales about the exaggerated value of Southeast Asia in U.S. policy that can then lead to a lack of attention to the region in successive years, while periods of undercommitment can raise questions that echo into the future in regional capitals including when future increases of commitment are pledged.

More fundamentally, at the heart of this ambivalence is a broader point about the extent to which Southeast Asia itself is important within broader U.S. Asia policy and American *vital* interests. The conundrum, as William Henderson rather prophetically observed back in 1963, was as follows: explaining Southeast Asia's importance too narrowly in terms of direct and actual impact on U.S. interests simply would simply not be sufficient to justify heightened U.S. commitment levels compared to other regions; speaking too broadly about its indirect and potential significance to Washington could lead to overcommitment; and vacillating between these two notions would lead to swings in U.S. commitment. "The great weakness of United States policy, which indeed may ultimately prove a fatal defect," Henderson wrote, "is that we have never been quite sure how serious we are about the whole business."[15]

Apart from the ambivalence in the nature of U.S. commitment to Southeast Asia, imbalance is also evident in terms of the level of U.S. commitment to the subregion. From the end of World War II, we have witnessed a near-persistent series of ebbs and flows in the level of commitment—measured by expansions or contractions in the resources devoted across various realms—that Washington has had toward Southeast Asia. The largest expansions and contractions in commitment can be seen over periods of a few decades, such as the period in the 1950s and 1960s where, under the Truman, Eisenhower, Kennedy, and Johnson administrations during the height of the Cold War, Southeast Asia quickly moved from the periphery to the center of U.S. foreign policy to a region that was crucial to the realization of vital American interests and to the preservation of U.S. credibility as a global power, with clearest manifestation of this being deepening U.S. involvement in the Vietnam War.[16]

[15] William Henderson, *Southeast Asia: Problems of United States Policy* (Cambridge: MIT Press, 1963), p. 252.

[16] George C. Herring, *America's Longest War: The United States and Vietnam, 1950–1975* (McGraw-Hill, 1996).

Yet there are also examples of shorter ebbs and flows as well—both across and at times even within U.S. administrations—especially if we focus on commitment as it pertains to not just security-related metrics such as U.S. troop levels, but other diplomatic and economic ones as well that became increasingly important as Washington's involvement in Southeast Asia became more broad-based following the end of the Vietnam War. For instance, during the 2010s, U.S. commitment to Southeast Asia went through an ebb and flow cycle, with the region initially experiencing a broad-based commitment increase under the Obama administration across realms but this then decreasing and narrowing during the Trump years, with a much greater focus around China and relatively less sustained attention to diplomatic, economic and people-to-people aspects.

A third feature is unevenness in Washington's commitment distribution to Southeast Asia. If one reviews the litany of issues in U.S.-Southeast Asia relations on this front over the past few decades, this is evident in five realms of what we might characterize as commitment imbalance: economics and security; ideals and interests; bilateralism and multilateralism; cooperative and confrontational approaches toward adversaries or competitors; and means and ends. For instance, certain periods have seen U.S. policymakers focus more on security rather than economic issues relatively speaking—with more extreme manifestations being the Vietnam War period or the period following the September 11 attacks—while others have seen them devote relatively greater attention to ideals like democracy such as the early stages of the Carter and Clinton administrations be it in terms of U.S. engagement with particular countries (like the Philippines during the Carter years or Singapore during the Clinton period) or broader issues such as the Asian values debate of the 1990s.[17]

Similarly, in terms of diplomatic approaches, the Obama years saw a greater prioritization of multilateralism relative to bilateral or unilateral approaches compared to the Bush II years in terms of U.S. commitment to Southeast Asia, while, on cooperative and confrontational

---

[17] For a regional perspective on the economics vs. security imbalance, see: Abdullah Ahmad Badawi, "Creating a Better Understanding of ASEAN-United States Relations," Speech at the Asia Society, New York, September 15, 2005, http://asiasociety.org/creating-better-understanding-asean-united-states-relations?page=0,3. For an elaboration on the imbalance between ideals and interests, see: Bilahari Kausikan, *Dealing with An Ambiguous World* (Singapore: World Scientific, 2017), Lecture 4.

approaches toward adversaries and competitors, developments such as Nixon's engagement of China or Trump's declaration of strategic competition against Beijing were significant aspects of Washington's commitment to the region.[18] All administrations have also been confronted with how to reconcile means and ends to avoid what the renowned journalist Walter Lippman pointed out and subsequently became known as "Lippman Gaps" between commitments and resources, evident in certain times such as the Vietnam War or with the U.S. pivot to Asia.[19]

As we have seen in this brief overview of U.S. commitment to Southeast Asia, there are near persistent ebbs, flows and imbalances in Washington's commitment to the region over the past seven decades that transcend individual administrations and discrete domestic, regional and global shifts. Any explanation of U.S. commitment to Southeast Asia would need to be able to explain this.

3   Two Existing Explanation Types

There are essentially two existing explanation types that try to account for the near persistent ebbs, flows and imbalances in the level and distribution of U.S. commitment to Southeast Asia: those focused primarily on externally driven factors and those that emphasize more internally driven ones.

3.1   External Explanations: Neorealism and Constructivism

External explanations argue that in order to understand variations in U.S. commitment, one needs to begin at the international or systemic level. Among these, structural realism or neorealism generates a plausible (and traditionally the most popular) explanation for variations in U.S. commitment in general and Southeast Asia in particular.[20] Neorealists would

---

[18] Jonathan Stromseth, "Don't Make Us Choose: Southeast Asia in the Throes of US-China Rivalry," Brookings Institution, October 2019; Amy Searight, "How ASEAN Matters in the Age of Trump," East Asia Forum, March 11, 2018.

[19] Samiel P. Huntington, "Coping with the Lippmann Gap," *Foreign Affairs*, Vol. 66, No. 3 (1987/1988), p. 453.

[20] Structural realism or neorealism is just one among several members of the broader family of realist theories, which includes classical realism not discussed here. There are also internal divisions among structural realists as well, principally between offensive and

argue that variations in both the level and distribution of U.S. commitment in Southeast Asia are a product of Washington's response to changes in the distribution of capabilities, or the balance of power, between it and other contending powers in the region.

The logic behind this is straightforward: one of the United States' primary objectives in Southeast Asia since the end of WWII has been to prevent the domination of the region by any power deemed hostile to Washington, lest it gain control of critical sea lanes, markets and raw materials that may allow it to mount a bid for hegemony as Japan once did.[21] It would thus follow from this that U.S. policymakers would adjust their commitment to the region based on Washington's position relative to its perceived rivals. For instance, some contend that the United States increased its commitment to Southeast Asia in the 1960s during the Vietnam War to blunt advances by the Soviet Union, and some have cast the Obama administration's "rebalance" to Asia as being designed to counter Chinese gains there since the 1990s.[22]

If neorealism is right, we should see changes in the regional balance of power in Southeast Asia and the U.S. position within it match well against variations in its commitment levels there. In fact, in several instances, we do not. While it is certainly true that Washington's commitment levels do change partly as a reaction to the distribution of capabilities, the timing, extent and manner in which this is done vary considerably because of other factors. There have been cases where the United States has been late in balancing, overbalanced or underbalanced its competitors in particular regions or has been unable to muster the resources to do so effectively because of a variety of factors including bureaucratic infighting and financial constraints.

Two examples with respect to U.S. commitment in Southeast Asia illustrate this point. Firstly, the real puzzle of the Vietnam War is why it took so long for the United States to realize that it *did not* need such a

defensive realists (with arguments like balance of threat theory). For a good overview of realism, see: James E. Dougherty and Robert L. Pfaltzgraff, Jr., *Contending Theories of International Relations* (New York: Longman, 2000), pp. 63–98.

[21] Richard Sokolsky, Angel Rabasa, and C. Richard Neu, *The Role of Southeast Asia in the U.S. Strategy Toward China* (Washington, DC: Rand Corporation, 2001), especially Chapter 2.

[22] See, for example: Sheldon W. Simon, "The US Rebalance and Southeast Asia," *Asian Survey*, Vol. 55, No. 3, pp. 572–595.

costly and bloody war effort to balance the Soviet Union, as some neore-alists themselves at the time had noted.[23] Secondly, the administrations of President Harry Truman and Dwight Eisenhower had to settle for SEATO instead of a more connected alliance network linking Southeast and Northeast Asia not because of balance of power dynamics involving the Soviet Union, but in part because of domestic-political opposition from the Department of Defense.[24] Thus, it is clear that while neorealism has its merits, it needs to be combined with other explanations that take into account state-level variables to fully describe changes in the level and distribution of U.S. commitment to Southeast Asia.

A second external explanation can be found in social constructivism. According to this line of thought, variations of American commitment to Southeast Asia are the product of not just U.S. calculations of its own interests, but also local attempts by Southeast Asian states to shape this calculus, chiefly via regional institutions. While these constructivist accounts do not dismiss or discount power as a factor in affecting U.S. foreign policy outcomes, they draw greater attention to ideational deter-minants (principally norms), the agency of local actors despite their smaller size, and the possibility of transformation via socialization and institution-building.[25]

Most constructivist arguments center on the prominent role of the Association of Southeast Asian Nations (ASEAN) and its related insti-tutions in embedding great powers like the United States and China into a shared normative institutional framework to bind their commit-ment to the region and mitigate future great power rivalry.[26] This could

[23] George C. Herring, *America's Longest War: The United States and Vietnam, 1950–1975* (McGraw-Hill, 1996).

[24] Victor Cha, *Powerplay: Origins of American Alliance System in Asia* (Princeton, NJ: Princeton University Press, 2016), pp. 40–65; Amitav Acharya, *Constructing a Security Community* (New York, Routledge, 2001), p. 220.

[25] See, for instance: Amitav Acharya and Richard Stubbs, "Theorizing Southeast Asian Relations: An Introduction," *The Pacific Review*, Vol. 19, No. 2 (June 2006), pp. 125–134; and Charmaine Misalucha, *The Problem of Describing Relations Between the United States and Southeast Asian Nations: A Study of Political Language Games* (Lampeter: Edwin Mellen Press, 2012), pp. 1–27.

[26] See: Alice Ba, "Between China and America: ASEAN's Great Power Dilemmas," in: Sheldon W. Simon and Evelyn Goh (eds.), *China, the United States, and South-East Asia: Contending Perspectives on Politics, Security and Economics* (New York: Routledge, 2008), pp. 107–127.

in turn affect both the level and the balance of U.S. commitment to Southeast Asia. For example, some have argued that retracting objections to the ASEAN-led proposal for a multilateral security institution in the Asia–Pacific in 1992 was part of the first Bush administration's broader strategy of reassurance that accompanied the planned reduction of U.S. military commitment in the region.[27] Others have pointed out that it was the growing salience of regional institutions like the East Asia Summit (EAS) that led the Obama administration to step up their commitment to multilateralism in Southeast Asia relative to more unilateral and bilateral approaches.[28]

While constructivism does have its merits, it is important not to overstate its influence on U.S. foreign policy in general and U.S. commitment to Southeast Asia in particular. For example, it would be premature to speak of a socialization of the United States or even a strong American bipartisan appreciation for regional multilateralism, since some U.S. policymakers still tend to view regional institutions with skepticism compared to their steadfast commitment to bilateral alliances and other close partnerships in Southeast Asia.[29] The Trump administration's lack of engagement in multilateralism relative to the Obama years also offers a cautionary tale for those who hope for a linear development in the level of U.S. investment in multilateralism across time.

3.2   Internal Explanations: Culture and Domestic Politics

Internal explanations, as the term suggests, argue that the reasons for variations in U.S. commitment to Southeast Asia lie at the domestic level rather than the international system, be it certain traits within U.S.

---

[27] See, for instance: Evelyn Goh, *The Struggle for Order: Hegemony, Hierarchy, and Transition in Post-Cold War East Asia* (Oxford: Oxford University Press, 2013), especially pp. 51–52.

[28] See, for example: Jurgen Haacke, "Paying Catch-Up: The United States and Southeast Asia," IDEAS Report, 2010, pp. 28–33. For an exploration of the connections made, see: Surin Pitsuwan, "ASEAN Central to the Region's Future," East Asia Forum, May 2, 2010.

[29] Even the Obama administration, arguably one of the administrations supportive of multilateralism, specified certain conditions under which the United States would embrace such initiatives in Southeast Asia and the Asia–Pacific more generally. See, for example: Hillary Clinton, "America's Pacific Century", Speech at the East–West Center, Honolulu, Hawaii, November 10, 2011.

strategic culture or the nature of political dynamics occurring within the United States.[30]

Cultural approaches would explain variations in U.S. commitment to Southeast Asia with reference to American strategic culture relative to that of Southeast Asia—or shared values, beliefs and assumptions held by the American public in general and the foreign policy elite in particular. For instance, some scholars have identified seemingly particular aspects of U.S. strategic culture that play into foreign policy, be it classical liberal assumptions that may favor the promotion of democratic governments and open markets, or a preference for limited liability to avoid costs and commitments in grand strategy irrespective of stated goals.[31] Other more informal characterizations also seek to draw differences between the diplomatic cultures of the United States and Southeast Asia such as divergences between formal and informal decision-making through the ASEAN Way, less of a focus on deliverables and a greater focus on face-saving mechanisms.[32]

These aspects of American strategic culture have been used by some to explain the level and distribution of U.S. commitment to Southeast Asia during certain periods. The commitment to liberal assumptions has been used to explain the gaps between Washington's rhetorical commitment to goals such as democracy and free markets and the limited capacity to actually pursue these objectives, whether these principles believed by policymakers or merely advanced as a cover for an American empire designed to exploit Southeast Asia.[33] The notion of limited liability has recurred

[30] Alternatively, it is also possible to subsume cultural arguments under domestic politics as well. For instance, James D. Fearon's categorization of two kinds of domestic political theories in: James D. Fearon, "Domestic Politics, Foreign Policy, and Theories of International Relations," *Annual Review of Political Science*, Vol. 1 (June 1998), pp. 289–313.

[31] Colin Dueck, *Reluctant Crusaders: Power, Culture and Change in American Grand Strategy* (Princeton, NJ: Princeton University Press, 2006), pp. 21–30.

[32] See, for example: Michael Antolik, *ASEAN and the Diplomacy of Accommodation* (London: Routledge, 1990).

[33] For an example from the Clinton years, see: Donald K. Emmerson, "US Policy Themes in Southeast Asia in the 1990s," in: David Wurfel and Bruce Burton (eds.), *Southeast Asia in the New World Order: The Political Economy of a Dynamic Region* (London: MacMillan, 1996), pp. 103–127. For an alternative perspective, see: James A. Tyner, *America's Strategy in Southeast Asia: From the Cold War to the Terror War* (Plymouth, UK: Rowman & Littlefield, 2007), especially pp. 1–27.

across the history of U.S. involvement in Southeast Asia such as in the American occupation of the Philippines, and it continues to manifest itself during periods of doubt in parts of the region about Washington can truly commit the necessary resources to sustain its commitment to the region given its past record.[34] It is also not merely a historical concern, as some in the region do reference this notion, if informally, as they worry period-ically about whether Washington can commit the necessary resources to sustain its engagement given its past record.[35]

While the cultural argument does have some merit in certain periods, the fact that cultural traits like limited liability or America's liberal creed are seen as inherent characteristics makes it difficult for them to predict or explain major changes in commitment. For instance, with respect to limited liability, given the fact that we have also seen instances where the United States has shown little regard for expanding resources over a prolonged period such as wars in Vietnam and Iraq, it would suggest that there is less of a single notion of limited liability that is culturally ingrained in the United States, and in fact significant variations in the interpretation of limited liability across administrations. It would seem that other factors, including the economic position of the United States at a particular time or the distribution of power in the international system, would be able to explain these significant variations than culture would.

The other internal explanation focuses on domestic politics. The argument here is that factors such as struggles between government bureaucracies or logrolling between domestic-political factions may lead to sub-optimal foreign policy outcomes in terms of the level and distri-bution of U.S. commitment to Southeast Asia.[36] This is because actors within specific bureaucracies or interest groups may pursue policies that

[34] See, for instance: Niall Ferguson, *Colossus: The Price of America's Empire* (New York: Penguin, 2004), pp. 48–51.

[35] Prashanth Parameswaran, *ASEAN's Role in a U.S. Indo-Pacific Strategy* (Washington, DC: Wilson Center Asia Program, 2018).

[36] These are only two examples of a multitude of factors mentioned in domestic political explanations. For a more comprehensive treatment, see: James McCormick's two books: Eugene R. Wittkopf and James M. McCormick (eds.), *The Domestic Sources of American Foreign Policy: Insights and Evidence* (Lanham, MD: Rowman & Littlefield, 2004); *James McCormick, American Foreign Policy and Process* (Belmont, CA: Thomas Wadsworth, 2005).

benefit the organizations or the factions they represent rather than the national or collective interests.[37]

Several authors have advanced that domestic-political arguments to explain U.S. commitment to Southeast Asia. Some focus on the role of interest groups like the U.S.-ASEAN Business Council and the U.S. Chamber of Commerce in advocating for a more robust American economic commitment to Southeast Asia in times where protectionism is the popular sentiment, while others highlight the triumph of particular bureaucracies over others in specific policy decisions, like the sidelining of the State Department in favor of the office of the U.S. Trade Representative and the U.S. Department of Commerce in the promotion of trade policy in the Clinton administration.[38] Still others have attributed the lack of sustained U.S. attention to Southeast Asia to several factors related to the U.S. political system, including fragmented mobilization efforts which make Southeast Asian Americans a less significant force collectively in U.S. politics relative to other single countries like Israel, India or Taiwan.[39]

As seductive as domestic-political explanations are, they also have their limits. While variations in U.S. commitment to Southeast Asia may be partly shaped by interest groups or factions domestically, it is often only through other factors such as their collusion with the foreign policy elite based on congruent threat perceptions or their growing clout under certain international conditions, which accords them greater influence in the decision-making process in some periods relative to others.

The preceding evaluation highlights the fact that while existing mono-causal explanations can explain some periods of or individual tendencies in U.S. commitment to Southeast Asia, they cannot fully account for

---

[37] Graham Allison's presentation of the bureaucratic politics model explains the first point quite well. See: Graham Allison, *Essence of Decision: Explaining the Cuban Missile Crisis* (Boston: Little, Brown and Company, 1971). For logrolling, see: Jack Snyder, *Myths of Empire: Domestic Politics and International Ambition* (Ithaca: Cornell University Press, 1991).

[38] For the former, see, for example: Hans H. Indorf, "The U.S.-ASEAN Dialogue: A Search For Procedural Improvements," *Contemporary Southeast Asia*, Vol. 8, No. 3 (December 1986), pp. 179–191. For the latter, see: Donald K. Emmerson, "US Policy Themes in Southeast Asia in the 1990s," in: David Wurfel and Bruce Burton (eds.), *Southeast Asia in the New World Order: The Political Economy of a Dynamic Region* (London: Macmillan, 1996), pp. 103–127.

[39] Alice Ba, "Systemic Neglect? A Reconsideration of US-Southeast Asia Policy," *Contemporary Southeast Asia*, Vol. 31, No. 3 (December 2009), pp. 369–398.

the persistent variations in ebbs, flows and imbalances in Washington's commitment to the region since the end of WWII. None of these explanations are sufficient as a systematic, standalone explanation of U.S. commitment to Southeast Asia and why balances of commitment keep proving so elusive. The next chapter proposes an alternative approach.

CHAPTER 3

The Argument: Balance of Commitment

The great weakness of United States policy, which indeed may ultimately prove a fatal defect, is that we have never been quite sure how serious we are about the whole business.[1]

—William Henderson, 1963

America, the time has not yet come for you to lay down the heavy burden of leadership.

—Ferdinand Marcos, Address to U.S. Congress, September 15, 1966[2]

An analysis of U.S. commitment to Southeast Asia requires the development of a new framework that can account for the recuring ebbs, flows and imbalances in Washington's commitment to the region. This chapter develops a new balance of commitment model which aims to address the absence of an existing theory by reconciling the existing external and internal approaches outlined in the previous chapter. The model argues that changes in U.S. commitment to Southeast Asia are rooted in how U.S. policymakers balance between adjusting to power shifts, perceiving threats among Washington and its competitors and

---

[1] William Henderson, *Southeast Asia: Problems of United States Policy* (Cambridge: MIT Press, 1963), p. 252.

[2] Ferdinand Marcos, "Address to Congress, September 15," *Department of State Bulletin*, October 10, 1966.

© The Author(s), under exclusive license to Springer Nature Singapore Pte Ltd. 2022
P. Parameswaran, *Elusive Balances*,
https://doi.org/10.1007/978-981-16-6612-4_3

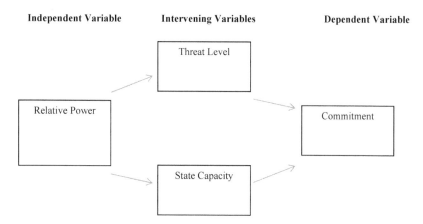

Fig. 1   The Balance of Commitment Model (*Source* Generated by Author)

extracting and mobilizing the necessary resources to respond to them. These balancing acts—both in terms of the level and distribution of commitment as well as internal and external considerations—help explain why achieving balances of commitment can prove so elusive.

This chapter develops the balance of commitment framework as a comprehensive explanation for changes to U.S. commitment to Southeast Asia. It sets out how to define and measure commitment level and distribution (dependent variable) and outlines the model as an inter-relationship between three key factors (independent and intervening variables): power shifts the United States experiences between itself and its competitors; U.S. policymakers' perceptions of threats; and the mobilization and extraction of resources necessary to respond. It also identifies how balance of commitment will be tested against the most popular explanation—balance of power—in the case studies in the book that follow (Fig. 1).

1 Dependent Variable: Defining and Measuring Commitment

1.1 Defining Commitment

The dependent variable in the balance of commitment model is foreign policy commitment. Foreign policy commitment is a product of broader considerations in foreign policy and grand strategy. If foreign policy is thought of as a program set up policymakers directed toward entities external to their jurisdiction, and grand strategy is a plan to provide national security by keeping national resources and external obligations in balance, then commitment is a consequence of these considerations manifested in various forms—be it military pacts, disbursements of development funds or trips by high-ranking officials.[3]

Although there is no shortage of scholarship on either individual components of commitment, such as military assistance or economic aid, or the consequences of commitment, like the literature on deterrence or reputation, comprehensive definitions of the concept of commitment itself are much rarer.[4] The balance of commitment model advanced in this book builds primarily upon Thomas Schelling's conception of commitment defined as "strategically becoming obligated to some course of

---

[3] For a definition of foreign policy, see: Charles F. Hermann, "Changing Course: When Governments Choose to Redirect Foreign Policy," *International Studies Quarterly*, Vol. 34, No. 1 (March 1990), pp. 3–21. For one on grand strategy, see: Charles Kupchan, *Vulnerability of Empire* (Ithaca: Cornell University Press, 1994), p. 3; John Lewis Gaddis, "What Is Grand Strategy?," Keynote Address at conference on "American Grand Strategy after War," sponsored by the Triangle Institute for Security Studies and the Duke University Program in American Grand Strategy. February 26, 2009, p. 7. For an elaboration of how these concepts relate in a practical sense, see: Charles Kupchan, "Grand Strategy for a Divided America," *Foreign Affairs*, August 1, 2007.

[4] On specific components of commitment, see for instance: William H. Mott, *United States Military Assistance: An Empirical Perspective* (Westport: Greenwood Press, 2002). The literature on the effects of commitment, particularly international commitments, is quite sizable. On the effects on reputation, see for example: Robert Keohane, *After Hegemony: Cooperation and Discord in the World Political Economy* (Princeton, NJ: Princeton University Press, 1984). On the signaling effects of commitment as an expression of state identity, see: Ian Johnstone, "Treating International Institutions as Social Environments," *International Studies Quarterly*, Vol. 45, No. 3 (December 2001). A related stream of literature deals with regime types and whether some may find it easier or harder to commit than others. See especially: Lisa Martin, *Democratic Commitments: Legislatures and International Cooperation* (Princeton, NJ: Princeton University Press, 2000); Brett Ashley Leeds, "Domestic Political Institutions, Credible Commitments, and International Cooperation," *American Journal of Political Science*, Vol. 43, No. 4 (October 1999), pp. 979–100; Kurt Taylor Gaubatz, "Democratic States and Commitment in international Relations," *International Organization*, Vol. 50, No. 1 (Winter 1996), pp. 109–139, 111. There are also a few other theoretical works on U.S. commitments more generally. See, for example: Bruce Jentleson, "American Commitments in the Third World: Theory vs. Practice," *International Organization*, Vol. 41, No. 4 (Autumn 1987), pp. 667–704.

(in)action or a constraint on future action in a way that restricts an actor's freedom of action and attempts to influence others."[5]

This definition has three critical elements. First and most fundamentally, commitment has to involve *being obligated to a certain course of action*. This means that an actor is contractually bound to it or obligated in some way, rather than just being emotionally impelled by it which is how it is often used in more casual discussions about foreign policy (e.g., administration X is "committed" to ensuring that state Y does not dominate Southeast Asia).[6]

Second, commitment involves *constraints on an actor's freedom of action*. In that sense, a test of whether commitment exists or not can be said to be contingent on whether or not it imposes a restriction on a committed nation in some way.[7] A case in point within U.S.-Southeast Asia relations is the 1951 U.S.-Philippine Mutual Defense Treaty (MDT), the anchoring document of the U.S.-Philippine alliance. The commitment is an American security guarantee to the Philippines, set out in Articles IV and V of the MDT where the parties pledge to "act to meet the common dangers" of "an armed attack on the metropolitan territory of either of the Parties, or on the island territories under its jurisdiction in the Pacific or on its armed forces, public vessels or aircraft in the Pacific."[8] The corresponding restriction would be the fact that if an armed attack occurs in areas such as the South China Sea, it would require Washington to act in

---

[5] Thomas C. Schelling, *Strategies of Commitment and Other Essays* (Cambridge: Harvard University Press, 2006), p. 1.

[6] This "binding" aspect of commitment has been a critical part of definitions even by early authors like Walter Lippmann, who defined commitment at its most basic level as "an obligation." This point was originally made in: Terry L. Deibel, *Commitment in American Foreign Policy* (Washington, DC: National Defense University Press, 1980), especially pp. 7–11.

[7] Ibid.

[8] The Avalon Project, "Mutual Defense Treaty Between the United States and the Republic of the Philippines," August 30, 1951: https://avalon.law.yale.edu/20th_cent ury/phil001.asp.

some way to counter that threat, a point of clarification sought within the alliance for decades.[9]

Third, commitment is a *strategic* move that *attempts to influence others.* The objective of commitment is to strategically surrender some control over one's future behavior in order to influence someone else's choices— be it the recipient of that commitment or other third parties.[10] In the case of U.S. commitment to Southeast Asia, U.S. policymakers engage in a process of attempting to convince core audiences—Southeast Asian elites and publics, and, secondarily, allies, competitors, potential adversaries and even some key domestic constituencies—that a course of action will be followed through. Receptiveness can then be discerned, both quantitatively through metrics such as public opinion polling, as well as qualitatively through expressed views of these audiences since power shifts can have a "psychological" as well as material aspects.[11]

Beyond these three critical elements, it is also important to specify how this definition will be operationalized in the balance of commitment model. First, the definition of U.S. commitment to Southeast Asia here refers primarily to that of the government of the United States. That does not mean that the commitment of other actors, such as the private sector or non-governmental organizations (NGOs) will not be considered at all: indeed, actors such as but not limited to the Center for Strategic

---

[9] The pursuit of clarity has gone through its own evolution through the decades. Assurance was given on this score in 1998 during the Clinton years by then-U.S. Defense Secretary William Cohen, but the Obama administration did not publicly restate this in unambiguous terms during its tenure despite the challenges that the Philippines faced in the wake of growing Chinese assertiveness. Clarity was then subsequently restated under Both Trump and Biden. See: Prashanth Parameswaran, "Managing the US-Philippines Alliance: The Limits of Commitment Clarity," *The Diplomat*, March 13, 2019, https://thediplomat.com/2019/03/managing-the-us-philippines-alliance-the-limits-of-commitment-clarity/; Gregory Poling and Eric Sayers, "Time to Make Good on the U.S.-Philippine Alliance," *War on the Rocks*, January 21, 2019, https://warontherocks.com/2019/01/time-to-make-good-on-the-u-s-philippine-alliance/; Richard Javad Heydarian, "The True Significance of Pompeo's South China Sea Statement," Asia Maritime Transparency Initiative, August 4. 2020, https://amti.csis.org/the-true-signif icance-of-pompeos-south-china-sea-statement/.

[10] Kurt Taylor Gaubatz, "Democratic States and Commitment in international Relations," *International Organization*, Vol. 50, No. 1 (Winter 1996), pp. 109–139, especially p. 111.

[11] Bilahari Kausikan, "Dodging and Hedging in Southeast Asia," *The American Interest*, January 12, 2017: https://www.the-american-interest.com/2017/01/12/dodging-and-hedging-in-southeast-asia/.

and International Studies, the Asia Foundation and the U.S.-ASEAN Business Council play important roles including feeding input into U.S. government thinking on commitment or functioning as implementing organizations for manifestations of U.S. commitment. Rather, the balance of commitment model will consider these actors to the extent that they are related to U.S. government policy in terms of strategy, planning and execution.

Second, as the focus of the balance of commitment model is regional, this book is primarily concerned with U.S. commitment to regions in general (or region-based commitment) and the U.S. commitment to Southeast Asia in particular. A region is thought of in this book as a group of states that can be defined as an interconnected subsystem, not only based on their geographical proximity, but also other notable common features such as their identity and the nature of their interactions with each other and with major power actors operating there.[12] Seen from this perspective, Southeast Asia is defined as composing eleven countries— Brunei, Cambodia, East Timor, Indonesia, Laos, Malaysia, Myanmar, Philippines, Singapore, Thailand and Vietnam.

Third, following from the first element of the definition which mentions being obligated to a course of action rather than being emotionally impelled by it, the primary focus of the balance of commitment model will be on commitments to Southeast Asia that are actually realized through the allocation of resources, with mechanisms ranging from memorandums of understanding or statements to troop deployments. For instance, verbal declarations by U.S. officials, including reaffirmations of the centrality of Southeast Asia to U.S. interests usually heard when a

---

[12] The definition is derived from: T. V. Paul, "Regional Transformation In International Relations," in: T. V. Paul (ed.), *International Relations Theory and Regional Transformation* (Cambridge, UK: Cambridge University Press, 2012), p. 4, where a region is defined as "a cluster of states that are proximate to each other and are interconnected in spatial, cultural and ideational terms in a significant and distinguishable manner." The conception of regions and subsystems draws on regional security complex theory (RSCT) advanced by Barry Buzan and the Copenhagen School, which view regions as subsystems. See: Barry Buzan, *People, States and Fear: The National Security Problem in International Relations* (Chapel Hill: University of North Carolina Press, 1983). For other interpretations, see: William R. Thompson, "The Regional Subsystem: A Conceptual Explication and a Propositional Inventory," *International Studies Quarterly*, Vol. 17, No. 1 (1973), pp. 89–117; and David A. Lake, "Regional Security Complexes: A Systems Approach," in: David A. Lake and Patrick M. Morgan (eds.), *Regional Orders: Building Security in a New World* (University Park: Pennsylvania State University Press, 1997), pp. 45–67.

new administration comes to office, matter in the sense that they signal future potential commitments or proposal to be followed through on, rather than being considered commitments in and of themselves. This helps distinguish between rhetoric and reality and places the emphasis on obligations that actually materialize.

Fourth, while discussions of commitment tend to focus on formal commitments such as alliances, the obligations to courses of action mentioned in this definition can either be formal or informal. Including both formal and informal notions of commitment is particularly important in the American context, since the United States has traditionally been reluctant to accept formal legal restrictions on its freedom of action and so commitment may manifest itself in other informal means beyond a binding agreement of some sort. For instance, within the context of the U.S.-Thailand alliance, the Rusk-Thanat joint statement inked in 1962 between the United States and Thailand did not have the same binding force or formality as the formation of the eventually short-lived Southeast Asia Treaty Organization (SEATO) of 1954, it is still considered an important indicator of U.S. commitment to its alliance with Thailand.[13]

Fifth, this definition adopts a broader conception of commitment that extends beyond the security dimension to include economic and diplomatic commitments. The case for this is clear. If U.S. commitment to Southeast Asia involves an American obligation to the region that restricts the former's freedom of action, various elements of relations can arguably create such a binding and restrictive effect. Just like a security guarantee in the U.S.-Philippines MDT may affect the U.S. military's actions, so too does a diplomatic commitment for a U.S. president to attend annual meetings at the East Asia Summit in a particular Southeast Asian state restricts the president's schedule, or an economic commitment to provide aid to countries in the Mekong subregion constrains the U.S. budget. While the lens of commitment has been broadened even further by some, the balance of commitment model focuses primarily on the security, economic and diplomatic aspects of commitment both because these

---

[13] U.S. Department of State, Foreign Relations, 1961–63, Vol. XXIIII, Southeast Asia, Office of the Historian, March 6, 1995; Justus Maria Van Der Kroef, *The Lives of SEATO* (Singapore: ISEAS, December 1976), pp. 10–11.

tend to be the main realms where contestations over level and distribution occur across and between administrations.[14]

1.2   Measuring Commitment Change

Given that the balance of commitment framework conceives of commitment in a multifaceted way and applied at the regional level, metrics for commitment change will need to be defined granularly and comprehensively to detect subtle shifts across various realms. Most of the current literature focuses on more aggregate dependent variables such as foreign policy change or grand strategy shifts, usually at the global level, which provide useful guidelines but limited in their ability to capture smaller shifts.[15] A useful start is focusing more narrowly on the concept of strategic adjustment, which can be defined as a process by which a state has expanded or contracted its overall capabilities and commitments.[16]

Drawing on the conception of strategic adjustment, the balance of commitment framework measures commitment change in two ways: commitment level as well as commitment balance. The attention to both commitment level and commitment balance is important because the experience of U.S. policy in Southeast Asia suggests that attention ought to be given not just to the extent to which the United States is committed, but *how* it is committed. To take just one example, while phases of the U.S. involvement in the Vietnam War and the U.S. rebalance to Asia may both be dubbed by some as high levels of commitment, commitment

---

[14] Some authors like Diebel also argue that commitment can extend even beyond this to ethnic ties that some groups in America have abroad.

[15] Several of these typologies currently exist, with Edward Luttwak contrasting "expansionist" with "status quo" strategies, Charles Kupchan distinguishing between "compellent," "deterrent," and "accommodationist," strategies, and Barry Posen and Andrew Ross assessing four primary strategies: neo-isolationism, selective engagement, cooperative security and primacy See, respectively: Edward Luttwak, *Strategy: The Logic of War and Peace* (Cambridge, MA: Belknap Press of Harvard University Press, 1987), p. 180; Charles Kupchan, *Vulnerability of Empire* (Ithaca: Cornell University Press, 1994), pp. 67–68; Barry Posen and Andrew Ross, "Competing Visions for US Grand Strategy," *International Security*, Vol. 21, No. 3 (1996/1997), pp. 3–4.

[16] Peter Trubowitz and Edward Rhodes, "Explaining American Strategic Adjustment," in: Peter Trubowitz, Emily Goldman, and Edward Rhodes (eds.), *The Politics of Strategic Adjustment: Ideas, Institutions and Interests* (New York: Columbia University Press, 1999), pp. 3–25.

balance in the latter case could be said to be relatively more evenly calibrated across security, economic and diplomatic realms, whatever its other
limitations.

Commitment level refers to the amount of resources devoted by the
committed state. Drawing on Colin Dueck, who measured changes in
U.S. commitment level across dimensions including military spending and
foreign aid, commitment level is measured by asking whether the United
States has expanded, contracted or in any way significantly changed
its overall commitments to Southeast Asia.[17] Expansions and contractions will be measured as "increases" or "decreases" to varying degrees
("minor," "moderate" and "major").

1. Alliances and partnerships: Are alliances and partnerships strengthened or weakened?
2. Military deployments: Are military deployments in the region
   expanded or reduced?
3. Economic engagement: Is economic engagement, which includes
   trade, investment and aid, increased or decreased?
4. Diplomacy: Does the administration engage in significant new diplomatic initiatives, or does it disengage from existing diplomatic
   initiatives?

Commitment balance, on the other hand, is concerned with the balance
of resources within different components or issue areas. The balance of
components within contemporary U.S. Asia policy deserves examination
in assessing how policymakers engage the region comparatively.[18] With
respect to U.S.-Southeast Asia relations in a more historical sense, one
can identify five realms of commitment balance in the post-WWII period
as mentioned in the previous chapter: economics and security; ideals

---

[17] Colin Dueck, *Reluctant Crusaders: Power, Culture and Change in American Grand
Strategy* (Princeton, NJ: Princeton University Press, 2006), p. 12.

[18] See, for instance: Kurt Campbell, Nirav Patel and Vikram J. Singh, "The Power of
Balance: America in iAsia," (Washington, DC. Center for a New American Security, June
11, 2011); See, for example: Senate Committee on Foreign Relations, *Rebalancing the
Rebalance: Resourcing U.S. Diplomatic Strategy in the Asia–Pacific Region*, Majority Staff
Report, April 17, 2014.

and interests; bilateralism and multilateralism; cooperative and confrontational approaches toward adversaries; and means and ends.[19] Accordingly, commitment balance can be measured by asking questions about the extent to which U.S. policymakers have shifted or toggled between the poles in the five realms of commitment balance, with changes measured as "increases" or "decreases" to varying degrees ("minor," "moderate" and "major").

1. Economics/Security: Does the administration devote greater attention to economic or security affairs?
2. Bilateralism/Unilateralism vs. Multilateralism: Does the administration tend to favor bilateral or unilateral approaches, or is it more inclined toward multilateral ones?
3. Ideals/Interests: Does the administration devote greater attention to ideals like democracy and human rights, or does it downplay them and focus more narrowly on just core national interests?
4. Cooperative/Confrontational: Does the administration adopt a more aggressive and confrontational stance toward its adversaries or competitors, or does it adopt a less confrontational stance?
5. Means/Ends: Does the amount of resources devoted by the administration match the goals and objectives it is trying to achieve?

2   INDEPENDENT AND INTERVENING VARIABLES: EXPLAINING COMMITMENT CHANGE

2.1   Independent Variable: Distribution of Power

The starting point of the balance of commitment model when it comes to explaining change—or the independent variable—is relative power. Relative power can be defined as the ability of political actors to shape outcomes within the international system compared to their competitors. Beginning with this variable, a key focus in the neorealist school of international relations as mentioned in the previous chapter, acknowledges that the international system sets the broad parameters for foreign policy outcomes.

---

[19] For a treatment of this, see: Prashanth Parameswaran, "The Power of Balance: Advancing US-ASEAN Relations Under the Second Obama Administration," *The Fletcher Forum on World Affairs*, Vol. 37, No. 1 (Winter 2013), pp. 123–134.

The relative power of a country is a function of its capabilities as well as its international environment.[20] As such, there are two measures of relative power. The first is *power degree*, which asks how an actor fares relative to others with respect to components of power. Though the balance of commitment framework acknowledges that power has several components, it also places an additional emphasis on two primary components—economic and military power, measured through indicators such as GDP per capita. The focus on these components also acknowledges the fact that different developments can have varying degrees of change with respect to relative power depending on various factors including magnitude, be it the defeat the United States faced in the Vietnam War or periodic global financial crises.

The second is *power distribution*, which refers to how an actor is positioned relative to others at various levels of the international system. Since the focus of the balance of commitment model is on explaining U.S. commitment variation in Southeast Asia, the model naturally focuses on both the global and the regional distribution of capabilities—an important distinction particularly for global powers like the United States that have to balance both aggregate international commitments as well as approaches across multiple regions.[21] Particular attention will be paid to metrics such as polarity—the number of poles in the international system—and the constraints those may pose on the United States. For instance, the end of the Cold War produced a unipolar system which imposed far less systemic constraints on the United States in terms of its commitment, while Soviet inroads into Southeast Asia in the late 1970s and early 1980s arguably helped reshape the regional distribution of power between Moscow and Washington.

Put together, the combination of power degree, which can be seen as an indicator of depth, and power distribution, which can be viewed as a measure of breadth, can tell us the extent to which relative power has

---

[20] These include theorists from Jean-Jacques Rousseau and David Hume to A. J. P Taylor, Arnold Toynbee and Raymond Aaron. For a broader treatment of this, see: William C. Wohlforth, *The Elusive Balance: Power and Perceptions During the Cold War* (Ithaca: Cornell University Press, 1993), p. 6.

[21] For more on the distinction between global and regional balances of power, see: Steve A. Yetiv, *The Absence of Grand Strategy: The United States in the Persian Gulf (1972–2005)* (Baltimore: Johns Hopkins University Press, 2008), especially Chapter 2.

been altered. These degrees can be scored as increases or decreases of different intensities "minor," "moderate" or "major."

2.2   Intervening Variables: Threat Level and State Capacity

While structural considerations like the relative distribution of power provide a useful starting point from which to begin understanding the external drivers of U.S. commitment to Southeast Asia, they need to be integrated with the internal dynamics of how policymakers build consensus around external threats and mobilize resources to respond to them in order to fully explain outcomes in strategic adjustment.[22] These balancing acts are ultimately what have helped shape U.S. commitment to the region, be it the shift in focus to the challenge of terrorism following the September 11 attacks or the resourcing constraints evident in some components of the U.S. rebalance to Asia.[23]

As such, the balance of commitment model acknowledges these balancing acts and adds two critical intervening variables to the equation in between the independent and dependent variables to explain balance of commitment outcomes—threat level and state capacity. This approach is consistent with a school of international relations theory called neoclassical realism, which attempts to merge the systemic factors outlined by neorealists—principally the relative distribution of capabilities—with unit-level intervening variables like elite perceptions in order to explain foreign

---

[22] For an example that makes a similar point but focuses on Britain rather than the United States, Aaron L. Friedberg, *The Weary Titan: Britain and the Experience of Relative Decline, 1895–1905* (Princeton, NJ: Princeton University Press, 2010), p. 8. For one focused around the United States, see: Fareed Zakaria, *From Wealth to Power: The Unusual Origins of America's World Role* (New York: Princeton University Press, 1999).

[23] See, for example: Senate Committee on Foreign Relations, *Rebalancing the Rebalance: Resourcing U.S. Diplomatic Strategy in the Asia–Pacific Region*, Majority Staff Report, April 17, 2014; Robert Sutter et al., *Balancing Acts: The U.S. Rebalance and Asia–Pacific Stability* (Washington, DC: Elliot School of International Affairs, August 2013).

policy outcomes of a country.[24] For neoclassical realists, while U.S. policymakers adjusting commitment levels to Southeast Asia may be attentive
to international imperatives such as changes in power between Washington and its competitors, domestic intervening variables such as how
the foreign policy elite perceives threats or mobilizes resources in the fact
of domestic constraints can complicate any attempted shifts.[25]

In doing so, the balance of commitment model also acknowledges
the critical importance of agency in the formulation of foreign policy
outcomes. In particular, it recognizes that the key actor in this intervening
process of calculating power and threats and mobilizing resources is the
foreign policy executive (hereafter FPE)—the group of people responsible for devising grand strategy and maximizing national security, located
primarily in agencies such as but not limited to the White House, the
State Department and the Department of Defense and the U.S. Treasury.[26] The role of the broader FPE in shaping U.S. Southeast Asia policy
is arguably even more important because within overall U.S. Asia policy,
Southeast Asia has not traditionally enjoyed as much attention as a standalone regional priority from the very top level of policymaking relative
to China or Japan.

The recognition of the FPE in the balance of commitment model
should not be confused for a singular focus on this group as drivers of
U.S. commitment to Southeast Asia. As we shall see from the case studies

---

[24] The term originated in an article by Gideon Rose in 1998. See: Gideon Rose,
"Neoclassical Realism and Theories of Foreign Policy," *World Politics*, Vol. 51, No. 1
(October 1998), pp. 144–172. For a more recent examination of contours, see: Steven
E. Lobell, Norrin M. Ripsman, and Jeffrey W. Taliaferro, *Neoclassical Realism, the State,
and Foreign Policy* (Cambridge, UK: Cambridge University Press, 2009), p. 7. For a take
on the integration of the internal and external, see: Robert D. Putnam, "Diplomacy and
Domestic Politics: The Logic of Two-Level Games," *International Organization*, Vol. 42,
No. 3 (Summer 1988), pp. 427–460.

[25] Ibid.

[26] In defining what I mean by FPE, I draw on Stephen Krasner's narrow conception
of "the American state," which consists only of "those institutions and roles that are relatively insulated from particularistic pressures and concerned with general goals (primarily
the White House, the State Department, and to a lesser extent the Treasury and Defense
Departments). See Stephen Krasner, "United States Commercial and Monetary Policy:
Unraveling the Paradox of External Strength and Internal Weakness," in: Peter J. Katzen-
stein (ed.), *Between Power and Plenty: Foreign Economic Policies of Advanced Industrial
States* (Madison: University of Wisconsin Press, 1978), p. 53. The logic for doing so is
because the FPE has access to more privileged information than the rest of the population.

in the book, in the practice of foreign policy, the FPE receives regular feedback from both other non-government domestic actors as well as other actors in Southeast Asia which can indirectly influence its views about regional conditions and responses to them. In addition to domestic debates, the FPE also interacts with government officials, scholars and publics in other regions of the world in various settings from official visits to think tank conferences and dialogues. While this point may seem obvious, it nonetheless bears emphasis because it reaffirms the fact that regions like Southeast Asia are not always merely "acted upon" in terms of U.S. foreign policy, but can have some degree of influence in shaping policy as well in an indirect sense.

The first intervening variable, *threat level*, focuses on elite perceptions about power and threats—or, more specifically, the extent to which the FPE thinks that changes in capabilities or dangers pose a challenge to the state.[27] The role of the FPE in perceiving power and threats is important because as real as shifts in the distribution of power in the international system might be in neorealist analyses, they also may fail to have a discernable impact on foreign policy outcomes unless and until they are actually perceived by individual actors.[28] For instance, as much as the September 11 attacks may have exacted a toll on the United States objectively speaking, it took a subjective heightened threat level perceived by the George W. Bush administration for this to translate into a shaping of Washington's commitment to Southeast Asia.

There are two ways to measure elite threat perception in the balance of commitment model. The first measure is *threat hierarchy*—or the calculations the FPE makes about how to prioritize or rank the series of challenges and threats based on the urgency, intensity and likelihood of dangers to U.S. interests. This measurement goes beyond the sense of whether the FPE can detect threats in general and down to specific and granular insights—whether right or wrong—about time horizons, magnitude and probability of occurrence. This is important because as other

---

[27] For a more comprehensive treatment of definitional issues, see: Janice Gross Stein, "Threat Perceptions in International Relations," in: Leonie Huddy, David O. Sears, and Jack S. Levy (eds.), *The Oxford Handbook of Political Psychology* (Oxford: Oxford University Press, 2013), pp. 364–394.

[28] Aaron L. Friedberg, *The Weary Titan: Britain and the Experience of Relative Decline, 1895–1905* (Princeton, NJ: Princeton University Press, 2010), p. 8.

studies have shown, there is a chance that parts of the FPE could misperceive or underestimate the intensity or time horizons of impending or ongoing power shifts or challenges, or focus on some components of power but not others, thereby reducing the overall threat level.[29]

The second measure is *threat consensus*—or the degree of shared understanding among the FPE about some facts in the world as being problems of a particular nature requiring certain remedies.[30] Such a shared understanding about the presence, nature and extent of threat can be even more difficult to forge in democracies like the United States because of the presence of veto players whose minds need to be changed, thereby leading to delayed and inefficient balancing of threats and a passing of the buck on who was ultimately responsible for a particular decision.[31] As a case in point, partly in reaction to the criticism of his administration's lack of response to the 1997 Asian Financial Crisis, Bill Clinton wrote in his memoirs that despite the fact that the White House, the State Department, the National Security Council and the Department of Defense all wanted to take a more aggressive approach to stemming the Asian financial crisis at the early stages when Thailand's economy was on the brink of collapse, the Treasury Department which was charged with "making the call" opposed it on economic and domestic-political grounds.[32]

Put together, the combination of threat hierarchy, which can be seen as an indicator of depth, and threat consensus, which can be viewed as a measure of breadth, can tell us the extent to which the FPE thinks that changes in capabilities or dangers pose a challenge to the state. They may

[29] Ibid.

[30] This definition is derived from: Randall Schweller, *Unanswered Threats: Political Constraints on the Balance of Power* (Princeton, NJ: Princeton University Press, 2006), p. 47.

[31] Schweller defines veto players as individual or collective actors whose mind needs to be changed in order for the status quo to shift. Randall Schweller, *Unanswered Threats: Political Constraints on the Balance of Power* (Princeton, NJ: Princeton University Press, 2006), p. 48. A notable example of threat consensus is Steven E. Lobell's study of London's threat assessment between 1933 and 1936 of Germany, Japan and Italy which was hamstrung by elite disagreement. Steven E. Lobell, "Threat Assessment, the State, and Foreign Policy," in: Steven E. Lobell, Norrin M. Ripsman, and Jeffrey W. Taliaferro (eds.), *Neoclassical Realism, the State, and Foreign Policy* (Cambridge, UK: Cambridge University Press, 2009), especially pp. 67–68.

[32] Bill Clinton, *My Life* (New York: Knopf, 2004), p. 656.

do so to varying degrees, which can be scored as "low," "medium" or "high" in terms of their concern about power shifts and rising dangers.

The second intervening variable is *state capacity*—or the ability of a state to extract or mobilize resources for its foreign policy goals in the face of domestic constraints.[33] State capacity is an important variable the within balance of commitment model because even after the FPE perceives certain power shifts or rising threats at various levels, it will need to secure the resources necessary to respond to those threats and eventually affect changes in commitment level and distribution.[34]

There are two primary ways to measure state capacity in the balance of commitment model. The first measure is *institutional cohesion*, which can be defined as the extent to which relevant entities are aligned on the allocation of resources toward a particular end.[35] Institutional cohesion takes on importance in a context like the United States, where resource mobilization requires the alignment of various bodies including not just the government, but private industry and other non-governmental organizations as well and can often be tied to the nature of the party in power.

The second measure is *elite autonomy* or the extent to which the domestic-political structure allows the FPE to pursue policies when faced with either public or legislative opposition.[36] More specifically, in the American context, we would be most concerned about potential opposition along partisan lines, from Congress, as well as public opinion at large. For instance, elite autonomy underwent a significant decline following

[33] Jeffrey W. Taliaferro, "State Building for Future Wars: Neoclassical Realism and the Resource-Extractive State," *Security Studies*, Vol. 15, No. 3 (July–September 2006), pp. 464–495.

[34] As Jeffrey Taliaferro puts it, "even if leaders make 'accurate' estimates of relative power and power trends, they do not always have complete access to the material resources of their own societies" See: Jeffrey W. Taliaferro, "Neoclassical Realism and Resource Extraction: State Building for Future War," in: Steven E. Lobell, Norrin M. Ripsman, and Jeffrey W. Taliaferro (eds.), *Neoclassical Realism, the State, and Foreign Policy* (Cambridge, UK: Cambridge University Press, 2009), p. 213.

[35] See *Fareed Zakaria, From Wealth to Power: The Unusual Origins of America's World Role* (New York: Princeton University Press, 1999).

[36] This definition is derived from: Norman Rippsman, *Peacemaking By Democracies: The Effect of State Autonomy on the Post-World War Settlements* (Pennsylvania: Penn State University Press, 2004), especially pp. 43–57; and Eric A. Nordlinger, *On the Autonomy of the Democratic State* (Cambridge, MA: Harvard University Press, 1981), especially pp. 209–211 on elite autonomy-enhancing options.

Independent Variable   Intervening Variables   Dependent Variable

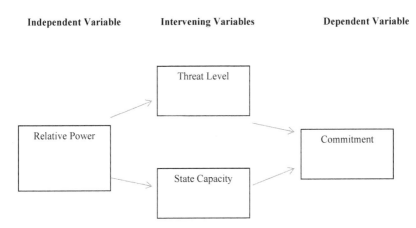

Fig. 2 Balance of Commitment Model (*Source* Generated by Author)

the Vietnam War, with increased congressional activism and a war-weary public making it difficult for the FPE under the administration of U.S. President Jimmy Carter to extract resources for new commitments and in some cases keep old ones. State capacity, like threat level, can be scored as "low," "medium" or "high" with various gradients in between as well.

Integrating the various pieces, the balance of commitment model holds that changes in relative power (independent variable), mediated by threat level and state capacity (intervening variables), lead to changes in U.S. commitment to Southeast Asia (dependent variable). The term balance of commitment is appropriate because of the balancing acts U.S. policymakers undergo in trying to navigate between external and internal dynamics as well as to shape individual components of foreign policy commitment (see Fig. 2). The title of this book, "Elusive Balances," reflects the fact that these multiple balancing acts can prove challenging for U.S. policymakers as they look to manage commitment with respect to Southeast Asia. William Wohlforth's book, "The Elusive Balance," examined the evolution of balance of power and perceptions during the Cold War.[37]

[37] William Wohlforth, *The Elusive Balance: Power and Perceptions During the Cold War* (New York: Cornell University Press, 1993).

According to the balance of commitment model, the most extreme changes in U.S. commitment level and balance in Southeast Asia are to be found when there are shifts in capabilities as well as threat levels and state capacity in the same direction. In these cases, a greater alignment between capabilities, threat perception and state capacity would facilitate greater changes in commitment levels, while the absence of offsetting conditions in any of these three variables would enhance the ability of policymakers to move squarely in the direction of favoring particular domains over the other, thereby resulting in bigger changes to commitment balance as well. For instance, if we see a decrease in relative power along with low threat perception and low state capacity, which approximates what U.S. policy-makers faced following the Vietnam War, then we are likely to see a major decrease in commitment level as well as a major decrease in commitment balance, with a greater propensity for an administration to move toward one domain vs. another (e.g., economics over security or multilateral over bilateral approaches).

However, if the changes in relative power and either or both threat levels and state capacity move in opposite directions in cases of U.S. commitment to Southeast Asia, we can expect the shifts in commitment level and distribution to moderate more from the extremes. In these cases, the misalignment between capabilities, threat levels and state capacity would moderate commitment levels and also offset potential commitment imbalances. For example, if we see a decrease in relative power with low state capacity but high threat perceptions, which can be said to approximate what U.S. policymakers faced during the post-2007–2008 Global Financial Crisis period, we can expect to see more moderate increases in commitment level and commitment balance. In this scenario, though the relative distribution of capabilities and state capacity may be limited, a sense of threat among policymakers would nonetheless play an important role in both pulling commitment level up from an otherwise depressed state and also moderating commitment imbalance that would otherwise be more pervasive with an alignment between all three of the independent and intervening variables in question.

3   Generating and Testing Competing Hypotheses

Having laid out the balance of commitment model derived from neoclassical realism as a new, alternative explanation for U.S. commitment in Southeast Asia, this section outlines how it will be tested against a popular existing explanation—neorealism or balance of power theory. This will be done with respect to four periods in U.S.-Southeast Asia policy from 1975 to the present: the post-Vietnam War period; the post-Cold War period; the post-9/11 period; and the post-Global Financial Crisis period.

The cases were selected to be representative of the recent history of U.S. commitment to Southeast Asia and the ebbs, flows and imbalances witnessed during this time. While they certainly do leave out certain developments—be it the Asian Financial Crisis, the Trump administration's approach to Southeast Asia or Covid-19's impact on U.S. commitment—they nonetheless do capture a series of broader, significant power shifts that cut across administrations to illustrate the role of broader structural and agential forces at play that extend beyond personality or party and can be applied to other periods as well.

The causal logic of balance of power and balance of commitment leads to different predictions with respect to U.S. commitment to Southeast Asia. According to a balance of power model, if U.S. capabilities increase, then Washington will boost the level of its commitment to Southeast Asia across military, economic and diplomatic realms. On the other hand, if Washington's capabilities decline, then the United States may reduce its level of commitment to Southeast Asia. While the balance of power model may not include as many granular implications for U.S. commitment distribution, one can see aspects of it affecting some components of this aspect of the dependent variable as well. For instance, increases in U.S. capabilities could facilitate the adoption of more unilateral mechanisms, while decreases in U.S. capabilities may affect the selection of more conciliatory rather than confrontational approaches toward adversaries or competitors.

According to the balance of commitment model, major adjustments in U.S. commitment levels and distribution require not just capability shifts, as a balance of power model would suggest, but also changes in intervening variables of threat perception and state capacity moving in the same direction as the independent variable. However, if these intervening variables move in different directions, then the level of U.S. commitment may be higher or lower and the balance of that commitment may be different than suggested under a balance of power model.

For instance, if Washington's capabilities increase and both threat perceptions and state capacity are high, then one would expect the alignment between capabilities, sense of threat and state capacity to make it easier for policymakers to boost commitment levels and toggle between commitment distributions, leading to an increase in commitment level and decrease in commitment balance—the former of which would have also been predicted by balance of power theory. However, if Washington's capabilities increase but this is accompanied by low threat perception and low state capacity, then one would expect a decrease in commitment level and increase in commitment balance. The commitment level would be much lower than would be suggested by a balance of power model which sees the increase in capabilities as more directly leading to higher commitment, and the implications for commitment distribution would also be more granular across realms (Fig. 3).

The key difference is that the balance of commitment model sees outcomes as emerging from the intersection of power differentials, threat levels and state capacity, rather than just power itself, and measures them in terms of both level and distribution. If neorealism is right, one should find a clear transmission belt between changes in the relative power and changes in the level and balance of U.S. commitment to the region which would confirm it. If, however, one finds that this relationship is in fact much more complex in various ways—be it time lags, miscalculations or disagreements with respect to threat perceptions, or congressional opposition or public opinion constraints leading to divergences from what neorealism expects the U.S. commitment level and distribution to be—then this could be read as support for neoclassical realism instead.

The testing of these two models in this book will combine a series of techniques, including process-tracing and the congruence method, to probe the causal connections between the independent, intervening and dependent variables across time. This testing approach requires attention to granularity. To successfully employ it, the book utilizes extensive

BALANCE OF POWER MODEL

Relative Power ——▸ Commitment Change

BALANCE OF COMMITMENT MODEL

Relative Power ——▸ Threat Perceptions + State Capacity ——▸ Commitment Change

Fig. 3 Balance of Power vs. Balance of Commitment (*Source* Generated by Author)

secondary sources, original conversations conducted with policymakers in both the United States and Southeast Asia and archival material where available.

CHAPTER 4

The Post-Vietnam Period

[W]e can't say that our treaty commitments are not going to be kept, and the Chinese better think they're gonna be kept. But the practical problem, that's what we've got to face, is that at the present time...there are damn few places where you would get support.
—U.S. President Richard Nixon, March 23, 1972[1]

The United States of America is the greatest power in the history of mankind. Certainly it is the most powerful military power in the world today. It has the capacity to wipe off the whole of humanity if it chooses to do so. But the Americans must remember the Vietnam War.
—Malaysia's former prime minister Mahathir Mohamad, 2020[2]

1   INTRODUCTION

Arguably the most dramatic change in U.S. commitment to Southeast Asia in the post-World War II period occurred as Washington began withdrawing from the Vietnam War and reshaping its role in the region. During what one might call the post-Vietnam period—which began to

---

[1] Richard M. Nixon, National Archives, Nixon Presidential Materials, White House Tapes, Recording of Conversation Among Nixon, Green, Haig, and Holdridge, March 23, 1972, 4:08–5:02 p.m., Oval Office, Conversation No. 692-3

[2] Mahathir Mohamad Twitter account, January 14, 2020.

© The Author(s), under exclusive license to Springer Nature   47
Singapore Pte Ltd. 2022
P. Parameswaran, *Elusive Balances*,
https://doi.org/10.1007/978-981-16-6612-4_4

take off once Richard Nixon announced what became known as the Nixon Doctrine in July 1969 and continued on under Gerald Ford and the first part of Jimmy Carter's administration up to the Vietnamese invasion of Cambodia in December 1978, we saw the transition to a low level and highly imbalanced commitment from the United States over this period.

What accounted for the sustained trend toward what might be termed imbalanced retrenchment that continued on for around a decade under three different presidents? This chapter will argue that the balance of commitment model offers a plausible explanation, and one that is more complete than the next best explanation which is balance of power.

To preview the argument, as the balance of commitment model would predict, a relatively minor decrease in U.S. relative capabilities, mediated by a low threat level as well as low state capacity, accounted for a major decrease in U.S. commitment level and balance during this period. U.S. policymakers felt that a decrease in American relative power in a more multipolar world dictated a fundamental reorientation in U.S. policy to deal with this new international setting, including in Southeast Asia where the perception had long been that Washington was overcommitted. This, combined with the deeply held belief among U.S. policymakers that they were operating in a low threat environment in Southeast Asia and the reality that the domestic climate made it difficult to mobilize and extract the resources that they needed, eventually led to a significantly reduced and highly imbalanced commitment to the region (Fig. 1).

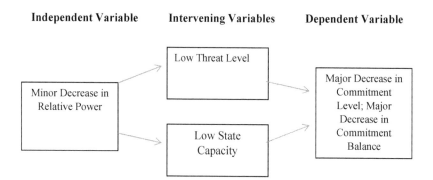

Fig. 1   The Balance of Commitment Model in the Post-Vietnam Period (*Source* Generated by Author)

If this case does fit with this more complex picture presented by the balance of commitment model, as opposed to a simpler one forecasted by balance of power with a strong, direct relationship between changes in the relative power and changes in the level and distribution of U.S. commitment to the region, this would be significant for the purposes of this book for three reasons.

First, the case is itself constitutes the most dramatic change in post-WWII U.S. commitment to Southeast Asia. Within a few years in the 1970s, declining U.S. commitment effectively relegated Southeast Asia from a region perceived as being tied to vital U.S. interests to one that was marginalized relative to other parts of the world. More broadly, perceptions about U.S. commitment also raised troubling questions about Washington's power, resolve and reliability, some of which continued to persist for decades and to a certain extent still do today.[3]

Second, though the post-Vietnam period might be admittedly viewed as an "easy" test for the balance of commitment model because of the intensity of the shifts witnessed in the case, it is also arguably the most representative of the four case studies because it deals with around a decade of U.S. foreign policy under three different administrations (of the other three cases, two deal with a single administration and the remaining case deals with two, and the time periods in all three cases are shorter than this one). Finding that these variables apply through different presidents during a continuous period would further prove their significance relative to more idiosyncratic explanations that have to do with the personalities of those in power.

Third and finally, confirmation of the balance of commitment model is also important in this case because this is the richest of the four case studies in terms of the available primary source documentary material. This case study was able to draw on archival material that has been made more available over the past few years. If a comprehensive analysis of both the private and public beliefs of U.S. officials during this period accords with the predictions expected from the balance of commitment model, then it would suggest that the explanation has even more traction.

An elucidation of this argument and analyzing its implications for the broader study requires three major tasks for this chapter. First, it

---

[3] One manifestation of the legacy of the Vietnam War is the idea of the "Vietnam Syndrome." For an explication of this, see: George C. Herring, "America and Vietnam: The Unending War," *Foreign Affairs*, Winter 1991/1992.

must provide evidence that U.S. commitment to Southeast Asia actually changed, and, more specifically, that both the level and balance of U.S. commitment declined significantly. Second, the chapter must verify that the balance of commitment model provides an explanation for this, and a superior one relative to balance of power theory. And third, it should then reflect on what this means for the broader study and the balance of commitment model, including previous predictions derived.

Accordingly, this chapter proceeds in three sections. The first section explores the shape of U.S. commitment to Southeast Asia during the post-Vietnam period, delving into the specific indicators and metrics set out in the introduction. The second section then explores the explanations for this level and balance of U.S. commitment, arguing that the balance of commitment model offers a good explanation and a better one than balance of power. The third and final section then evaluates the findings from the chapter and sieves out key insights that were gained.

2   The Shape of U.S. Commitment in the Post-Vietnam Period

As the United States sought to reshape its role in Southeast Asia, its commitment level and balance in Southeast Asia both unsurprisingly underwent significant changes under the Nixon, Ford, and early Carter years. In particular, both Washington's level and balance of commitment underwent a major decrease during this period.

These shifts in commitment level and distribution were captured most clearly by the so-called Nixon Doctrine, first announced on July 25, 1969, at a press briefing in Guam, and then developed in subsequent speeches and reports delivered by the administration. Though the Nixon Doctrine was misinterpreted by some as withdrawal, what Nixon actually laid out, and what would come to be the challenge for U.S. policy, would be how the United States would adjust the level and distribution of its commitment to Southeast Asia over time to reflect a changing world, its declining capabilities and a reduced willingness from the American public and Congress to commit resources for foreign policy objectives.[4]

---

[4] For the original Guam speech, see: Richard Nixon, "Informal Remarks in Guam with Newsmen," July 25, 1969. For the 'Nixon Doctrine' speech later that year, see: Richard Nixon, "Address to the Nation on the War in Vietnam," November 3, 1969. Available online by Gerhard Peters and John T. Woolley, The American Presidency Project. Good

As administration officials were fond of telling their Southeast Asian counterparts, the principal objective was "to reverse a feeling widely shared by
Americans that the United States is over-involved...in order to avoid a
reaction which would lead to under-involvement."[5]

This task of reshaping U.S. commitment would also continue on
through the Ford as well as the early Carter administrations as well. And
beyond the vague rhetorical pledges we heard from top U.S. officials
about continued U.S. commitment, a deeper analysis of specific metrics
indicates that there were clearly dramatic changes in the level and balance
of American commitment to Southeast Asia during this period.[6]

2.1 Major Decrease in Commitment Level

U.S. commitment to Southeast Asia underwent a major decrease during
the post-Vietnam period; the product of a significant level of contractions.
This was evidenced in a series of retrenchments across the board with
respect to U.S. alliances and partnerships, military deployments, economic
engagement and diplomatic initiatives.

2.1.1 Military Deployments

Perhaps the most visible of this was a significant reduction in military
deployments. Though this happened in other cases as well, most notably
in South Korea, for Southeast Asian states the clearest manifestation
of this was in the withdrawal of U.S. troops from Vietnam as well as

analyses of the Nixon Doctrine can be found in: Heiko Meiertons, *The Doctrines of
US Security Policy: An Evaluation Under International Law* (Cambridge, UK: Cambridge
University Press, 2010), pp. 142–143; and Henry Kissinger, *Diplomacy* (New York: Simon
and Schuster, 1995), pp. 707–708. See also: Earl G. Ravenal, "The Nixon Doctrine and
our Asian Commitments," *Foreign Affairs*, January 1971.

[5] Leonard Unger, "Telegram From the Embassy in Thailand to the Department of
State (Eliot) to the President's Assistant for National Security Affairs (Kissinger): Assistant
Secretary Green's Call on NEC Chairman Thanom," Bangkok, March 10, 1972. Foreign
Relations of the United States, 1969–1976, Volume XX, Southeast Asia, 1969–1972.

[6] For an example of a rhetorical statement reiterating U.S. commitment to Southeast
Asia during the Nixon administration, see: Henry Kissinger, "America and Asia," Speech,
July 22, 1976, Seattle, Washington, DC (US Department of State, Bureau of Public
Affairs, Office of Media Services). For an example from the Ford administration, See also
Gerald R. Ford Presidential Library and Museum Website, "Address by President Gerald
R. Ford at the University of Hawaii," December 7, 1975. Available online: http://www.
fordlibrarymuseum.gov/library/speeches/750716.asp.

decreases in troop numbers in Thailand and the Philippines, which were both U.S. treaty allies.

The level of reduction in military deployments was quite dramatic from the announcement of the Nixon Doctrine. Within a year, Nixon was reporting to Congress that, in East Asia alone, reductions were at 165,000 in Vietnam; 20,000 in South Korea; 6,000 in Thailand; and 6,000 in the Philippines.[7] This would continue on out to the Carter administration in the late 1970s. Indeed, by 1978, the United States only had around 103,000 troops in East Asia, down from the highest level of just over 769,000 in 1968 and lower than the level it had had even before the outbreak of the Korean War.[8]

To be sure, the way in which these reductions in military deployments occurred differed on a case-by-case basis. In Vietnam, where the level of U.S. troops had reached a height of 543,000 troops by April 1969, a phased withdrawal of U.S. troops was conducted in fifteen announced increments between June 1969, when he saw the first reduction of 25,000 troops under Nixon, and January 1973, when the last U.S. personnel departed following the signing of the Paris Peace Accords, which marked the official end of U.S. involvement in Vietnam War. Though the process was far from linear, as illustrated by Nixon's costly intervention in Cambodia, the overall trend was unmistakable.

In Thailand, a phasedown of U.S. forces began in 1969 but was accelerated in March 1975 when the Thai government stated that it wanted all U.S. troops to be removed by March 1976 (which was then later extended to July 1976). As a result, a high of 46,277 troops in 1969 were reduced to less than 250 by July 20, 1976.[9] In the Philippines, the reduction was much less dramatic, and, amid multiple rounds of basing negotiations, the reduction was eventually from around 28,000 troops in 1968 to around 14,000 by 1979.[10]

---

[7] Richard Nixon, "Presidential Statement to Congress: Nixon's Message on Additional Foreign Aid," November 18, 1970.

[8] The Heritage Foundation, "Global US Troop Deployment Dataset, 1950–2003," October 27, 2004.

[9] General Accounting Office, "Withdrawals of US Forces From Thailand: Ways to Improve Future Withdrawal Operations," June 3, 1977.

[10] The Heritage Foundation, "Global US Troop Deployment Dataset, 1950–2003," October 27, 2004. Apart from troop withdrawals, U.S. efforts to turn over Philippine

2.1.2   Alliances and Partnerships

The post-Vietnam period also witnessed a weakening in U.S. commitments in its alliances and partnerships. Specifically, relatively speaking U.S. policymakers during this period tended to invest less in their alliances and partnerships than they needed to and were much more equivocal about their commitments than they had to be.

In terms of investment, U.S. policymakers during this period tended to prefer playing a more hands-off role in alliances and partnerships, investing less and shifting more of the burden to regional states despite the attendant risks therein and eroding the level of commitment to them. This was evident early on in the post-Vietnam period, when the Nixon Doctrine was implemented in Southeast Asia in a way that would mean a much less robust role for Washington. As one U.S. official put it in a memo in May 1971 on the U.S.-Thailand alliance, a U.S. role that placed more of an emphasis on "local initiative" while downplaying U.S. security commitment to Thailand and Bangkok's dependence on it, despite its risks, would serve U.S. interests in the post-Vietnam era of reduced U.S. interests, limited U.S. resources and congressional support, and a focus on normalizing ties with China.[11]

U.S. policymakers were also much more focused on eluding commitment tests than they were in providing reassurances to countries that they were willing to uphold them. Though U.S. policymakers of course continued to affirm the strength of these commitments in public, in private their chief concern was ensuring that provocations by their Southeast Asian allies did not put Washington's commitments to a test it might not pass and embroil the United States in conflicts in Indochina and with Beijing. A case in point was Washington's unwillingness to clarify whether its treaty commitments to the Philippines covered the Spratly Islands in the South China Sea as base negotiations were ongoing in the 1970s,

---

bases back to the Philippines was a process that begun in 1971 with the turnover of Sangley Point in September.

[11] John B. Dexter, "Thoughts on US-Thai Relations," May 12, 1971. Foreign Relations of the United States, 1969–1976, Volume XX, Southeast Asia, 1969–1972. Stamped notation on the document shows that Green saw this, and copies were circulated to other U.S. officials as well As U.S. ambassador to Thailand Leonard Unger would note, Thai policymakers clearly detected this level of U.S. commitment, which accounted for their own partial disengagement from the alliance relationship. See: Letter from the US Ambassador to Thailand (Unger) to the Assistant Secretary of State for East Asian and Pacific Affairs (Green), FRUS, 1969–1976, Volume XX, Southeast Asia 1969–1972.

despite the fact that China's conquest of the Western Paracels in January 1974 had heightened Philippine fears in this respect.[12]

This trend extended even to limiting the development of partnerships that the United States actively wanted to cultivate in line with its interests. Indonesia was a case in point. Realizing at the outset that Indonesia was a key center of power in Southeast Asia and that its leader Suharto was quite aligned with the United States on key issues, Washington did take steps to step up its engagement with Jakarta, with steps such as the setting up of a U.S.-Indonesia Joint Consultative Commission in 1975.[13] But even as U.S. policymakers sought to do so, they deliberately limited any commitments to Jakarta lest this would contradict Washington's desire to demonstrate a low posture in the region.[14]

2.1.3   Diplomatic Initiatives

The period also saw a United States that was only engaged in a limited sense in diplomatic initiatives in the region. Despite the rhetoric from U.S. policymakers, in reality, Washington was primarily focused on initiatives that were either tied closely to its own narrow interests or those that demanded a response following a crisis or prolonged neglect.

As one might expect in the post-Vietnam period, U.S. engagement was overwhelmingly focused on efforts to scale down and reshape its level of involvement in Southeast Asia. Initiatives—be they within Southeast Asia like negotiating a settlement to pull itself out of Vietnam or outside of it like normalizing relations with China—tended to consume most of the attention of U.S. policymakers, who were already working with limited bandwidth and resources. And of course, Washington was also preoccupied with responding periodic diplomatic crises in the region as well, with the Indochina refugee crisis that emerged in the mid-1970s being a case in point.

---

[12] See, for instance: Minutes of the Secretary of State's Staff Meeting, Washington, DC, January 31, 1974. Foreign Relations of the United States, 1969–1976, Volume E–12, Documents on East and Southeast Asia, 1973–1976. For the broader context within the base negotiations, see: Central Intelligence Agency, "1979 Amendment of the Military Base Agreement with the Philippines," November 1, 1983.

[13] Henry A. Kissinger, "US-Indonesia Consultative Arrangements," November 1, 1975. Volume E–12, Documents on East and Southeast Asia, 1973–1976.

[14] "Telegram From Secretary of State Rogers to the Department of State: Indonesian Reaction to Presidential Visit," Bali, August 5, 1969. Foreign Relations of the United States, 1969–1976, Volume XX, Southeast Asia, 1969–1972.

But beyond this, there were almost no instances of proactive diplomatic engagement on Washington's part. A case in point was the slow and tentative U.S. involvement in the development of Southeast Asian regionalism, which had been on the uptick with the development of the Association of Southeast Asian Nations (ASEAN). Though U.S. policymakers in the post-Vietnam period were quick to welcome ASEAN's development as a show of growing self-reliance from Southeast Asian nations as Washington's own commitment was ebbing, the Nixon and Ford administrations were slow to directly support it, even through basic moves such as the funding of ASEAN industrial projects.[15] Even under the Carter administration, when U.S. commitment to ASEAN rose, there was still the sense that Washington was too occupied with Vietnam in Southeast Asia at the expense of ASEAN, and that there was still an insufficient acknowledgment of the genuine importance of the organization regionally speaking.[16]

At times, diplomatic initiatives that the United States could undertake in Southeast Asia were subordinated to bigger concerns when seen from a narrower perspective of U.S. conduct. A case of this was normalization with Vietnam in the late 1970s. During the Carter years, efforts to pursue normalization with Hanoi, which initially held promise, were subordinated to broader concerns about China and the Soviet Union.[17] Indeed, some U.S. officials actively worked to undermine the diplomatic process of normalizing ties with Vietnam because they prioritized normalizing relations with Beijing, even though this may not have been the overall consensus position within the administration itself.[18] In private conversations among themselves, Carter administration officials admitted

---

[15] "Until at least the end of the Vietnam War, American relations with ASEAN consisted mainly of moral and verbal support for the idea of regional cooperation without a corresponding willingness to treat the five countries as a group in any other than a symbolic way." See: Kai Dreisbach, "Between SEATO and ASEAN," in: Mark Frey et al. (eds.), *The Transformation of Southeast Asia* (Armonk: Sharpe, 2003), pp. 255–256.

[16] Russel Hunt Fifield, *National and Regional Interests in ASEAN: Competition and Cooperation in International Politics* (Singapore: ISEAS, 1979), p. 69.

[17] For more on this point, see: Franklin B. Weinstein, "US-Vietnam Relations and the Security of Southeast Asia," *Foreign Affairs*, July 1978.

[18] For more on this broader 'China-first' tendency that characterized this period, see: Robert G. Sutter, *U.S.-Chinese Relations: Perilous Past, Pragmatic Present* (Lanham, MD: Rowman & Littlefield, 2010), p. 81.

that their reluctance to be involved in such initiatives was due to the low priority attached to the region and the limited resources that Washington would have to follow through.[19]

2.1.4   Economic Engagement

The post-Vietnam period also saw a more tentative approach to U.S. economic engagement with Southeast Asian states. Even though Southeast Asian states were looking for more U.S. engagement in the 1970s with a variety of issues—including slow growth, rising unemployment, and inflation—and the United States did recognize the subregion's growing importance, Washington's own economic woes, coupled with strong protectionist tendencies, created a challenging environment that made it difficult to even keep existing commitments, let alone negotiate new ones.[20]

U.S. policymakers understood the reality of Southeast Asia's economic importance to the United States and the broader region. Indeed, through the Nixon, Ford and Carter administrations, U.S. policymakers comprehended that as U.S. economic linkages were being increasingly tied with Asia than with Europe, Southeast Asia's longtime role as a source of key commodities and as a region of significant growth potential began to play out, albeit in a slow and uneven way across countries.[21] The statistics during this period bear this out. Trade-wise, U.S. exports to ASEAN increased from about $1 billion in 1970 to $6.8 billion in 1979, an annual growth rate of 22.4% for the 1970s which made it the fifth-largest U.S.

[19] See: Michael Oksenberg, "China Policy Since Mid-1978," December 19, 1980. Foreign Relations of the United States, 1977–1980, Volume XIII, China. Oksenberg admits "the low priority we attached to the region at the time" and the resource problem for following through on major diplomatic initiatives. These factors, he says, led to the U.S. decision to let ASEAN take the lead on the Indochina situation.

[20] For a broader, contextual explanation of this point, see: Cheong Kee Cheok, "Review of the Southeast Asian Economies, 1979," Southeast Asian Affairs 1980 (Singapore: Institute of Southeast Asian Studies, 1979).

[21] For a more in-depth look at the variations between countries, see: Lawrence B. Krause, U.S. Economic Policy Towards the Association of Southeast Asian Nations: Meeting the Japanese Challenge (Washington, DC: The Bookings Institution, 1982).

trade partner.[22] Investment also rose, with U.S. government data indicating that service business in ASEAN countries rose from around $60 million in 1966 to $92 million in 1977.[23]

But the recognition of that reality did not remove the constraints that U.S. policymakers had in trying to pursue further economic engagement. Indeed, repeatedly during this period, U.S. policymakers would reiterate to their Southeast Asian counterparts in private—even key allies and partners—the familiar refrain that the domestic situation made it difficult for the United States to even sustain its current level of economic assistance, let alone undertake fresh economic incentives. U.S. policymakers during this period tended to expend considerable time just resolving a number of economic concerns among Southeast Asian states to prevent ties from worsening further, be it cuts to various forms of assistance including Public Law 480 (PL 480); exclusion from the Generalized System of Preferences (GSP); and acquiring Most-Favored Nation (MFN) status for commodities.

To be sure, there were certain instances where U.S. policymakers were able to secure funding despite these challenges. Particularly during the Carter administration, where Southeast Asian states were viewed through the broader lens of Washington's desire to improve relations with developing countries and North–South relations, there were also some initiatives advanced.[24] This included the setting up of the U.S.-ASEAN Business Council, investment missions by Overseas Private Investment Corporation (OPIC) and the Export–Import Bank (EXIM Bank), as well as the addressing of some commodity issues which were important to Indonesia and Malaysia.[25] But protectionism still largely continued to

[22] Data calculated from International Monetary Fund Direction of Trade statistics.

[23] Data from U.S. Department of Commerce censuses taken abroad for years 1966 and 1977, which provide an estimate of the growth of U.S. service business in ASEAN countries.

[24] Indeed, in some of the administration's explanations of its policy, diplomacy with ASEAN states was grouped under the heading of "The Developing Countries," with issues such as the North–South Dialogue and the Conference of International Economic Cooperation (CIEC). See, for instance: Jimmy Carter, "Public Papers of the Presidents of the United States," 1978, p. 120.

[25] Edward E. Masters, "Telegram From the Embassy in Indonesia to the Department of State: Conference of the US Ambassadors to ASEAN," Jakarta, April 24, 1979. Foreign Relations of the United States, 1977–1980, Volume XXII, Southeast Asia and the Pacific.

Table 1 Summary of Findings on Commitment Level in the Post-Vietnam Period

Category	Choices	Finding
Military deployments	Expanded or reduced?	Reduced
Alliances and partnerships	Strengthened or weakened?	Weakened
Diplomatic initiatives	Active, reactive, or inactive?	Largely reactive
Economic engagement	Increased or decreased?	Decreased
Overall level	Increased or decreased?	Major decrease

Source Generated by Author

limit economic engagement on trade and investment in general as well as on specific issues.[26]

In sum, with reduced military deployments, weakened alliances and partnerships, largely reactive diplomatic initiatives and a relatively depressed level of economic engagement despite the best efforts of policy-makers, it was clear that U.S. commitment level to Southeast Asia during the period had experienced a major decrease, as illustrated by Table 1.

2.2   Major Decrease in Commitment Balance

Apart from a low level of commitment, there was also a major decrease in commitment balance during the post-Vietnam period as well. Specifically, all of the five areas set out in this study saw a shift toward greater imbalance within them, most of them quite significant.

2.2.1   Means/Ends

The first imbalance was seen with respect to means and ends. In theory, U.S. policymakers in the immediate post-Vietnam era, as Nixon and Kissinger were fond of repeating, were aiming to use less available means

Letter of Secretary Vance to General Romulo, Washington, DC, 19 August 1978. As seen in: Pamphlet on The Second US-ASEAN Summit, ISEAS, Singapore.

[26] Ronald D. Palmer and Thomas J. Reckford, *Building ASEAN: 20 Years of Southeast Asian Cooperation* (New York, 1987), especially discussions in pp. 47 and 134–135.

to serve more limited ends.[27] In practice, however, U.S. policymakers in the Nixon, Ford and Carter administrations all found that the means were not quite available even for the more limited ends that they sought, creating an imbalance that was difficult to address.

Throughout the post-Vietnam period, U.S. policymakers grappled with this imbalance between available means and intended ends. This manifested itself in several forms, including restrictions to ongoing foreign assistance, scrutiny over existing American security commitments to its allies and partners, and even outright Congressional overriding or undermining of key military decisions that were made by the executive branch.

Whether it be finding ways to support Thai forces in Laos or accept more Indochinese refugees by getting around restrictions or contending with the Symington Committee scrutinizing U.S. defense commitments, the post-Vietnam era was replete with cases of deep constraints. Often, these constraints were so severe such that it seemed that instead of getting from defining ends to then summoning the necessary means, U.S. policy-makers were instead forced to do things in reverse; starting from limited budgets to then determining what manpower they had and then piecing together some sort of approach.[28]

The imbalance between means and ends was clearly recognized by U.S. Asia hands and by Southeast Asian states alike. In a fairly typical assessment of U.S. Asia policy during the period, Philip Habib, the U.S. Assistant Secretary of State for East Asian and Pacific Affairs, noted upon his return from a Southeast Asia trip in June 1975 that in every country, there was a uniform desire to see the United States play a role in the region but "a deep suspicion that the U.S. will fail to provide the type financial and security resources the ASEAN countries perceive as essential." "It's going to take some resources," Habib admitted in assessing whether Washington could fulfill this role. "And I think it is going to take both economic and military resources".[29]

---

[27] For works with broader discussions on this point, see: Franz Schurmann, *The Foreign Politics of Richard Nixon: The Grand Design*, 3 vols (Berkeley: University of California, Institute of International Studies, 1987); Robert E. Osgood, *Retreat From Empire? The First Nixon Administration* (Baltimore: Johns Hopkins University Press, 1973).

[28] Earl G. Ravenal, "The Nixon Doctrine and Our Asian Commitments," *Foreign Affairs*, January 1971.

[29] Minutes of the Acting Secretary of State's Staff Meeting, Washington, DC, June 13, 1975, 8–9:05 a.m. https://history.state.gov/historicaldocuments/frus1969-76ve12/d15.

2.2.2   Interests/Ideals

There were also clear imbalances between ideals and interests during the
post-Vietnam period. Though there were moderations over time, within
the period of less than a decade, there was initially a clear tilt toward a
focus on interests during the Nixon administration, but then a dramatic
reversal toward a focus on ideals during the initial Carter years.

The Nixon and Ford administrations saw a clear tilt toward a focus
on narrow national interests. Under both administrations, it was clear
that the promotion of American ideals was of secondary priority to the
pursuit of American interests.[30] As Kissinger put it during a July 1975
speech during the Ford presidency, though the United States needed
moral strength and a sense of purpose to navigate its way in a complex
and turbulent world, it also needed "a mature sense of means" lest it
"substitute wishful thinking for the requirements of survival."[31]

In Southeast Asia, the United States during this period saw no issue in
supporting strongmen in the region that were seen as critical geopolitical
allies, be it Suharto in Indonesia or Ferdinand Marcos in the Philippines.
But Washington also tended to turn a blind eye to democracy and human
rights flashpoints when they occurred.[32] A case in point was the Indonesian annexation of East Timor in 1975, which the Ford administration
knew about ahead of time but did not act on despite this fact.[33]

Under the Carter administration, by contrast, things were tilted toward
ideals. Carter not only emphasized human rights and democracy, but

[30] Michael Stohl, David Carleton, and Steven E. Johnson, "Human Rights and U.S.
Foreign Assistance from Nixon to Carter," *Journal of Peace Research*, Vol. 21, No. 3
(September 1984), pp. 215–226.

[31] Henry A. Kissinger, "The Moral Foundations of Foreign Policy," Address by Secretary Kissinger at Minneapolis, July 15, 1975, Department of State Bulletin, No. 1884
(August 4, 1975), pp. 161–172.

[32] In fact, Nixon tended to warn about the perils of democracy imposition with respect
to both cases. For Nixon warning about not imposing democracy on the Philippines, see:
"Memorandum of Conversation San Clemente, February 10, 1973, 10:05–11:30 a.m.:
Vice-President Agnew's Return from His Southeast Asian Trip," Foreign Relations of the
United States, 1969–1976, Volume E-12, Documents on East and Southeast Asia, 1973–
1976. For his take on the U.S. need to keep Suharto in power despite concerns, see:
"322: Editorial Note," in Foreign Relations of the United States, 1969–1976, Volume
XX, Southeast Asia, 1969–1972.

[33] William Burr and Michael L. Evans (eds.), "East Timor Revisited: Ford, Kissinger,
and the Indonesian Invasion, 1975–76," National Security Archive Electronic Briefing
Book No. 62, December 6, 2001.

made it, in his words, "a fundamental tenet of our foreign policy."[34] The setting up of new institutions such as the Bureau of Democracy, Rights, and Labor (DRL) in 1977 and the Interagency Group of Human Rights and Foreign Assistance (called the Christopher Group) by the NSC to examine military and economic assistance proposals showed that this tendency directly impacted decision-making in the administration. There was also clearly both a greater concern for humanitarian issues, such as the worsening Indochina refugee crisis, as well as more scrutiny on human rights practices of states like Indonesia and the Philippines.

Yet the tilt toward ideals over interests was not nearly as dramatic of an imbalance as is often portrayed in more superficial accounts. Opposition from other departments and bureaus, including the State Department, over time led to a more calibrated, case-by-case approach in dealing with rights concerns, leading to more moderation in the criticism of strategically significant countries like the Philippines.[35] And there were some striking exceptions made beyond this period, most notably when Carter elected to support Pol Pot's United Nations recognition bid for his genocidal government in exile for fear of angering Beijing and disrupting the normalization process.[36] Nonetheless, though the implementation was far messier than the rhetoric suggested, the general trend here was unmistakable.

2.2.3   Cooperative/Confrontational

A second clear imbalance in the post-Vietnam period was the one favoring a cooperative over a confrontational approach to American adversaries and competitors. During this period, as part of a broader effort to shape a balance of power in a more multipolar world that was more favorable to the United States, U.S. policymakers were pursuing détente toward the

[34] Jimmy Carter, Speech at Notre Dame University, Jimmy Carter, Public Papers of the Presidents of the United States: Jimmy Carter, Vol. 1 (1977), 954.

[35] The strongest opposition within the State Department against rights advocate Patricia Derian came from Holbrooke. After Derian traveled to the Philippines in early 1978 and criticized Marcos, Holbrooke persuaded the White House to send Mondale to Manila to smooth maters over with the Philippine leader.

[36] Burton Ira Kaufman, "Presidential Profiles: The Carter Years," 2006. pp. 154–156.

Soviet Union, opening ties with China, and, later on, even exploring the possibility of normalizing relations with Vietnam.[37]

This imbalance in favor of cooperation over confrontation meant boldly exploring opportunities for collaboration with these adversaries and competitors, which had significant implications for Southeast Asia. Southeast Asian leaders witnessed a succession of events of note on this score in quick succession, which included Nixon's historic visit to China, the continued pursuit of détente with the USSR, including Strategic Arms Limitations Talks/Treaty (SALT), and normalization talks with Vietnam that were opened in 1977 before stalling.

But the imbalance of cooperation over confrontation also manifested itself in what the United States did not do with its allies and partners in Southeast Asia. Most prominently for Southeast Asian states, U.S. policymakers were repeatedly concerned that any security moves they made, even basic ones such as robustly supporting their allies and partners in the region, would jeopardize a more cooperative relationship with China. As Robert Sutter notes, this was part of a broader trend during the period where U.S. leaders focused on "doing what was needed to advance the new China relationship and gave secondary attention to longstanding U.S. allies and other close relationships in East Asia or manipulated them in ways that would accord with the China-first emphasis in U.S. policy".[38]

To be sure, the imbalance of cooperation over confrontation, as with the other imbalances in this period, is not as extreme as it might seem. The United States was not afraid to use force when necessary against its adversaries, as evidenced by Ford's decision to send a rescue mission after Khmer Rouge forces seized the U.S. container ship *Mayaguez* in May 1975 as well as Nixon's bombing of Cambodia earlier in the decade. U.S. policymakers also were still conscious of gains that American adversaries were making even as they refused to abandon their cooperative endeavors, be it Soviet access to Sembawang Naval Base in Singapore or China's taking of the Paracel Islands.[39]

---

[37] Evelyn Goh, "Nixon, Kissinger, and the Soviet Card in the U.S. Opening to China, 1971–1974," *Diplomatic History*, Vol. 29, No. 3 (June 2005), p. 475.

[38] Robert G. Sutter, *U.S.-Chinese Relations: Perilous Past, Pragmatic Present* (Lanham, MD: Rowman & Littlefield, 2010), p. 81.

[39] A review was conducted on U.S.-Singapore relations in part due to Soviet concerns. See: "Memorandum From W.R. Smyser of the National Security Council Staff to Secretary of State Kissinger, Washington, DC, January 30, 1975: Proposed NSSM on US Military

Nonetheless, the non-communist Southeast Asian states in particular clearly and nervously noted this imbalance in favor of cooperation over cooperation and what that meant for U.S. commitment to the region. Summarizing their views in a trip report following his return from an Asia trip in April 1977, Richard Holbrooke wrote that these nations "fear we are moving into an era of concentration solely on the communist adversary nations, including China and Vietnam, and the trilateral nations."[40] While the view of China as an "adversary" was not as evident in the earlier part of the period, evolved over time, and was not shared equally strongly by members of the administration, the pattern within the broader balance between cooperation and conflict was nonetheless quite clear.

2.2.4   Bilateralism/Multilateralism

The third imbalance was the one in favor of multilateralism over bilateralism. Though Washington did focus its attention on cultivating ties with allies like Thailand and the Philippines and partners such as Indonesia and Singapore, there was a tilt in favor of multilateralism that was evident as well. U.S. policymakers recognized this as a way to conserve resources, to cultivate self-reliance among states and to deal with complex problems in what was perceived to be a more multipolar world.

This tilt toward multilateralism was admittedly less prominent during the Nixon and Ford years. Even here, though, we clearly did see instances of this. In his second foreign policy report to Congress in February 1971, Nixon devoted an entire section to Asian multilateralism, noting that "Asian regionalism has an essential role to play in the future structure of Asia." The report contained specific examples of this that Washington was involved in, whether it be the attention to subregional cooperation among Mekong countries, contributions to the World Bank or involvement in the Intergovernmental Group for Indonesia.[41]

Access to Singapore," Foreign Relations of the United States, 1969–1976, Volume E-12, Documents on East and Southeast Asia, 1973–1976.

[40] Richard Holbrooke, "Briefing Memorandum From the Assistant Secretary of State for East Asian and Pacific Affairs (Holbrooke) to Secretary of State Vance: My Trip to Asia," Washington, DC, April 21, 1977, Foreign Relations of the United States, 1977 1980, Volume XXII, Southeast Asia and the Pacific.

[41] For Nixon's remarks on Asian regionalism, see: Richard Nixon, "US Foreign Policy for the 1970s, a Report to the Congress," February 25, 1971.

During the Carter years, this imbalance intensified further. The Carter administration did not just see multilateral approaches as a way to manage challenges, such as the economic concerns of Southeast Asian states or the Indochina refugee crisis, but as an opportunity to support Southeast Asian regionalism more vigorously.[42] Most notably, U.S. support for ASEAN, which was largely only at the rhetorical stage during the Nixon and Ford years, under Carter was given some reality, particularly with the commencement of the U.S.-ASEAN Dialogue which was first held in 1977, with the second iteration held in Washington, DC the following year.[43]

2.2.5   Security/Economics

There was also an imbalance in favor of economics over security in the post-Vietnam period. While it was certainly true that U.S. policymakers were trying to cobble together resources for the realization of limited commitments in both the economic and security domains, it was also true that there was a tilt toward a focus on the economic realm, particularly given the recent withdrawal from the Vietnam War.

The focus on the economic domain was evident in the areas of prioritization under the Carter administration. Despite resource constraints, under the Nixon administration, U.S. policymakers sought creative avenues to secure some economic assistance for allies and partners and backed Asian-led institutions and proposals for regional and subregional development. Under the Carter administration, there were also some additional efforts made in terms of promoting stabilization in commodity prices, the dispatching of aid for ASEAN industrial projects and the sending of investment missions to Southeast Asian states.[44]

This focus and creativity were less evident in the security realm. To be sure, policymakers still worked hard to retain a military footprint in

---

[42] Zbigniew Brzezinski, Memorandum From the President's Assistant for National Security Affairs (Brzezinski) to Secretary of State Vance: Indochinese Refugees, Washington, DC, November 9, 1977. Foreign Relations of the United States, 1977–1980, Volume XXII, Southeast Asia and the Pacific.

[43] Letter of Secretary Vance to General Romulo, Washington, DC, August 19, 1978. As seen in: Pamphlet on The Second US-ASEAN Summit, ISEAS, Singapore.

[44] A lot of focus on economic issues in the Second US-ASEAN Dialogue 1978. Letter of Secretary Vance to General Romulo, Washington, DC, August 19, 1978. As seen in: Pamphlet on The Second US-ASEAN Summit, ISEAS, Singapore.

Table 2 Summary of Findings on Commitment Balance in the Post-Vietnam Period

Category	Choices	Finding
Means/ends	Are resources commensurate with goals and objectives?	Imbalance (no means)
Interests/ideals	Is attention on ideals or more narrowly on core interests?	Imbalance (both sides)
Cooperative/confrontational	Is approach to adversaries and competitors cooperative or confrontational?	Imbalance (cooperative)
Bilateralism/multilateralism	Is bilateral & unilateral or multilateral approach favored?	Imbalance (multilateral)
Security/economics	Is there a greater attention on security or economics?	Imbalance (economics)
Overall balance	Increase or decrease	Major decrease

Source Generated by Author

the Philippines, provided assistance to allies and partners to the extent possible and even agreed to some new initiatives such as setting up a plant in Indonesia for Southeast Asian military modernization.[45] Yet the focus was primarily on preserving the remnants of a declining U.S. military presence rather than advancing new ideas to strengthen it. And unlike the economic domain, several of the ideas floated did not end up materializing in practice and translating from rhetoric into reality.

In sum, U.S. commitment to Southeast Asia during the post-Vietnam period saw a major decrease in commitment balance, with all five of the five categories witnessing changes toward imbalances. Despite the best efforts of U.S. policymakers, calibration proved to be elusive given the domestic and international environment that they were operating in (Table 2).

[45] John H. Holdridge, "Memorandum From John H. Holdridge of the National Security Council Staff to the President's Assistant for National Security Affairs (Kissinger): Indonesian Request for U.S. Assistance in Furthering Southeast Asian Regional Military Cooperation," Washington, DC, October 13, 1970.

3   EXPLAINING U.S. COMMITMENT
DURING THE POST-VIETNAM PERIOD

Having detailed the shape of U.S. commitment during the post-Vietnam period, where commitment level and balance both underwent major decreases, we can now move to explaining how and why this occurred. This section argues that, as the balance of commitment model would predict, we witnessed a case where a decline in U.S. relative power, mediated by a low threat perception as well as low state capacity, accounted for major decreases in U.S. commitment level and balance in Southeast Asia.

3.1   Minor Decrease in Relative Power

The distribution of military and economic power between the United States and its competitors both globally and regionally certainly played into the shape of its commitment during this period. U.S. policymakers recognized that as U.S. relative power had undergone a minor decrease materially speaking given the post-Vietnam realities, they were living in an increasingly multipolar world, and that such a reality called for the United States to adjust to a new equilibrium premised on an understanding of the limits of its own power. That affected both the level and the distribution of U.S. commitment to Southeast Asia.

Despite their disagreements, U.S. policymakers through the Nixon, Ford and Carter years all perceived that the world was becoming more multipolar and that U.S. power was in relative decline. These administrations understood that the ascendance of Western Europe, Germany and Japan had created more centers of world power; the split in the communist world between the Soviet Union and an increasingly influential China had shattered simplistic notions of bipolarity; and that the emergence of new nations in the developing world had added complexity to the world.

They also comprehended the fact that the combination of U.S. economic problems at home and shrinking defense spending in the face of Soviet advances meant that Washington had to deal with a more complex world.[46] As Kissinger put it in December 1969, the challenge

---

[46] U.S. defense spending shrunk significantly in the 1970s from 8.1.% of GDP in 1970 to 4.9% in 1977 even as Soviet defense spending increased dramatically, reaching parity in surface combatants with the U.S. navy (except for carriers) and growing the Red

was "helping to build international relations on a basis which may be less unilaterally American".[47] He also later reflected in his book *Diplomacy* that the broad context for the post-Vietnam period was that a major reassessment of U.S. foreign policy was required "for the age of America's nearly total dominance of the world stage was drawing to a close."[48]

Southeast Asia was not exempt from this view. U.S. policymakers felt that the Vietnam War had done nothing less than fundamentally distort their view of Asia, and that, in the wake of declining capabilities and changing realities, they had to rescale their commitments to take advantage of bigger opportunities in the region including the Sino-Soviet split—part of a broader notion of how "triangular diplomacy" was perceived especially under the Nixon administration.[49] And given the growing emergence of nations within Southeast Asia as well as other key external powers, they sought to create more balanced and diversified relationships that tied countries within the region together and connected them to multiple centers of power including the United States.[50]

That in turn affected both the level of U.S. commitment as well as its distribution. With respect to its level, it was clear that this meant that there would be some decline in the overall level of U.S. commitment in some areas as the United States, as Kissinger noted, would seek to "navigate between overextension and abdication," with that vacuum filled by other powers as well as by Southeast Asian states themselves.[51] As Nixon

Army to over twice the size of the U.S. army Michael J. Green, *By More Than Providence: Grand Strategy and American Power in the Asia–Pacific Since 1783* (New York: Columbia University Press, 2017), pp. 363–364; Sheldon Simon, *The ASEAN States and Regional Security* (Stanford, CA: Hoover Institution Press, 1982), pp. 114–115; Melvyn Leffler, *For the Soul of Mankind: The United States, the Soviet Union, and the Cold War* (New York: Hill and Wang, 2007), p. 263.

[47] White House Background Press Briefing by the President's Assistant for National Security Affairs (Kissinger), December 18, 1969. https://history.state.gov/historicaldocuments/frus1969-76v01/d47.

[48] Henry Kissinger, *Diplomacy* (New York: Simon & Schuster, 1994), p. 703.

[49] As Nixon put it, "The war in Vietnam has for so long dominated our field of vision that it has distorted our picture of Asia. A small country on the rim of the continent has filled the screen of our minds; but it does not fill the map." See: Richard M. Nixon, "Asia After Viet Nam," *Foreign Affairs*, October 1967

[50] Office of the Historian, "Foreign Relations of the United States, 1969–1976, Volume 1: Foundations of Foreign Policy, 1969–1972."

[51] Henry Kissinger, *Diplomacy* (New York: Simon & Schuster, 1994), p. 708.

clarified to Philippine Foreign Secretary Carlos P. Romulo in 1973, Washington's view was that though other external powers like Japan might be able to fill any perceived vacuum left by the United States, the main U.S. objective was to "help others to help themselves."[52] During the post-Vietnam period, U.S. policymakers would repeatedly wrestle with the balance of committing just enough resources—be it in terms of troops, assistance or diplomatic support—for Southeast Asian states to help themselves but not too much such that it would run contrary to the U.S. objective of maintaining a lower profile.[53]

It also meant that there would be some hesitancy on the part of U.S. policymakers to increase their commitment level in some areas given their worldview. For instance, in their pursuit of closer ties with China, which was a key priority, U.S. policymakers tended to play up positive changes in Beijing's conduct, downplay worrying signs and hesitate in undertaking moves with allies and partners that might be seen as jeopardizing these ties. Repeatedly during this period, top U.S. policymakers elected not to pursue what were perceived as more assertive positions such as heavily arming Thailand to play a stronger military role in Southeast Asia or firmly backing the Philippines in its South China Sea claims because they tended to conclude that Beijing currently did not have an intention of undertaking actions hostile to the United States and that the main impetus for such actions would be provocations by the United States, either directly or through emboldened allies.[54]

[52] "Memorandum of Conversation, Washington, DC, January 5, 1973, 3:30 p.m." Washington, DC, January 5, 1973. Foreign Relations of the United States, 1969–1976, Volume E-12, Documents on East and Southeast Asia, 1973–1976.

[53] For an example of fears of overcommitting financial resources to the U.S.-Indonesia relationship, see: "Telegram From Secretary of State Rogers to the Department of State: Indonesian Reaction to Presidential Visit," Bali, August 5, 1969. Foreign Relations of the United States, 1969–1976, Volume XX, Southeast Asia, 1969–1972. For an example of fears of overcommitting diplomatic attention to Southeast Asia, see: W. Richard Smyser, "Memorandum from W.R. Smyser of the National Security Council Staff to Secretary of State Kissinger: The Situation in Asia," Washington, DC, July 15, 1975, Foreign Relations of the United States, 1969–1976, Volume E-12, Documents on East and Southeast Asia, 1973–1976.

[54] John B. Dexter, "Thoughts on US-Thai Relations," May 12, 1971. Foreign Relations of the United States, 1969–1976, Volume XX, Southeast Asia, 1969–1972.

With respect to commitment balance, it was also clear that this could lead to several imbalances in the shape of U.S. commitment in Southeast Asia as well. Greater U.S. comfort with a more multipolar world and a heavier focus on exploiting fissures within the communist bloc meant there was likely to be a tilt toward cooperation rather than confrontation with U.S. adversaries like China and the Soviet Union, irrespective of what might look like worrying behavior by Beijing and Moscow to Southeast Asian states.[55] It also meant that a more low-profile United States may seek to either invest more in a few bilateral alliances and partnerships to get a better bang for its buck or place more of an emphasis on multilateral initiatives with other major powers and indigenous ASEAN states to share the burden. As Nixon put it, the future of the United States' role in Asia was rooted in the broader context of two pillars for the region's prospects: "the collective interests of Asian nations acting in regional groupings, and the policies of the four major powers concerned with the region."[56]

But although relative power does give us a sense of the broad thinking behind and general contours of U.S. commitment to Southeast Asia as balance of power theory would expect, it tells us much less about the specifics of the level and balance of that commitment based on the metrics laid out in the preceding section. For a better sense of how U.S. policymakers reacted to opportunities and challenges they faced domestically, regionally and globally during this period as well as how they managed the limited military, economic, political and diplomatic resources at their disposal, we need to delve into their calculations about power and threats (threat level) as well as their ability to mobilize resources (state capacity)—the two intervening variables that are key to the balance of commitment model.

[55] As Richard Holbrooke wrote on his inaugural Asia trip in April 1977, Southeast Asian states perceived that the United States was "moving into an era of concentration solely on the communist adversary nations, including China and Vietnam, and the trilateral nations." See: "Trip Report," Washington, DC, April 21, 1977, Foreign Relations of the United States, 1977–1980, Volume XXII, Southeast Asia and the Pacific.

[56] See: Richard M. Nixon, "Second Annual Report to Congress on United States Foreign Policy," February 25, 1971.

3.2   Low Threat Level

While the relative distribution of capabilities no doubt played a role in shaping U.S. commitment to Southeast Asia during this post-Vietnam period, this was also filtered through the lens of elite calculations about power and threats, or, put more simply, threat level. Specifically, during this period, we witnessed a low threat level among the U.S. foreign policy elite with respect to Southeast Asia. This trend of low threat perceptions continued on through most of period, at times despite events that ran to the contrary to what was the belief among U.S. policymakers who were familiar with regional developments as well as Southeast Asian observers.

For most of this period, U.S. policymakers saw the threat level in Southeast Asia, and relatedly, the broader region and world, as being low, and this would not change even as some realities did. Globally, as was mentioned in the previous section, the Nixon, Ford and Carter administrations espoused a general worldview premised on low threat levels, where, despite their differences, the world's major powers could work together for global peace and stability.[57] Indeed, it was this line of thinking that led them to reduce America's commitments overseas while also extending an olive branch to Washington's two communist enemies—China and then the Soviet Union. Throughout this period, U.S. policymakers sought to create a broader framework for international cooperation with allies and adversaries in a rapidly changing world that attempted to transcend past divides.

This worldview affected how U.S. policymakers assessed opportunities and challenges in the post-Vietnam war context. Broadly speaking, such a low threat level tended to be relatively more accepting of greater autonomy and some animosity in U.S. relations with allies, partners and friends in the context of a reduced U.S. presence and a more complex world; more tolerant of gains made by China and the USSR in a context of multipolarity; and more tentative about the U.S. role in the context of economic turmoil and political transitions which were viewed as both

---

[57] For instance, Nixon spoke of an "enduring structure of peace" between major powers, while Carter spoke of an effort "to create a wider framework of international cooperation suited to the new and rapidly changing historical circumstances." See: Richard M. Nixon, "Second Annual Report to Congress on United States Foreign Policy," February 25, 1971; Jimmy Carter, "Address at Commencement Exercises at the University of Notre Dame," May 22, 1977.

partly cyclical in nature and more a consequence of structural conditions in countries and regions rather than anything that Washington had control over.[58]

Southeast Asia was not immune from this worldview during this period.[59] Reactions to U.S. withdrawals in Southeast Asia, including greater independence and even partial disengagement by U.S. allies and partners that generated alarm in ASEAN capitals, were read as not being as dramatic or not concerning since there was still demand for Washington's presence. Chinese and Soviet gains—be it the Soviets seeking more naval access in Southeast Asia or the Chinese inroads with respect to the Paracels—were viewed as less worrisome, both given the significant inroads the United States had made in terms of normalization with China (which Beijing would be keen to preserve and was at Moscow's expense) and the belief that Washington should not undertake moves that would jeopardize relations with China. And issues that Southeast Asian countries faced, including economic upheaval and domestic insurgencies, were seen more as internal issues for them to sort out rather than problems the United States could help address.[60]

Winston Lord, then the director of the Policy Planning Staff at the Department of Defense, captured this well in one of his assessments of the region, delivered six months after the fall of Saigon which had generated serious anxiety in Southeast Asia and could have generated a rethink among U.S. policymakers. At a time when Southeast Asian states were facing economic turmoil and were seriously questioning their alignment choices, Lord wrote in October 1975 that while the U.S. position in Southeast Asia was being transformed, "our basic interests are not in serious jeopardy," with ASEAN states eager to keep the United States

---

[58] For a reflection of this line of thinking, see: Central Intelligence Agency, "National Intelligence Estimate: Southeast Asia After Vietnam," November 1968.

[59] Robert J. McMahon, *The Limits of Empire: The United States and Southeast Asia Since World War II* (New York: Columbia University Press, 1999), p. 185.

[60] For a broader explication of this view, see: Melvin Gurtov, "Southeast Asia After Withdrawal from Vietnam," RAND Corporation, 1970. Reflecting this point of view, Gurtov argued that Southeast Asia would continue to endure tests, and that the special character of each country's history, social, and economic conditions and politics would provide the setting for these tests that they would then endure—and these were areas over which all major foreign powers can have little control. Seen from this perspective, Gurtov argued, even a dramatic withdrawal would not have catastrophic consequences.

involved politically and economically.[61] He then went on to downplay threats posed by the USSR and China in what he himself termed an "upbeat assessment," arguing that while the Soviets may have gained in Southeast Asia, they were losing as much in Northeast Asia, and that though China had doubted U.S. political will and staying power, "the strategic factors underlying the PRC's interest in closer ties with us remain valid."

That in turn affected both the level of U.S. commitment as well as its balance. With respect to its level, a lower threat perception meant that U.S. policymakers were more risk-prone with respect to reducing the level of commitment in Southeast Asia militarily, economically and diplomatically, which they tended to justify through various means, be it their skepticism about the capacity of other competing powers to fill it or a greater confidence in the ability of resident ASEAN countries to individually and collectively work to fill the gaps as well. This was a belief that was hard to shake even amid growing regional anxiety. Even after the fall of Saigon, periodic regional assessments continued to insist that U.S. withdrawal from the region was gradual and sufficiently coordinated enough to not threaten U.S. interests, with some Southeast Asian states willing to pick up the slack and Moscow and Beijing both continuing to face challenges of their own.[62] U.S. policymakers repeatedly referenced that a rough equilibrium among major powers was being preserved instead of drawing attention to specific relative gains made in certain areas.[63]

Low threat level also affected the balance of U.S. commitment to Southeast Asia as well. It played into the inclinations of U.S. policymakers to tilt more toward cooperative rather than confrontational views with respect to their adversaries and competitors, whether it be Beijing, Moscow, or even Hanoi at some stages following the Vietnam War. It also

[61] Winston Lord, Memorandum from the Director of the Policy Planning Staff (Lord) to Secretary of State Kissinger, Washington, DC, October 16, 1975: US Strategy in Asia: Trends, Issues, and Choices," Foreign Relations of the United States, 1969–1976, Volume E-12, Documents on East and Southeast Asia, 1973–1976.

[62] Memorandum from W.R. Smyser of the National Security Council Staff to Secretary of State Kissinger, Washington, DC, July 15, 1975.

[63] See: "Memorandum From Michael Armacost and Michel Oksenberg of the National Security Council Staff to the President's Assistant for National Security Affairs (Brzezinski) and the President's Deputy Assistant for National Security Affairs (Aaron): East and Southeast Asian Policy," February 18, 1977, Foreign Relations of the United States, 1977–1980, Volume XXII, Southeast Asia and the Pacific.

gave them greater room to pursue multilateral initiatives, which, though they required less resources, also needed more time and effort to play out and were riskier bets to make relative to bilateral ones with U.S. alliances and partnerships where Washington exerted more control. Lastly, in some cases, it even afforded U.S. policymakers an opportunity to focus more on democracy and human rights, as was the case under the Carter administration. As Bilahari Kausikan, one of Singapore's most prominent diplomats during his tenure in government, has recounted, strategic realities have occasionally had the habit of disciplining American ideological tendencies on this score in practice.[64]

3.3 Low State Capacity

The other filter in the balance of commitment model, in addition to threat perceptions, is state capacity. During the post-Vietnam period, we witnessed a period of low state capacity where it was difficult for U.S. policymakers to mobilize resources for their intended goals. Specifically, increased congressional activism and a war-weary public combined to produce an environment of low institutional cohesion and low elite autonomy, which made it difficult for the foreign policy elite to get the commensurate capability and willingness to keep old commitments, let alone pursue new commitments as well.

The post-Vietnam period saw a trend where the power of the executive branch was curtailed by several forces at home, most notably public opinion and congressional activism. Though the trend reached its peak in the early 1970s, with domestic protests rocking the United States, Congress passing the War Powers Resolution following the Nixon administration's bombing of Cambodia and Nixon himself resigning following the Watergate scandal, public scrutiny and legislative curbs on the executive branch to use military force and dole out economic and security assistance persisted through the Ford and Carter years too.[65] As a

---

[64] See: Bilahari Kausikan, "The Myth of Universality: The Geopolitics of Human Rights," in *Dealing With an Ambiguous World* (Singapore: World Scientific, 2017), p. 113.

[65] Andrew L. Johns. *Vietnam's Second Front: Domestic Politics, the Republican Party, and the War* (Lexington: The University Press of Kentucky, 2010), pp. 293–294. This led Kissinger to famously fret that things would have turned out differently "if we didn't have this damn domestic situation." Henry Kissinger, *Years of Upheaval* (Boston, 1982).

result, the scholar Richard Melanson wrote, "After Vietnam, presidents delivered their foreign policy messages in a domestic environment of relative dissensus."[66] Noting this level of dissensus, Kissinger himself later reflected extensively in his own book, *Diplomacy*, that the post-Vietnam period constituted the "most fractious domestic circumstances since the Civil War."[67]

Low state capacity contributed to both the level and balance of the U.S. commitment to Southeast Asia. In terms of the level, given both a climate where it was difficult to get the necessary public approval and legislative authorization for resources as well as the fact that Southeast Asia had been so tied to a previous period of perceived overcommitment with the Vietnam War, it was no surprise that we now saw reductions in the level of U.S. military, diplomatic and economic engagement to varying degrees to Southeast Asia.

For instance, low state capacity made resource extraction and mobilization much more difficult. In private discussions among themselves and in conversations with Southeast Asian states, U.S. officials repeatedly mentioned that protectionist sentiment, economic difficulties and Congressional scrutiny had meant restrictions on both economic and military assistance. This applied not just to U.S. manpower in terms of troops or new defense sales, but even U.S. economic, technical and logistical help where multi-year certainty was often required for planning purposes.[68] Summarizing where several key Southeast Asian states were in their ties with the United States at the time, Indonesian Foreign Minister Adam Malik bluntly told Kissinger at one of their Joint Consultative Group meetings that Jakarta appreciated U.S. goodwill, Washington's constraints

As cited in: Walter LaFeber. *The American Age: US Foreign Policy at Home and Abroad, 1750 to the Present* (London: W. W. Norton, 1994), pp. 640–641.

[66] Richard A. Melanson, *American Foreign Policy Since the Vietnam War: The Search for Consensus from Richard M. Nixon to George W. Bush* (New York: Routledge, 2005), p. 24.

[67] Henry Kissinger, *Diplomacy* (New York: Simon & Schuster, 1994), p. 675.

[68] Memorandum From W.R. Smyser of the National Security Council Staff to Secretary of State Kissinger, Washington, DC, July 18, 1974. https://history.state.gov/historicaldo cuments/frus1969-76ve12/d10.

meant that Indonesia was "still waiting" for what he called a "translation to reality."[69]

The challenge of mobilization applied not just to material resources, but commitments as well. U.S. policymakers had to repeatedly publicly reassure allies about the applicability of their commitments even though they were privately unsure about their validity. To take just one example, during the U.S.-Philippines base negotiations, which dragged on for much of the 1970s, U.S. policymakers had to repeatedly rebut the claim that the lack of support of Congress and the wider public, manifested by curbs on the executive branch like the War Powers Act of 1973, reduced or eliminated the value of an American treaty commitment to defend the Philippines. Nixon summarized the problem that low state capacity presented for Washington's commitments to its allies and partners rather bluntly in reference to the U.S.-Thai alliance in a conversation with U.S. officials back in March 1972:

> "Suppose that we just—suppose the Chinese thing made a run at Thailand. And suppose the Thais said, "Look, we have a treaty with you." Do you see an American President going down to the Congress and saying, "We're going to declare war on China to keep our treaty commitments with Thailand?" Huh? We've got to let them think that. I mean we can't say that our treaty commitments are not going to be kept, and the Chinese better think they're gonna be kept. But the practical problem, that's what we've got to face, is that at the present time, except for Western Europe there are damn few places where you would get support. You wouldn't even get it now on Israel. Not today."[70]

Low state capacity also affected the distribution of U.S. commitment in the post-Vietnam period. Most clearly, as noted previously, though the Nixon, Ford and Carter administrations all tried to calibrate means for a more limited set of ends, low state capacity made it difficult for them to get the resources even for those limited ends, creating an imbalance that

---

[69] Memorandum of Conversation, Washington, DC, June 29, 1976, 2:30 p.m.: US-Indonesia Consultations, Foreign Relations of the United States, 1969–1976, Volume E-12, Documents on East and Southeast Asia, 1973–1976.

[70] Richard M. Nixon, National Archives, Nixon Presidential Materials, White House Tapes, Recording of Conversation Among Nixon, Green, Haig, and Holdridge, March 23, 1972, 4:08–5:02 p.m., Oval Office, Conversation No. 692-3.

was difficult to address. This resulted in gaps in the way U.S. commitment shaped up, be it gulfs between rhetoric and reality or shortfalls in terms of manpower or money required. This was problematic, because, as Singapore's Lee Kuan Yew had noted, "repeating…assurances to friends and allies is not as effective as a visible and credible American capacity to respond to crises anywhere in the region."[71]

Low state capacity also affected the choices and trade-offs that U.S. policymakers had to make when it came to the balance of commitment. For instance, at times Washington would play up multilateral solutions rather than bilateral approaches to get others to pitch in on initiatives and share the burden. As the scholar Michael Antolik has argued, ASEAN initiatives in particular served "to prime the pump" when the U.S. political situation and mood would not permit Washington to launch initiatives of its own in the region as much as it would like.[72] Other times, administrations would try to rebalance aid packages for key allies and partners to ensure that economic and security considerations were calibrated in accordance with available domestic resources, to the point where assistance trade-offs and offset mechanisms imposed by legal restrictions confused U.S. allies and partners, as U.S. policymakers privately were aware.[73]

Southeast Asian states too clearly recognized the effects that low state capacity had on the shape of U.S. commitment and the arduous task for U.S. policymakers. In a fairly typical assessment of regional perceptions during the period, Philip Habib, the U.S. Assistant Secretary of State for East Asian and Pacific Affairs, noted upon his return from a Southeast Asia trip that in every country, there was a uniform desire to see the United States play a role in the region but "a deep suspicion that the U.S. will fail to provide the type financial and security resources the ASEAN countries perceive as essential." "ASEAN doubts," Habib continued "are rooted

---

[71] Far Eastern Economic Review, *Interview with Lee Kuan Yew*, October 26, 1979, http://www.nas.gov.sg/archivesonline/data/pdfdoc/lky19811016.pdf.

[72] Michael Antolik, *ASEAN and the Diplomacy of Accommodation* (New York: Routledge, 1990), p. 113.

[73] John N. Irwin II, "Telegram From the Consulate in Hong Kong to the Department of State," May 29, 1971, Foreign Relations of the United States, 1969–1976, Volume XX, Southeast Asia, 1969–1972.

Table 3 Summary of Findings on Balance of Commitment Model in Post-Vietnam Period

Variable	Type	Finding	Predicted?
Relative power	Independent	Minor decrease	Yes
Threat perceptions	Intervening	Low	Yes
State capacity	Intervening	Low	Yes
Overall commitment level and distribution	Dependent	Major decrease; Major decrease	Yes

Source Generated by Author

in the concern that the U.S. Congress will not join in an Administration policy of a continued active interest and role in the region."[74]

From the above exploration into the reasons behind the shape of U.S. commitment during the post-Vietnam period, it is clear that, as the balance of commitment model predicted, we did indeed witness a case where a decline in U.S. relative power, mediated by low level as well as low state capacity, accounted for a major decrease in commitment level and commitment balance during this period. Table 3 summarizes the findings with respect to the one independent variable and two intervening variables.

4   EVALUATING U.S. COMMITMENT DURING THE POST-VIETNAM PERIOD

The post-Vietnam period offers confirming evidence of the balance of commitment explanation in the U.S. commitment to Southeast Asia through the Nixon, Ford and early Carter administrations. While changes in the strategic environment certainly shaped the general level and balance of U.S. commitment, as balance of power theory would suggest, threat perceptions and state capacity accounted for the specific manifestations of components and categories of that commitment and explain why policy-makers ended up adopting the course they did as opposed to others that they may have preferred or considered.

---

[74] Memorandum From Secretary of State Kissinger to President Ford, Washington, DC, June 13, 1975. https://history.state.gov/historicaldocuments/frus1969-76ve12/d16.

In terms of the dependent variable, both commitment level and distribution experienced major decreases. Notably, a couple of differences were also observed within discrete components. For instance, some U.S. engagement on certain fronts were unable to offset the "major decrease" designation in commitment level, which one might otherwise predict to be a "moderate decrease." Additionally, the ideals/interests balance on the commitment distribution aspect was more contested across administrations albeit still discernable.

Turning to the independent and intervening variables, there was no clear transmission belt observed directly between relative power and commitment level and balance, which would have been the case if balance of power theory were correct. Instead, the contours of debates that U.S. policymakers had, such as over how robust Washington should look for its alliances to be in the region to preserve security or what was the right balance between equipping partners and facilitating their own independent objectives, were largely around the intervening variables of threat level and state capacity emphasized in the balance of commitment model. And at times, as mentioned earlier, even though actual capabilities of Beijing and Moscow did change, U.S. policymakers did not deviate from their approach either because of the "stickiness" of threat perceptions or the stubborn realities of state capacity.

Given all this, the balance of commitment model can be said to have passed its first test of the four cases in the context of U.S.-Southeast Asia relations—the one that is richest in terms of documentary evidence and the most expansive in terms of the administrations it covers. Now that this is clear, we can move on to the next case that occurs in an arguably more complex post-Cold War context—where the balance of power was more diffuse, the intensity of the intervening variables was not quite as high, and where the conception of Southeast Asia was itself changing with a melding of the non-communist states and the former communist nations and the expansion of ASEAN.

CHAPTER 5

The Post-Cold War Period

I think it's fair to say that as the world has changed dramatically, as the cold war is over, the threat that existed between the Soviet Union and the United States is certainly way, way, way down. And I think our friends in Asia see it that way. But I think everyone recognizes that there can be untoward happenings.
—U.S. President George H. W. Bush, January 4, 1992[1]

With the end of the Cold War, however, the national priorities of the U.S. and its allies have changed. It seems that greater attention is now accorded to domestic interests. Demands and pressures of domestic lobbies and specific interest groups are growing. Human rights, the environment and humanitarian interests are now active players in the U.S. foreign policy process. These have complicated U.S. interests with some countries in Asia, and distracted the U.S. from its longer-term strategic interests in engaging Asia.
—Former Singapore Prime Minister Goh Chok Tong[2]

---

[1] "The President's News Conference with Prime Minister Goh Chok Tong in Singapore," in: *Public Papers of the Presidents of the United States: George H.W. Bush* (U.S. Government Printing Office, 1992), pp. 20–25.

[2] Goh Chok Tong, "ASEAN-U.S Relations: Challenges," Speech at the Asia Society, New York, September 7, 2000.

© The Author(s), under exclusive license to Springer Nature   79
Singapore Pte Ltd. 2022
P. Parameswaran, *Elusive Balances*,
https://Doi.org/10.1007/978-981-16-6612-4_5

1   INTRODUCTION

Apart from the post-Vietnam war period, another significant period of change to U.S. commitment to Southeast Asia occurred as the Cold War ended and Washington began attempting to reshape its commitment to the subregion. During what one might term the post-Cold War period—which began under George H. W. Bush's presidency in 1989 and continued on during Bill Clinton's first term up to 1995—we saw a minor decrease in commitment level and a moderate decrease in commitment balance from the United States over this period.[3]

This outcome for U.S. commitment in Southeast Asia was far from guaranteed. The end of the Cold War produced tectonic shifts that could have led U.S. policymakers in the Bush and Clinton administrations to retreat completely into isolationism or crusade more internationally. What, then, accounted for a more modest reduction in commitment level and balance? This chapter will argue that the balance of commitment model offers a plausible explanation, and one that is more complete than the next best explanation which is balance of power theory.

To preview the argument, as the balance of commitment model would predict, a major increase in U.S. relative power, mediated by a low threat level perceived by the American foreign policy elite as well as moderately low state capacity, accounted for a minor decrease in commitment level and major decrease in commitment balance during this period. For U.S. policymakers, despite the major increase in U.S. relative power brought about by the demise of the Soviet Union which created a unipolar world, the lack of an imminent threat and a difficult domestic climate to mobilize and extract resources meant more constraints to actively shape outcomes in Asia in general and Southeast Asia in particular. That led to a minor decrease in commitment level and a major decrease in commitment balance to the region. The argument is visually illustrated with Fig. 1.

If this case does fit with the more complex picture of the balance of commitment model, as opposed to a simpler one forecasted by balance of power theory with a stronger, more direct relationship (or "clear transmission belt") between changes in relative power and changes in the level

---

[3] The period in question was selected with several considerations in mind, including needing to account for the period that led up to the end of the Cold War during the Bush years to observe changes at play as well as including enough of the Clinton years to get a sense for the administration's thinking. 1995 takes the case up to the end of the midterm election that occurred in November 1994.

Independent Variable   Intervening Variables   Dependent Variable

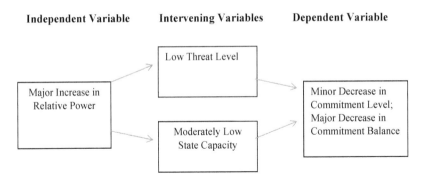

Fig. 1 Balance of Commitment in the Post-Cold War Period (*Source* Generated by Author)

and distribution of U.S. commitment to the region as balance of power theory would suggest, this would be significant for the purposes of this study for three reasons.

First, the case itself constitutes a significant change in post-WWII U.S. commitment to the world in general and Southeast Asia in particular for both international relations theory as well as foreign policy practice. The end of the Cold War brought about historic changes to relative power in the international system and produced fierce debates regarding the implications for how the United States behaved at home and abroad in a rare period of extreme preponderance.[4] Southeast Asia was no exception, and the post-Cold War shifts in American priorities generated high levels of anxiety about how Washington would employ its power and pursue its strategic interests, some of which still remain today.[5]

Second, the case appears to be a difficult and complex test for the balance of commitment model to pass, and doing so would thus be

[4] See, for instance: William C. Wohlforth, "The Stability of a Unipolar World," *International Security*, Vol. 24, No. 1 (Summer 1991), pp. 5–41. Another article that is usually cited to capture this is: Charles Krauthammer, "The Unipolar Moment," *Foreign Affairs*, 1990, pp. 23–33.

[5] As an example, former Prime Minister Goh Chok Tong lamented in a discussion on US-ASEAN relations that the post-Cold War era saw the United States get distracted from its strategic interests with the greater attention devoted to domestic interests. See: Goh Chok Tong, "ASEAN-U.S. Relations: Challenges," Speech at the Asia Society, New York, September 7, 2000.

a robust confirmation of the framework advanced in this book. Most notably, unlike the post-Vietnam period, where the effects of the two intervening variables of threat level and state capacity both seemed quite extreme relative to the change in relative power, in the post-Cold War period, the more dramatic change would appear to have come in terms of relative power instead, suggesting that balance of power theory might thus have more of an influence on outcomes than balance of commitment. Adding to the complexity here as well is the fact that the U.S. conception of Southeast Asia was itself in flux due to the melding of two parts of the region kept separate during the Cold War: the non-communist states and the former communist nations. Given such realities, if this case does nonetheless prove to go more in favor of the balance of commitment model, it would mark a significant advance.

Third and finally, in terms of sourcing, though much of the period still lacks the extensive declassified documentation that the post-Vietnam period had, this post-Cold War period case study has been buttressed with interviews with some key policymakers with firsthand accounts of what occurred at the time. If enough individuals familiar with U.S. decision-making at the time are able to confirm some of the dynamics at play that balance of commitment would predict and their accounts can be adequately corroborated with other forms of evidence, it would constitute an even clearer confirmation of the model's validity.

An elucidation of this argument and analyzing its implications for the broader study requires three major tasks. First, it must provide evidence that U.S. commitment to Southeast Asia actually changed, and, more specifically, that the level of U.S. commitment increased moderately and that the distribution of U.S. commitment was moderately imbalanced. Second, it must verify that the balance of commitment model provides an explanation for this, and a superior one relative to balance of power theory. And third and finally, it must then reflect on what this means for the broader study and the balance of commitment model, including previous predictions derived from the framework.

Accordingly, this chapter proceeds in three sections. The first section explores the shape of U.S. commitment to Southeast Asia during the post-Cold War period, delving into the specific indicators and metrics set out in the introductory chapter. The second section then explores the explanations for this level and distribution of U.S. commitment, arguing that balance of commitment model offers a good explanation and a better one than balance of power theory. The third and final section then evaluates the findings from the chapter and sieves out key insights that were gained.

2   THE SHAPE OF U.S. COMMITMENT
DURING THE POST-COLD WAR PERIOD

As the United States sought to fashion its role in Southeast Asia in the post-Cold War period, its commitment level and distribution both unsurprisingly underwent significant changes under the Bush and initial Clinton years. Absent a single, imminent threat, U.S. policymakers viewed Southeast Asia as part of a broader approach of recalibrating U.S. primacy for a new world.[6] The general shape of U.S. commitment during the post-Cold War period that emerged was one around preserving the tools of U.S. dominance in the region while promoting the vision of a new Pacific Community that both the Bush and Clinton administrations referred to, which linked the three goals of securing U.S. access to Asian markets, countering a wider range of traditional and non-traditional security threats, and advancing democracy and human rights.[7]

During the period, U.S. policymakers tended to define goals broadly, with the list including resolving the problems of the past, creating a system for Asia–Pacific integration to flourish and reinforcing bilateral ties with multilateral mechanisms to foster peace.[8] Nonetheless, a closer analysis of specific metrics clearly indicates that there were some deeper tendencies with respect to the level and distribution of American commitment to Southeast Asia during this period. Specifically, the U.S. commitment level underwent a minor decrease while commitment balance saw a moderate decrease.

[6] For a good overview of some of the scenarios that were put forth at the time, see: Charles Morrison, "US Security Relations with Southeast Asia: Possibilities and Prospects for the Clinton Administration," *Australian Journal of International Affairs*, Vol. 47, No. 2 (1993), pp. 239–249.

[7] For accounts on the struggle to define a post-Cold War U.S. role, see: James M. McCormick, "Foreign Policy Legacies of the Clinton Administration for American Administrations in the Twenty-First Century," Iowa State University, Digital Repository, 2002; and Charles William Maynes, "America Without the Cold War," *Foreign Policy*, March 19, 1990. Though Bush administration officials had made reference to a new Pacific Community, the first public articulation of it is credited to Clinton himself, who first unveiled the vision during remarks at Waseda Universiy in Tokyo in July 1993. See: William J. Clinton, "Remarks and a Question-and-Answer Session at Waseda University in Tokyo," July 7, 1993.

[8] William Clark, Jr, "The Asia Pacific Area Needs a Stronger Sense of Community," Address to the Mid-America Committee Chicago, December 4, 1992. See also: Baker, as seen in Evelyn Goh, *The Struggle for Order: Hegemony, Hierarchy, and Transition in the Post-Cold War East Asia* (Oxford: Oxford University Press, 2013), p. 43.

2.1   Minor Decrease in Commitment Level

U.S. commitment to Southeast Asia underwent a minor decrease during the post-Cold War period: the product of a mix of expansion and contraction. Some expansion in economic engagement and diplomatic initiatives were unable to entirely offset major contractions in some military deployments and alliances and partnerships.

2.1.1   Military Deployments

There was a decrease in the overall level of U.S. military deployments in Southeast Asia during the post-Cold War period. This was part of a broader story in East Asia where the U.S. policymakers examined various plans and then moved to reduce American personnel stationed regionally in the early 1990s.

Specifically, all in all, between 1990 and 1994, the number of U.S. military personnel in the Asia–Pacific was reduced from approximately 135,000 to about 100,000 personnel.[9] Much of this was the product of both preexisting legislative concerns on this front as well as broader U.S. policy considerations for planned reduction and adjustment of U.S. military forces in the region set out in the Department of Defense East Asia Strategic Initiative (EASI), outlined in two reports from 1990 and 1992.[10] But it was also coupled with other regional developments as well that led to some unexpected withdrawals.

In Southeast Asia, the most dramatic example of this during the post-Cold War period was the unexpected withdrawal of around 8,100 U.S. troops from bases in the Philippines in 1992 following the Philippine Senate's rejection of a new military base treaty with the United States in September 1991. The event had a dramatic impact because it essentially meant that for the first time in a century, the United States effectively had no formal military bases of that kind in Southeast Asia. It was not until the renegotiation of the Visiting Forces Agreement (VFA) with the Philippines, which came into force in 1999, that this would be rectified.

[9] Statistics calculated from: Department of Defense, Office of International Security Affairs, *The United States Security Strategy for the East Asia–Pacific Region*, Washington, DC, February 1995.

[10] For accounts of those reports, see: CQ Almanac, "Burden-Sharing Conditions for Allies Relaxed in 1989 Military Construction Budget," 1988. See also: Les Aspin, US Secretary of Defense, *The Bottom-Up Review: Forces for a New Era* (Washington, DC: US Department of Defense, September 1, 1993).

To be sure, the level of decrease in military deployments was much more limited than some of the sensationalism that the headlines generated about U.S. "withdrawal" during the early 1990s. The troop reductions that were eventually adopted were tempered from some higher end estimates that had been initially floated. In addition, there were also attempts to negotiate some new military presence arrangements with other Southeast Asian states like Singapore, Malaysia and Brunei for the United States to operate more there.[11]

The 1992 agreement worked out with Singapore was particularly notable in this respect. The 1990 Memorandum of Understanding (MOU) reached between the United States and Singapore under the Bush administration gave Washington access to Singapore facilities in Paya Lebar Airbase and Sembawang Wharves, and both sides worked toward the effective transfer of the U.S. logistics command for the western Pacific from the Philippines to Singapore in 1992.[12]

Yet those posture changes did not reverse the overall picture for U.S. military deployments in Southeast Asia, which could be summarized as one of contraction. U.S. government officials and experts alike understood that even if all the new defense arrangements that had been discussed with regional states were to be added up, they would still constitute a significant reduction in the U.S. military presence given the significance and unique advantages that the Philippine facilities that afforded Washington for decades.[13]

2.1.2   Alliances and Partnerships

The post-Cold War period also saw some contraction in alliances and partnerships as the United States adjusted its traditional alliances and emerging partnerships in the face of new realities. Though expansions

---

[11] For a broader context around these deployments, see: James A. Baker III, "America in Asia: Emerging Architecture for a Pacific Community," *Foreign Affairs*, Vol. 70, No. 5 (Winter 1991), pp. 1–18.

[12] An agreement was reached "in principle" for the transfer of the command during Bush's visit to Singapore in 1992, but the groundwork had been laid by both sides for months. For a public version of events, see: "The President's News Conference with Prime Minister Goh Chok Tong in Singapore," in: *Public Papers of the Presidents of the United States: George H.W. Bush* (U.S. Government Printing Office, 1992), pp. 20–25.

[13] Sheldon W. Simon (ed.), *East Asian Security in the Post-Cold War Era* (New York: Routledge, 1993), pp. 20–22.

were seen in some areas and relationships, overall, the picture was one of limited contractions.

The clearest examples were with respect to Washington's two Southeast Asian treaty alliances in Thailand and the Philippines. Among these two, the relationship with the Philippines was a clearer picture of contraction, with the base closure in 1992 being just the clearest manifestation of strains in ties.[14] This is despite the fact the two sides also quickly begun looking at ways to refashion ties following the fallout on that front, with Ramos visiting the United States in 1993 and Clinton visiting the Philippines in November 1994—the first in two decades—concretizing efforts at revival and expansion, particularly on the economic side.[15]

Some contraction was also evident in the U.S.-Thailand alliance, albeit in a less dramatic fashion. A string of issues simmered during the post-Cold War period exposed this, including tensions between the United States and the new military regime following a coup that initially resulted in the suspension of some exercises and assistance. Efforts to expand the relationship were also fraught with issues, with a case in point being the Thai rejection of U.S. requests to preposition military equipment during the Clinton administration in the form of a U.S. navy depot flotilla in the Gulf of Thailand, which was also opposed by other regional states such as Malaysia.[16]

Contraction was evident in some relationships beyond alliances as well. Indonesia is a case in point. Though partly kicked off by Indonesian human rights abuses in East Timor in 1991 and subsequent Congressional pressure, the initial part of the period in question saw the suspension of some U.S. assistance to Indonesia, primarily in the military realm, that complicated the bilateral relationship and only exacerbated existing anxieties in the region about the ability of U.S. domestic pressures to shape the trajectory of Washington's regional alignments more broadly.

---

[14] For an account of U.S.-Philippines alliance management during this period, see: Renato Cruz de Castro, "Special Relations and Alliance Politics in U.S.-Philippine Security Relations, 1990–2002," *Asian Perspective*, Vol. 27. No. 1 (2003), pp. 137–164.

[15] Jim Mann, "Clinton Visit Revives Ties with Philippines After Pullout," *Los Angeles Times*, November 14, 1994. This trend was evident earlier on as well. For instance, the Bush administration launched a multilateral assistance initiative for the Philippines in coordination with Japan, Europe, and other states.

[16] Donald Weatherbee, "Southeast Asia at Mid-Decade: Independence Through Interdependence," in: Daljit Singh and Liak Teng Kiat (eds.), *Southeast Asian Affairs* (ISEAS: Singapore: 1995), p. 16.

To be sure, this is not to suggest that contraction in alliances and partnerships were unidirectional and uniform across the board. Cooperation with Thailand expanded in some non-traditional security realms such as law enforcement, which several former policymakers who were interviewed stressed was important for wider U.S. efforts in Southeast Asia as well.[17] Some expansion was also seen in certain existing U.S. partnerships as well such as Singapore and Malaysia, even though these relationships too were not immune from the pressures on rights and protectionism.[18] And U.S.-Vietnam relations continued down a path toward normalization beginning under the Bush administration and then accelerated during the Clinton years, with steps including the lifting of the economic embargo in 1994 and the establishment of diplomatic relations subsequently in 1995.[19]

That said, this did not detract from the fact that the overall picture in terms of alliances and partnerships was still one of contraction. Several key U.S. relationships in Southeast Asia faced growing strains under both the Bush and Clinton administrations amid the broader changes of the post-Cold War period.

[17] For an outlook on the alliance at the end of the Cold War, see: Clark D. Neher and Wiwat Mungkandi (eds.), *US-Thailand Relations in a New International Era* (University of California at Berkeley, 1989), especially Introduction. For a broader and more contemporary perspective, see: Kitti Prasirtsuk, "An Ally at the Crossroads: Thailand in the US Alliance System," as seen in Michael Wesley, *Global Allies: Comparing US Alliances in the 21st Century* (Canberra: ANU Press, 2017), pp. 115–132. See, for instance, the Thailand chapter in: CSIS Southeast Asia Initiative, "U.S. Alliances and Emerging Partnerships in Southeast Asia: Out of the Shadows," Center for Strategy and International Studies, Washington, DC, July 2009, pp. 4–16. Note: The author participated in the drafting of this report. See also: National Bureau for Asian Research, "The United States-Thailand Alliance: Reinvigorating the Partnership," Washington, DC, 2010.

[18] The choice of these countries also reflects the more limited lens through which relationships were viewed in terms of high-level attention. State visits in the White House during the period or visits to the region were confined to these three countries apart from U.S. bilateral alliances. In the case of Bush, his only trip to Southeast Asia in January 1992 included a stopover in Singapore. In the case of Clinton, during this period, he made trips to the Philippines and Indonesia. Other trips made were outside of the period covered in this chapter: Thailand and Philippines (1996) and Brunei and Vietnam (2000). Author's examination of presidential travel records.

[19] For general overviews of the evolution of ties, see: Mark E. Manyin, "The Vietnam-US Normalization Process," (Washington, DC: Congressional Research Service, 2005); and Eleanor Albert, "The Evolution of US-Vietnam Ties," Council on Foreign Relations, March 7, 2018.

2.1.3   Diplomatic Initiatives

The post-Cold War period saw a limited expansion in terms of U.S. diplomatic initiatives in the region. Whether it be with respect to specific bilateral countries, broader peace settlements or regional diplomatic mechanisms, Washington remained committed to advancing this aspect of its Southeast Asia engagement despite the challenges inherent in doing so and some limits.

Bilaterally, the clearest instance of this was the attention given to progress regarding the gradual normalization of relations with Vietnam mentioned earlier. Though this was part of an ongoing effort that had begun back during the Carter years and then subsequently suspended, advancing political and economic collaboration was a diplomatic priority under both the Bush and Clinton administrations, and particularly during the Clinton years, there was a significant acceleration on this front, and former administration officials stressed that much time and attention was devoted to its pursuit.[20]

Beyond this, there were also attempts by Washington to be involved more in a subregional and regional sense as well. Subregionally, the main example is with respect to Cambodia, which held the key to broader peace and engagement with mainland Southeast Asia.[21] Here, the United States played an important role in shaping the process that led to a comprehensive peace settlement reached in October 1991 via the United Nations Security Council that gave the UN full authority to organize a transition in that country, including supervising a ceasefire, disarmament and preparations for elections.[22] The United States also continued to push for assistance to Cambodia into the mid-1990s and remained diplomatically

[20] For a deeper discussion, see: Jonathan R. Stromseth and Chadwick Bolick, "US-Vietnam Relations: An Overview," in: Jonathan Stromseth (ed.), *Dialogue on US-Vietnam Relations: Domestic Dimensions* (Washington, DC: The Asia Foundation, 2003), pp. 6–17. For a firsthand account from Congress, see: John Kerry, "Looking Ahead: The United States and Vietnam," *Harvard International Review* (Winter 1997).

[21] Peter Grier, "Washington Intensifies Effort to Restore Peace in Southeast Asia Region," *The Christian Science Monitor*, April 16, 1991.

[22] For a firsthand account of the U.S. role, see: Richard H. Solomon, *Exiting Indochina: U.S. Leadership of the Cambodia Settlement and Normalization with Vietnam* (Washington, DC: United States Institute of Peace Press, 2000), especially pp. 40–48 on the general UN multilateral context.

engaged, with Warren Christopher eventually becoming the first secretary of state to visit the country since John Foster Dulles.[23]

The post-Cold War period also saw the United States invest more in the development of multilateral regional organizations as well, which was a major focus of discussion within Southeast Asia at the time. Both the Bush and Clinton administrations supported the Asia–Pacific Economic Cooperation grouping (APEC) as a way to advance regional economic multilateralism in the Asia–Pacific, while also actively opposing exclusivist regional mechanisms that left the United States out of it such as the East Asia Economic Group (EAEG) advocated by Malaysian Prime Minister Mahathir Mohamad.[24] Under Clinton, U.S. engagement in multilateral institutions was elevated to a key pillar of the administration's new "Pacific Community." The administration not only attended regional multilateral fora, but also actively supported the development of forums such as the ASEAN Regional Forum (ARF), a multilateral security forum that got underway in 1994, as part of the rollout of its Pacific Community in contrast to Washington's previous ambivalence.[25]

Yet there were also limits to the extent of this diplomatic engagement that was evident during the post-Cold War period. A case in point was with respect to the South China Sea disputes, particularly as the situation showed signs of deteriorating in the 1990s following developments such as Beijing's passage of a unilateral law in February 1992 despite its participation in multiple informal ASEAN workshops led by Indonesia where participants agreed to self-restraint and cooperation, and the Mischief Reef incident with the Philippines. The United States did react to some degree, with moves such as the issuance of a formal five-point statement on the South China Sea in May 1995. But as one former U.S. official

[23] Winston Lord, Remarks before the U.S. House Committee on Asia and the Pacific, September 21, 1995.

[24] For a discussion of the EAEC within the context of Mahathir's thinking, see: Robert Stephen Milne and Diane K. Mauzy, *Malaysian Politics Under Mahathir* (New York: Routledge, 1999), pp. 128–130. For a sense of U.S. opposition to the initiative during the period, see: Shim Jae Hoon and Robert Delfs, "Block Politics: APEC Meeting Clouded by Fears of Regionalism," Far Eastern Economic Review, November 28, 1991, pp. 26–27, 30.

[25] *Los Angeles Times*, "China 'Rendezvous With Freedom' Will Come, Baker Says," June 27, 1989. https://www.latimes.com/archives/la-xpm-1989-06-27-mn-4376-story.html?_amp=true; Clayton Jones, "Clinton Gets Asian Economic Summit, but Only at a Price," *The Christian Science Monitor*, July 28, 1993.

familiar with the thinking at the time put it, beyond this, the general sense was one of "deliberate ambivalence" where Washington was unwilling to be drawn into the South China Sea disputes beyond reaffirming its general interests.[26]

2.1.4   Economic Engagement

The post-Cold war period also witnessed some increase in economic engagement as part of the level of U.S. commitment to Southeast Asia. During this period, despite a narrowing focus at home and grievances among some regional states, U.S. policymakers nonetheless attempted to advance some economic initiatives in the subregion and the level of economic activity between the United States and Southeast Asia also increased.

Bilaterally, U.S. officials did try to continue to push for some economic assistance where possible despite constraints. In 1989, the United States formally launched the Multilateral Assistance Initiative for the Philippines in 1989 involving Washington along with Japan, Europe and other nations, even though Washington's initial contribution when it was launched was just $1 billion over five years. The Bush administration advanced ties with Singapore through a trade and investment framework agreement in 1991 and then an agreement in principle for a bilateral investment agreement in 1992, modest steps which would lay the groundwork for the eventual establishment of a free trade agreement. The Clinton administration also pressed into the mid-1990s for pathways to boost economic ties with Cambodia even though this was a tough sell in Congress, including the inking of agreements with organizations such as OPIC and the granting of Most-Favored Nation status.[27]

At the multilateral level, some ideas were broached at various levels in the United States and Southeast Asia under the U.S.-ASEAN umbrella

---

[26] An additional irritant came when, in May 1992, Creston Energy Corp, a U.S. company, signed an agreement with the Chinese Offshore Petroleum Corporation and obtained a right to explore for oil and gas, with a U.S. government official present at the signing ceremony held in Beijing. The move resulted in Vietnam charged Washington with connivance, irrespective of the denials of U.S. officials. See: Susumu Awanohara, "South China Sea," *Far Eastern Economic Review*, August 13, 1992, p. 18.

[27] Winston Lord, Remarks before the U.S. House Committee on Asia and the Pacific, September 21, 1995.

that had first taken off under the Carter administration.[28] While some of the bolder initiatives, such as a U.S.-ASEAN free trade agreement, were unsurprisingly not realized, there was nonetheless movement in some areas. A case in point was the US-ASEAN Alliance for Mutual Growth (AMG), a joint government and private sector program that was initially unveiled in 1994 to boost trade and investment with the subregion.[29]

These initiatives took shape as the level of economic activity between the United States and Southeast Asia was increasing. In terms of trade data for instance, per statistics from the International Monetary Fund (IMF), two-way trade between the United States and ASEAN member states rose from $48 billion in 1990 to $141 billion in 2000, despite the advent of the Asian Financial Crisis (AFC) in the late 1990s.[30] Similarly, U.S. investments to the region were on the uptick as well through the early to mid-1990s, rising from $11.8 billion in 1990 to $37.5 billion in 1997 before steep decline following the AFC.[31]

To be sure, there were still limits to the extent of U.S. economic engagement, be it in terms of its overall level or its distribution across different Southeast Asian countries or specific industries in each of these individual states.[32] Furthermore, at times, more attention seemed to be paid in boosting the attention to economic engagement domestically within bureaucracies rather than with individual foreign partners

---

[28] For instance, with government support, a joint committee by the East–West Center and the Institute of Southeast Asian Studies examined various proposals for greater U.S.-ASEAN economic engagement, including initial outlines of a U.S.-ASEAN free trade agreement. See: Seiji Naya et al. (eds.), *ASEAN-US Initiative: Assessment and Recommendations for Improved Economic Relations* (Singapore: Institute of Southeast Asian Studies, 1989).

[29] Stephen Haggard, *Developing Nations and the Politics of Global Integration* (Washington, DC: Brookings Institution Press, 1995), p. 73.

[30] Author's calculations from IMF Direction of Trade statistics. Separately, data from the U.S. Department of Commerce also indicates a similar albeit more gradual rise in terms of trade data: it went from $45.9 billion in 1990 to $118 billion in 1999.

[31] Author calculations of data from U.S. Department of Commerce. For a broader overview of the FDI picture for Southeast Asia, see also: Friedrich Wu et al., "Foreign Direct Investments to China and Southeast Asia: Has ASEAN Been Losing Out?" Economic Survey of Singapore, Third Quarter 2002.

[32] For a thorough account of U.S. economic stakes in Southeast Asia by country and by industry during this period, see: John Bresnan, *From Dominoes to Dynamos: The Transformation of Southeast Asia* (New York: Council on Foreign Relations Press, 1994), especially pp. 17–29.

Table 1 Summary of Findings on Commitment Level in the Post-Cold War Period

Category	Choices	Finding
Military deployments	Expanded or reduced?	Reduced
Alliances and partnerships	Strengthened or weakened?	Weakened
Diplomatic initiatives	Active, reactive, or inactive?	Active
Economic engagement	Increased or decreased?	Minor increase
Overall level	Increase or decrease?	Minor decrease

Source Generated by Author

in Southeast Asia, which, as was the case with the APEC summit, led to concerns among some that was subordinating regional designs to its domestic-political imperatives.[33] Nonetheless, it was clear that during the post-Cold War period, the United States was working to expand economic engagement in the subregion.

In sum, given the fact that the United States was active in terms of diplomatic initiatives, increased its economic engagement, and strengthened alliances and partnerships, even while military deployments were contracting, U.S. commitment to Southeast Asia during the post-Cold War period can be said to have experienced a minor decrease, as illustrated by Table 1.

2.2   Major Decrease in Commitment Balance

The minor decrease in commitment level was accompanied by a major decrease in commitment balance during the post-Cold War period as well. Specifically, all five of the five areas set out in the balance of commitment framework witnessed imbalances within them, and most of them were quite significant as well.

---

[33] For a sense of this sentiment, see, for instance: Yoji Akashi, "An ASEAN Perspective on APEC," Working Paper #240, The Helen Kellogg Institute for International Studies, August 1997; and Clayton Jones, "Clinton Gets Asian Economic Summit, but Only at a Price," *The Christian Science Monitor*, July 28, 1993. For a broader evaluation, see: Sheldon Simon and Richard Ellings, "A Postscript on US Policy," in: Simon and Ellings (eds.), *Southeast Asian Security in the New Millenium* (Routledge, 1996).

2.2.1 Means/Ends

There was an imbalance with respect to means and ends during the post-Cold War period. While U.S. policymakers appeared to be adjusting their general ends to whatever specific means were at their disposal, they still found it difficult to prevent a discrepancy between the goals they were trying to accomplish and the ends available to them to avoid an imbalance in this domain.

During the post-Cold War period, U.S. ends in Southeast Asia remained quite general, which increased the risk that they would be quite imbalanced relative to ends. With the end of the Cold War and the dissolution of the Soviet threat that had served as a source of strategic discipline, U.S. policymakers defined ends in Southeast Asia in terms of the more general vision of a "Pacific Community" that they were seeking to promote, with ambitious and mutually reinforcing goals in the security, economic and democratic domains.[34] As referenced earlier, despite adaptations that were attempted, this resulted in multiple instances of gaps between the general vision and the means available—be it available economic or military resources themselves or the political capital or will to summon them.

This tendency was evident in both the Bush and Clinton administrations. In the case of the Bush administration, it adopted a more reactive and restrained approach to the subregion, so the imbalance was relatively less.[35] Even here though, while it acted when it needed to—such as on the Cambodia peace settlement or reshaping the post-Cold war military presence—is also quickly succumbed to the usual bouts of Congressional opposition or domestic pressure when it encountered it, be it in the U.S. reaction to Indonesian rights abuses in East Timor or increasing assistance to Southeast Asian states.

---

[34] The "Pacific community" language was evident in both the Bush and Clinton administrations. For an example from the Bush years, see: James A. Baker III, "America in Asia: Emerging Architecture for a Pacific Community," *Foreign Affairs*, Vol. 70, No. 5 (Winter 1991), pp. 1–18. See also, Council on Foreign Affairs Report, "U.S.-Asia Relations," April 11, 1996: https://www.c-span.org/video/?71171-1/us-asia-relations.

[35] This was also evident in Bush's broader Asia policy. As Michael Green notes, despite knowing more about the region than any of his predecessors before coming to office, Bush "never publicly articulated a longer-term vision for Asia and the Pacific." See: Michael J. Green, *By More Than Providence: Grand Strategy and American Power in the Asia–Pacific Since 1789* (New York: Columbia University Press, 2017), p. 432.

The Clinton administration was more ambitious, particularly in its pursuit of democracy and human rights and multilateralism, and that in turn increased the gaps between means and ends.[36] Though the administration would stick to its guns on some core issues like normalization with Vietnam, it would also retreat or refashion its objectives depending on the pressures it encountered from at home or abroad, trying and sometimes unsuccessfully so at "adapting ends to means rather than means to ends," as Christopher Hemmer has put it.[37] The Clinton administration's Pacific Community, which spoke grandly about the promotion of greater security, prosperity and democracy—what Donald K. Emmerson calls the "Three Good Things"—led to a series of cases which exposed the challenges of not only pursuing these simultaneously, but also in a mutually reinforcing way which betrayed the realities of trade-offs that policymakers knowingly were making in practice.[38]

2.2.2   Interests/Ideals

There were also clear imbalances witnessed between ideals and interests during the post-Cold War period. Though there were of course changes over time and an overall lack of consistency, the broad trend was that the United States placed a greater emphasis on ideals over interests in its approach to Southeast Asia.

Under the Bush administration, U.S. policymakers tried their hardest to restrict idealism to rhetoric. Consistent with his predecessors, Bush spoke about the rise of democracy in his public statements and speeches, and in his last National Security Strategy, there was even reference to creating an "age of democratic peace."[39] But in practice, Bush and his administration itself largely resisted the urge to crusade in Asia in line

[36] Interview with former U.S. official, Washington, DC, October 2018.

[37] Christopher Hemmer, *American Pendulum: Recurring Debates in U.S. Grand Strategy* (New York: Cornell University Press, 2015), p. 128.

[38] Donald K. Emmerson, "US Policy Themes in Southeast Asia in the 1990s," in: David Wurfel and Bruce Burton (eds.), *Southeast Asia in the New World Order: The Political Economy of a Dynamic Region* (New York: St. Martin's Press Inc., 1996), pp. 103–128.

[39] George H. W. Bush, "Statement on the National Security Strategy Report," in *Public Papers of the Presidents of the United States: George H. W. Bush*, Book 2 (1992–1993), pp. 2263–2264.

with its overall restraint, even when events like the Tiananmen Square massacre occurred that presented such opportunities.[40]

Even so, the Bush administration struggled to prevent a tilt toward ideals over interests in Southeast Asia. In the face of key democratic setbacks in Southeast Asia and Congressional pressure, the administration moved to impose restrictions on regional states ranging from Myanmar to Indonesia and at times even pressured other states to follow suit.[41] Though the hardline approach to Myanmar's military junta was less surprising given the relatively little strategic stake that Washington had there, Washington's line with respect to Jakarta and the atrocities in East Timor was notable because of the oft-cited strategic importance it had for U.S. interests and the sharp contrast from the Nixon administration which had turned a blind eye to the same issues before in the 1970s, something which Indonesian policymakers did not hesitate to point out.[42]

During the initial Clinton years, the balance in favor of ideals became much clearer, with the administration taking a forward-leaning approach to promoting democracy and human rights.[43] As a result, the United States took even more aggressive steps against its partners on a whole variety of issues ranging from labor conditions to media restrictions, and its messianic zeal directly conflicted with the emerging Asian values debate

[40] Richard Haass, who served on the National Security Council, characterized the approach adopted by the administration as being one of hoping that some of what was best about the United States would rub off on others. See: Richard Haass, *War of Necessity, War of Choice: A Memoir of Two Iraq Wars* (New York: Simon & Schuster, 2009), p. 102.

[41] For example, U.S. Undersecretary Robert Zoellick fiercely criticized ASEAN's quiet diplomacy approach in the face of the situation in Myanmar. For an account of the incident, see: Alice Ba, *Renegotiating East and Southeast Asia: Region, Regionalism, and the Association of Southeast Asian Nations* (Stanford, CA: Stanford University Press, 2009), p. 118.

[42] For an examination of this episode, see: Larry Niksch, *Report RS20332: East Timor Crisis: U.S. Policy and Options*, CRS Report, November 5, 1999.

[43] For an account of the Clinton administration's record (relative to its predecessor in the George W. Bush administration), see: Barbara Ann J. Reiffer and Kristan Mercer, "US Democracy Promotion: The Clinton and Bush Administrations," *Global Society*, Vol. 19, No. 4 (2005), pp. 385–408.

that had taken hold in some Southeast Asian capitals.[44] The most high-profile case during this period was the U.S.-Singapore spat over the caning of U.S. citizen Michael Fay for vandalism, which brought Washington's relationship with a key strategic partner to a crisis.

Beyond individual actions with respect to Southeast Asian states, the Clinton administration also acted proactively at home to tilt the balance in favor of ideals. Among other things, Clinton created a new post of Assistant Secretary of Defense for Democracy and Human Rights, and, in a longer-lasting move, paved the way for the creation of Radio Free Asia, an organization that would broadcast pro-U.S. messaging into authoritarian or non-democratic regimes in the region.

2.2.3   Cooperation/Confrontation

Another clear imbalance in the post-Cold War period was one favoring a cooperative over a confrontational approach to American adversaries, rivals and competitors. During this period, U.S. policymakers tended to place greater emphasis on the fashioning of more cooperative arrangements to manage relationships with such actors where they could in contrast to some of the more adversarial and divisive approaches taken during the Cold War.

Southeast Asia was not immune from this imbalance. With the Cold War over, U.S. policymakers during both the Bush and Clinton administrations descriptively chose to place less emphasis on the "sword" of Washington's military battles with the Soviet Union and its allies, and more on the "shield" that it had provided to Southeast Asian states that had facilitated the emergence of the subregion as a locus of peace and prosperity.[45] Prescriptively, both administrations spoke of a cooperative U.S. approach to the region directed at furthering Southeast Asia's role as a locus of peace and prosperity through various means, from Washington's role in pursuing a peace settlement in Cambodia to the normalization

---

[44] For additional context regarding the Asian values debate, see: Diane K. Mauzy, "The Human Rights and 'Asian Values' Debate in Southeast Asia: Trying to Clarify the Key Issues," *The Pacific Review*, Vol. 10, No. 2 (1997), pp. 210–236.

[45] In one instance, in the middle of a Congressional testimony in June 1996, U.S. Assistant Secretary of State Winston Lord directly referenced the "shield" analogy, linked it to a lecture that had recently been given by Singapore Foreign Minister Jayakumar on the subject, and asked for a copy of Jayakumar's speech to be entered in the record. See: Winston Lord, "Opportunities for Peace, Stability and Prosperity," Bureau of Public Affairs, June 11, 1996.

process with Vietnam to its support of multilateral economic and security institutions.

The Cambodian peace process in particular was viewed by U.S. policymakers as not only an end in and of itself but a catalyst that would further enable regional cooperation. Baker at one point even spoke of it creating the possibility of "a new era in Southeast Asia," with the integration of Cambodia, Vietnam and Laos into the regional mainstream and the normalization of U.S. relations with Indochinese states.[46] Similarly, viewed from the lens of a broader cooperative approach, U.S. officials likened the normalization with Vietnam to a similar process that had been in place with respect to China in terms of the impact it would have in terms of Washington's approach to Southeast Asia relative to the confrontation of the Cold War era.[47]

But the imbalance of cooperation over confrontation also manifested itself in what Washington did not do with respect to its adversaries, rivals and competitors in Southeast Asia and beyond. Most prominently for Southeast Asian states, U.S. policymakers remained concerned that any moves they made would jeopardize ties with China, which Washington was seeking to cultivate as a constructive strategic partner.[48] In that context, the largely muted U.S. response to China's growing assertiveness in the South China Sea in the early- to mid-1990s, manifested most clearly in its occupation of Mischief Reef beginning in 1994, was a clear source of concern for the region in the post-Cold War period.[49]

[46] James A. Baker III, "America in Asia: Emerging Architecture for a Pacific Community," *Foreign Affairs*, Vol. 70, No. 5 (Winter 1991), pp. 1–18.

[47] These comparisons were made even early on during the Bush years. See for instance: Richard Solomon, "US-Vietnam Relations: Requirements for Normalization," Address before the conference Vietnam Today, Vietnam Tomorrow: Prospects for US Business, Washington, DC, December 5, 1990.

[48] For a deeper treatment of U.S.-China relations during this period, see: David M. Lampton, *Same Bed, Different Dreams: Managing US-China Relations, 1989–2000* (Berkeley: University of California Press, 2001); and Robert Sutter, *US-China Relations: Perilous Past, Uncertain Present* (London: Rowman & Littlefield, 2010), especially Chapter 5, pp. 91–119.

[49] Several interviewees emphasized that the United States did take some actions on this front, including issuing a clear policy statement in 1995 that was appreciated in Southeast Asian capitals. Nonetheless, with more forward-leaning initiatives not taken, the response was nonetheless widely viewed as muted. For examples, see: Diane K. Mauzy and Brian L. Job, "US Policy in Southeast Asia: Limited Reengagement After Years of Benign Neglect,"

To be sure, the imbalance of cooperation over conflict did not mean that the United States was not preparing for contingencies that might lead it to take a tougher approach further down the line. Indeed, documents such as the 1992 Defense Planning Guidance clearly indicate that U.S. policymakers during the post-Cold War period were very much concerned about the prospect of the potential emergence of a rival such as the Soviet Union or China that might undermine the U.S.-led order and American primacy.[50] Nonetheless, during the period in question, this cooperative approach tended to dominate the U.S. approach to Southeast Asia.

2.2.4   Bilateralism/Multilateralism

The third imbalance was one in favor of multilateralism over bilateralism. Though Washington continued to focus its efforts on preserving and expanding relations with key allies and partners, there was a tilt in favor of more multilateralism that was evident as well.

Both the Bush and Clinton administrations gave multilateralism a prominent place in their overall foreign policies as well as in their Asia approaches. Bush's "New World Order" and Clinton's "Engagement and Enlargement" both included multilateral institutions and collective action more generally as a component, which was viewed as part of tackling complex problems in what was perceived to be a more multipolar world. Similarly, the "Pacific Community" that both administrations spoke of in Asia had a diplomatic leg that stressed the virtue of multilateral approaches in addition to bilateral ones. In an address to the Asia Society in June 1989 before heading on a trip to Asia, Baker spoke of the need for a "framework for a new Pacific partnership," noting that, unlike Europe, there were inadequate regional mechanisms to manage the effects of interdependence.[51]

Asian Survey, Vol. 47, No. 4, pp. 622–641; and Stephen W. Bosworth, "The US and Asia in 1992: A New Balance," *Asian Survey*, Vol. 33, No. 1 (January 1993), pp. 103–113.

[50] For a detailed account of the Defense Planning Guidance and its wider significance, see: Hal Brands, "Choosing Primacy: US Strategy and Global Order at the Dawn of the Post-Cold War Era," *Texas National Security Review*, Vol. 1, Issue 2, No. 6 (February 2018).

[51] *Los Angeles Times*, "China 'Rendezvous with Freedom' Will Come, Baker Says," June 27, 1989. https://www.latimes.com/archives/la-xpm-1989-06-27-mn-4376-story.html?_amp=true.

In practice, during the Bush administration, though there was already some evidence of growing U.S. tilt toward multilateralism, there was also a hint of skepticism and a lack of clarity.[52] Initially, some leading administration officials questioned the value of multilateral security approaches relative to U.S. bilateral alliances, viewing them as at best a distraction and at worst a guise for excluding Washington from the region.[53] But over time, U.S. policymakers began to see complementarity between these approaches and became open to helping to shape them, particularly in the economic realm with APEC as an example. Baker summarized the administration's position when he said Washington ought to remain attentive to flexible and ad hoc multilateral engagement but not lock itself into any overly structural approach.[54]

During the Clinton years, the increasing emphasis on multilateralism was much clearer and the commitment to it was much firmer. Investment in multilateral institutions was laid out as one of ten goals for U.S. policy in Asia by Winston Lord in his confirmation hearing.[55] Administration officials not only attended multilateral fora consistently, but also actively supported the creation of new institutions such as the ASEAN Regional

[52] For one account, see: Robert B. Zoellick, "An Architecture of U.S. Strategy After the Cold War," in: Melvyn P. Leffler and Jeffrey W. Legro (eds.), *In Uncertain Times: American Foreign Policy After the Berlin Wall and 9/11* (New York: Cornell University Press, April 2011), pp. 26–43. For a summary in broader perspective, see: Victor D. Cha, "Complex Patchworks: US Alliances as Part of Asia's Regional Architecture," *Asia Policy*, No. 11 (January 2011), pp. 27–50.

[53] For instance, Richard Solomon once famously described Asian multilateral security institutions as a "solution in search of a problem." See: Richard H. Solomon, "Asian Security in the 1990s: Integration in Economics, Diversity in Defense," Address at the University of California San Diego, October 30, 1990. Baker also saw Mahathir's EAEC as an attempt to draw a line down the middle of the Pacific to leave the United States out, and worked hard to kill the proposal as he noted in his memoirs. See: James A. Baker III, *The Politics of Diplomacy* (Putnam: 1995), pp. 609–611. For a different take that argues that there existed far more division between so called "community builders" and alliance strengtheners," see: Harry Harding, "Contending American Views of the Asian Security Order," Symposium Paper, 2000, http://www.nids.mod.go.jp/english/event/symposium/pdf/2000/sympo_e2000_6.pdf.

[54] James A. Baker III, "America in Asia: Emerging Architecture for a Pacific Community," *Foreign Affairs*, Vol. 70, No. 5 (Winter 1991), pp. 1–18.

[55] Winston Lord, "A New Pacific Community: Ten Goals for American Policy," *Foreign Policy Bulletin*, Vol. 3, No. 6 (May–June 1993), pp. 49–53.

Forum (ARF).[56] The administration even proactively elevated the U.S. role in some institutions, with Clinton himself convening the first-ever summit meeting of APEC leaders in Seattle back in 1993 in a historic move.

2.2.5   Security/Economics

The post-Cold War period also saw a greater imbalance in favor of economic over security considerations. With the end of the Soviet Union as a singular security threat and rising domestic imperatives of economic growth, U.S. policymakers tended to place greater emphasis on the economic aspects of U.S. policy and geoeconomic considerations at times even subsumed geostrategic considerations altogether.

During the post-Cold War period, the reality of Asia's growing economic prosperity, the desire for a greater U.S. role in the construction of the emerging regional order and the necessity of synching foreign policy considerations abroad with domestic economic considerations at home led U.S. policymakers to elevate the role of economics in foreign policy. Administration officials never failed to emphasize the economic imperative of U.S. involvement in the world in general and Asia in particular, and there were also direct references to the growing role of economics in foreign policy relative to security considerations and even a whole new "era of geoeconomics".[57] At his confirmation hearing in March 1993, Winston Lord, the future Assistant Secretary of State for East Asia and Pacific Affairs, typified this worldview quite clearly in his opening statement:

> Economics is increasingly supplanting military considerations on our foreign policy agenda. More than ever our national security depends on our economic strength. With domestic renewal now America's highest

---

[56] This was amid the evolution of the thinking of Southeast Asian states as well. See: Yuen Foong Khong, "Coping with Strategic Uncertainty: The Role of Institutions and Soft Balancing in Southeast Asia's Post-Cold War Strategy."

[57] I. M. Destler, "Foreign Economic Policymaking Under Bill Clinton," as seen in: James M. Scott (ed.), *After the End: Making US Foreign Policy in the Post-Cold War World* (Durham: Duke University Press, 1998), p. 89. The "geoeconomics" era was mentioned by Richard Solomon. See: Richard H. Solomon, "America and Asian Security in an Era of Geoeconomics," Address before the Pacific Rim Forum, San Diego, California, U.S. Department of State Dispatch, Vol. 3, No. 21 (May 1992), p. 410.

priority, trade and investment are critical. And no region is more central for American economic interests than the world's most dynamic one – Asia.[58]

The imbalance in favor of economics was not just rhetorical but also evident in the reality of U.S. foreign policymaking during the post-Cold War period, including in Southeast Asia. The subregion was not immune from the broader tendencies in U.S. policy, including the greater attention paid to economic affairs within the U.S. government, with new staff positions created and U.S. diplomats assuming more economic responsibilities as part of their portfolio.[59] A particularly vivid case in point was Clinton's visit to Indonesia in November 1994 ahead of APEC, where he delivered remarks to the international business community in Jakarta laying out the outlines of U.S. economic strategy in the region and noted that while Washington would continue to pay attention to security affairs, "it's also a fact, and a healthy one, that the balance of our relationship with Asia has tilted towards trade."[60]

More generally, it was also no coincidence that many of the key U.S. policy initiatives in Southeast Asia during this period—from normalization with Vietnam to the growing emphasis to APEC—had an economic basis. Writing for *The Washington Post* on the emphasis on economics over security in the post-Cold War period in March 1992, the journalist Stuart Auerbach noted that this was emblematic of the fact that, in the minds of policymakers, U.S. policy was adjusting to the fact that "global economic competition replaces the Cold War and economic strength becomes a significant part of the currency of power."[61]

[58] Winston Lord, "A New Pacific Community: Ten Goals for American Policy," Opening statement at confirmation hearing, Senate Foreign Relations Committee, March 31, 1993.

[59] Renato Cruz de Castro, "Whither Geoeconomics? Bureaucratic Inertia and U.S. Post-Cold War Foreign Policy Towards East Asia," *Asian Affairs*, Vol. 26, No. 4 (Winter 2000), pp. 201–221.

[60] William J. Clinton, "Remarks to the International Business Community in Jakarta," November 16, 1994. https://www.govinfo.gov/content/pkg/WCPD-1994-11-21/pdf/WCPD-1994-11-21-Pg2404.pdf.

[61] Stuart Auerbach, "U.S. Ambassadors Making Business Their New Business," *The Washington Post*, March 20, 1992.

Table 2   Summary of Findings on Commitment Balance for the Post-Cold War Period

Category	Choices	Finding
Means/ends	Are resources commensurate with goals and objectives?	Imbalance (ends)
Interests/ideals	Is attention on ideals or more narrowly on core interests?	Imbalance (ideals)
Cooperative/confrontational	Is approach to adversaries and competitors cooperative or confrontational?	Imbalance (cooperative)
Bilateralism/multilateralism	Is bilateral & unilateral or multilateral approach favored?	Imbalance (multilateral)
Security/economics	Is there a greater attention on security or economics?	Imbalance (economics)
Overall balance	Increase or decrease?	Major decrease

Source Generated by Author

In sum, U.S. commitment to Southeast Asia during the post-Cold War period saw a high level of imbalance, with all of the five categories witnessing imbalances. The summary of the findings is illustrated in Table 2.

3   Explaining U.S. Commitment During the Post-Cold War Period

Having detailed the shape of U.S. commitment during the post-Cold War period, which was found to have experienced a minor decrease in commitment level and a major decrease in commitment balance, we can now move to explaining how and why this occurred. This section argues that, as balance of commitment would predict, we witnessed a case where a major increase in U.S. relative capabilities, mediated by a low threat level perceived by the American foreign policy elite as well as a moderately low state capacity, accounted for a minor decrease in commitment level and a major decrease in commitment balance during the post-Cold War period.

3.1   Major Increase in Relative Power

The distribution of military and economic power between the United States and its competitors both globally and regionally certainly played into Washington's commitment to Southeast Asia during the post-Cold

War period, as neorealism would predict. U.S. policymakers recognized that the winding down of the Cold War and the demise of the Soviet Union meant that the relative capabilities of the United States had increased despite the domestic challenges that it continued to confront, and that this thereby gave Washington an increased ability to sustain U.S. primacy while shaping the broader multipolar order in Asia in general and Southeast Asia in particular; that affected both the level and the distribution of U.S. commitment to Southeast Asia.

In terms of relative capabilities, globally, the end of the Cold War left the United States in a position of what the scholar Stephen Walt termed "unprecedented preponderance."[62] Despite being weighed down by rising budget and trade deficits from the Reagan era and some contractions in economic growth, with the fall of the Soviet Union, the United States' economy was nonetheless 40% larger than that of its nearest rival, with Washington continuing to enjoy significant leads in terms of higher education, scientific research and advanced technology, as Walt noted.[63] Similarly, despite increasing pressures to cut the defense budget, U.S. defense spending was still equal to that of the next six countries combined (four of which were close U.S. allies).[64] Given these realities, it was little wonder that there was much talk about U.S. capabilities in a new era of unipolarity.[65]

That favorable picture in terms of relative capabilities from a U.S. perspective was clear in Southeast Asia as well. Despite lingering concerns about the growing economic influence of actors like Japan and China, the bigger picture was that the demise of the Soviet Union as a capable power in Asia, followed by other related capability shifts as well such as the withdrawal of Vietnamese troops from Cambodia, further reinforced Washington's dominant position in the subregion. It also removed a source of instability that had emphasized Southeast Asia's geopolitical

[62] Stephen M. Walt, "Two Cheers for Clinton's Foreign Policy," *Foreign Affairs*, March–April 2000. For a comparative perspective of U.S. capabilities, see: William C. Wohlforth, "The Stability of a Unipolar World," *International Security*, Vol. 24, No. 1 (Summer 1991), pp. 5–41.

[63] U.S. economic growth contracted from 3.53% in 1989 to 0.19% in 199, followed by a period of recovery in 1992, per World Bank data.

[64] U.S. defense spending from 1990 to 1995 was reduced by over 5% per year in real terms, which represented a fall from 5.5% of GDP to 3.9% of GDP, per World Bank data.

[65] Charles Krauthammer, "The Unipolar Moment," *Foreign Affairs*, 1990, pp. 23–33.

significance but also at times complicated or undermined Southeast Asia's true economic and political potential.

U.S. policymakers in both the Bush and Clinton administrations understood the dominant position that the United States was in with respect to its capabilities both globally and regionally, in spite of its domestic challenges. "We are...the world's sole remaining superpower," General Colin Powell, the chairman of the Joint Chiefs of Staff during the Bush administration, plainly told a Congressional hearing in 1992. "Seldom in our history have we been in a stronger position relative to any challengers we might face. This is a position we should not abandon."[66] Echoing this sentiment, in a September 1993 address, Clinton's National Security Adviser Anthony Lake said that, even though there was work to be done in terms of U.S. "domestic revival," the defining feature of the post-Cold War era "is that we are its dominant power."[67]

For U.S. policymakers, beyond rhetoric, the boost in relative capabilities meant that despite the domestic challenges Washington continued to confront at home, it nonetheless had an increased ability to sustain U.S. primacy in a unipolar world while shaping the broader multipolar order. Given that, rather than retreat into isolationism or crusade unilaterally, both the Bush and Clinton administrations, with their "New World Order" and "Engagement and Enlargement" foreign policy approaches, worked to preserve U.S. leadership while at the same time engaging with other actors to highlight the indispensability of American leadership in an uncertain world.

In Asia in general and Southeast Asia in particular, this was advanced through the "Pacific Community" both administrations referred to, which rested on shaping the emerging regional order by confronting a whole host of traditional and non-traditional security threats, increasing U.S. access to Asian markets, and promoting democracy and human rights. While there continued to be questions about the degree of coherence in the overall approach, by the time that the Clinton administration had taken office, the idea of mutually reinforcing priorities focused around prosperity, stability and democracy was well laid out in speeches the

---

[66] Colin Powell, Remarks at "The Future of U.S. Foreign Policy in the Post-Cold War Era: Hearings Before the Committee on Foreign Affairs," *House of Representatives* (Washington, DC: Government Printing Office, 1992), p. 367.

[67] Anthony Lake, "From Containment to Enlargement," Address at Johns Hopkins University, September 21, 1993.

president himself had laid out in speeches to Korean National Assembly in Seoul and Waseda University in Tokyo about the "The New Pacific Community".[68]

The way relative capabilities were perceived and employed in turn affected both the level of U.S. commitment as well as its distribution in Southeast Asia. With respect to its level, this meant that there would be some increases in the level of attempted U.S. commitment in the region as we saw in diplomacy and economic engagement as Washington, in view of the favorable picture with respect to its relative capabilities, sought to shape the emerging order in Southeast Asia with what Warren Christopher characterized as "the opportunity to create a new strategy that directs America's resources at something other than superpower confrontation." Reflecting on their time in office, Christopher and Deputy Secretary of State Strobe Talbott equated the post-Cold War period with the rare shaping moment of the post-WWII period in U.S. foreign policy which Dean Acheson had presided over, jokingly characterizing the problems they dealt with and their role in them as being "present at the recreation"—from Acheson's memoir "Present at the Creation."[69]

With respect to the distribution of commitment, it also meant that there would be imbalances in some areas that would result as well now that the United States was in a more powerful position in Southeast Asia with the collapse of the Soviet Union. The imbalance in favor of ideals over interests was a case in point. "The case for tolerating dictatorships so long as they lined up with the 'Free World' against the USSR had vanished, along with the USSR itself," the scholar Donald Emmerson observed. That the post-Cold War period saw an imbalance in favor of ideals over interests given the relative capabilities that the United States

---

[68] William J. Clinton, Speech to Korean National Assembly, Seoul, July 10, 1993; William J. Clinton, Speech at Waseda University, Tokyo, July 6, 1993. For an evaluation of the strategy, see: Richard Cronin, "The United States and Asia in 1993: Year of Asia and the Pacific," *Asian Survey*, Vol. 34, No. 1 (January 1994), pp. 98–109. Laure Paquette, *Security for the Pacific Century: National Strategy in a Multilateral Setting* (NOVA, 2002); and Hideki Kan, "The Clinton Administration's Policies in the Asia–Pacific Region," Sophia University, Working Paper, 1993. Michael J. Green, *By More than Providence: Grand Strategy and American Power in the Asia–Pacific Since 1789*, (New York: Columbia University Press, 2017), especially pp. 453–464.

[69] University of Virginia Miller Center, "Warren Christopher and Strobe Talbott Oral History," Presidential Oral Histories: Bill Clinton Presidency," April 2002. See also: Strobe Talbott, "Post-Victory Blues," *Foreign Affairs*, 1991.

enjoyed, Emmerson continued, "was not inevitable, but it was opportune."[70] The lack of a rival or threat to U.S. primacy also afforded policymakers more room to think about building up the foundations of economic power rather than just responding to security threats, leading to a greater prioritization of promoting economic and business interests to better position Washington for global economic competition.[71]

But although relative power does give us a sense of the broad thinking behind and general contours of U.S. commitment to Southeast Asia in the post-Cold War era as balance of power theory would expect, it tells us much less about the specifics of the level and distribution of that commitment based on the metrics laid out in the preceding section. For a better sense of how U.S. policymakers reacted to opportunities and challenges they faced domestically, regionally and globally during this period as well as how they managed the limited military, economic, political and diplomatic resources at their disposal, we need to delve into their calculations about power and threats (threat perceptions) as well as their ability to mobilize resources (state capacity)—the two intervening variables that are key to balance of commitment.

3.2   Low Threat Level

While relative power no doubt played a role in shaping U.S. commitment to Southeast Asia during this post-Cold War period, this was also filtered through the lens of elite calculations about power and threats, or, put more simply, threat perceptions. Specifically, during this period, we witnessed a low threat level among the U.S. foreign policy elite with respect to Southeast Asia. This trend of low threat perceptions continued on through most of period in question, even amid concerns among some in Southeast Asia and even in the U.S. foreign policy community about growing threats in the subregion.

Through the post-Cold War period, the Bush and Clinton administrations operated under low threat perceptions. Though U.S. policymakers did recognize and would consistently argue that there were a range of

[70] Donald K. Emmerson, "US Policy Themes in Southeast Asia in the 1990s," in: David Wurfel and Bruce Burton (eds.), *Southeast Asia in the New World Order: The Political Economy of a Dynamic Region* (New York: St. Martin's Press Inc., 1996), pp. 103–128.

[71] Stuart Auerbach, "U.S. Ambassadors Making Business Their New Business," *The Washington Post*, March 20, 1992.

smaller or longer-term threats to U.S. interests, such as regional conflict, human rights violations, authoritarian regimes and the future rise of another competing hegemon, there was nonetheless no single, imminent threat that could compare to that of the Soviet Union during the Cold War.

Bush himself typified this reality when he was asked about the rationale for a strong U.S. military presence with the end of the Cold War while on his visit to Singapore in 1992, where he became the first sitting U.S. president to visit the country. "We see less imminent threat," he acknowledged, noting that, relative to the level of threat that existed during the Cold War, it was "certainly way, way, way down".[72] "We are not in a war frame of mind," Bush went on in his contrast between the Cold War and the post-Cold War period. "We're in a peace frame of mind, but we're keeping our eyes open." The Clinton administration concurred with this general sense, too, and was more forthright in describing the post-Cold War period as one of low threat perceptions. In a public address early in the administration, Lake noted that there was no "credible near-term threat to America's existence," and that while other serious threats remained, "none of these threats holds the same immediate dangers for us."[73]

Low threat perceptions affected both the level and distribution of U.S. commitment to Southeast Asia during the post-Cold War period. With respect to the level of U.S. commitment, the best example was the reduction in military presence. With the demise of the Soviet threat, U.S. policymakers were more willing to tolerate a reduced U.S. military presence within limits. A case in point was with respect to the closure of U.S. bases in the Philippines. Though the development was viewed with alarm in Southeast Asia, the reality was that the end of the Cold War had given rise to a reduced U.S. threat perception that made the bases, once considered *indispensable*, to merely being *desirable*. "The Philippine facilities," read one striking report that directly reflected this

---

[72] "The President's News Conference with Prime Minister Goh Chok Tong in Singapore," in: *Public Papers of the Presidents of the United States: George H.W. Bush* (U.S. Government Printing Office, 1992), pp. 20–25. This was reflected in the defense realm as well. See, for instance: Report to Congress, "A Strategic Framework for the Asian Pacific Rim: Looking Toward the 21st Century," April 1990.

[73] Anthony Lake, "From Containment to Enlargement," Speech at Johns Hopkins University, Washington, DC, September 21, 1993.

sentiment, "while being extremely desirable, are *not vital* to American ability to fulfill Washington's defense commitments in the Pacific Theater" [emphasis added].[74] In another striking comment, William Clark noted in an address in Chicago in December 1992 that the closure of these bases was part of a recalibration to a post-Cold War framework that could be beneficial with "very healthy aspects," including redefining the relationship on the basis of shared commercial and political interests and focusing the region on "mutual security responsibilities."[75]

Changing threat perceptions also affected commitment balances in several ways. For one, a low threat environment created the conditions conducive for the greater focus on cooperative rather than confrontational approaches. As Richard Solomon has acknowledged in his firsthand account of the Cambodia peace settlement, an agreement was only truly made possible in a lowered threat environment that was brought about by the decline of the Soviet Union and its ending of support for Vietnam that catalyzed the subsequent withdrawal of Vietnamese troops from Cambodia.[76] In a similar vein, lowered threat perceptions following the fall of the Soviet Union made the prospects for normalization with Vietnam brighter even though it continued to face significant challenges.

A lower threat environment also facilitated greater U.S. investment in multilateralism relative to bilateral or unilateral mechanisms. While U.S. foreign policymakers were often more skeptical about the role of multilateral institutions to address the Communist threat during the Cold War, those same institutions were now more appealing in the post-Cold War environment where they could play a role in addressing a variety of lesser non-traditional security threats.[77] Both the Bush and Clinton administrations acknowledged the role of multilateralism in individual

---

[74] U.S. Congress, House Committee on Foreign Affairs, *Hearings: Philippine Bases Treaty*, 102nd Congress, 1st Session, 1991, p. 45. For a sense of the wider regional discussion, see: Philip Bowring and John McBeth, "Basis of Dependence: Military Facility Row Stirs Debate on U.S. Regional Role," *Far Eastern Economic Review*, April 12, 1990, pp. 22–23.

[75] William Clark, Jr., "The Asia Pacific Area Needs a Stronger Sense of Community," Address to the Mid-America Committee Chicago, December 4, 1992.

[76] Richard H. Solomon, *Exiting Indochina: U.S. Leadership of the Cambodia Settlement and Normalization with Vietnam* (Washington, DC: United States Institute of Peace Press, 2000), especially pp. 14–37.

[77] Richard Solomon, "Asian Architecture: The US in the Asia–Pacific Community," *Harvard International Review*, Vol. 16, No. 2 (Spring 1994), pp. 26–29.

cases, from the Cambodia peace process to Indonesia's South China Sea workshops, but counseled flexibility to preserve U.S. room to act unilaterally or bilaterally.[78] Under Clinton, this expanded even further, with the president declaring that the United States should "develop multiple new arrangements to meet multiple threats and opportunities," with those arrangements functioning "like overlapping plates of armor, individually providing protection and together covering the full body of our common security concerns."[79]

A lowered threat environment also helped facilitate an imbalance in favor of economic issues relative to security considerations. At home, in an environment of low threat levels, officials could claim, as Lake did, that the greatest threat to the United States was "sluggish economic growth." Even early on during the period in the Bush administration, there was a clear tendency to view economic strength as being a relatively more significant part of overall competition and power dynamics, which was an underlying reason why Baker and his deputy Lawrence S. Eagleburger made it a top priority for U.S. embassies to advance the interests of American business as global economic competition.[80] Abroad, with a low threat level, Washington could ask more of its partners in terms of economic concessions. In a comment that did not escape the attention of Southeast Asian elites, Clinton made that direct link at the 1993 APEC meeting in Seattle when he said: "We do not intend to bear the cost of our military presence in Asia and the burdens of regional leadership only to be shut out of the benefits of growth that stability brings...".[81]

To argue that threat levels were low is not to say that threat perceptions were entirely absent during the post-Cold War period. Indeed, U.S. policymakers during the post-Cold War period were very much concerned about not just a range of potential threats, but also the potential emergence of a rival such as the Soviet Union that might undermine the

---

[78] James A. Baker III, "America in Asia: Emerging Architecture for a Pacific Community," *Foreign Affairs*, Vol. 70, No. 5 (Winter 1991), pp. 1–18.

[79] William J. Clinton, Speech to Korean National Assembly, Seoul, July 10, 1993.

[80] Stuart Auerbach, "U.S. Ambassadors Making Business Their New Business," *The Washington Post*, March 20, 1992. https://www.washingtonpost.com/archive/politics/1992/03/20/us-ambassadors-making-business-their-new-business/402dc0cf-7cb2-4eb9-8e08-adeacf9a681f/.

[81] William J. Clinton, *Remarks by the President to Seattle APEC Host Committee* (Seattle: White House, November 9, 1993).

U.S.-led order, ways that the United States could prevent those threats from disrupting a broadly favorably environment, and, more broadly, how to maintain and extend American primacy.[82] Documents such as the 1992 Defense Planning Guidance clearly illustrate that at least some branches of government were thinking about these considerations.[83] Nonetheless, the dominant trend was one of low threat perceptions with respect to Southeast Asia during the post-Cold War period.

3.3   Moderately Low State Capacity

The other filter in the balance of commitment model, in addition to threat perceptions, is state capacity. During the post-Cold War period, we witnessed a period of moderately low state capacity, where U.S. policymakers found it more difficult to mobilize resources for intended goals. With pressures from Congress, public opinion and other sources more generally, the Bush and Clinton administrations struggled to get the commensurate capability and willingness to maintain commitments and at times even pursue new ones.

The post-Cold War period certainly produced its own share of structural factors that constrained the ability of U.S. policymakers to mobilize resources. As Robert Sutter has noted, the post-Cold War period produced a rise in near-isolationist sentiment with respect to U.S. foreign policy that manifested itself in a range of ways, including electoral outcomes.[84] As Sutter observes, the growth of "pluralism" produced a greater range of agencies within the executive branch involved in foreign policy; more reallocation of power to Congress; much greater participation by non-governmental organizations and lobby groups; and much less consensus within Congress; all of which compounded the constraints that would go into the state capacity variable.[85]

---

[82] Interview with former U.S. defense official, Washington, DC, October 2020.

[83] For a detailed account of the Defense Planning Guidance and its wider significance, see: Hal Brands, "Choosing Primacy: US Strategy and Global Order at the Dawn of the Post-Cold War Era," *Texas National Security Review*, Vol. 1, Issue 2, No. 6 (February 2018).

[84] The relatively growing traction witnessed with respect to Ross Perot was one prominent manifestation of this.

[85] Robert Sutter, *The United States in Asia* (London: Rowman & Littlefield, 2009), p. 25.

To be sure, this environment was not one of pure isolationism within public opinion which prevented U.S. government commitment entirely: indeed, the congruence between opinion change and policy change during the period is not quite as clear as might be suggested, and, indeed, the majority of the U.S. public was still supportive of U.S. involvement in world affairs and even supported some military interventions, including Bush's forays into Somalia and Iraq.[86] Additionally, Congressional constraints during this period in question, while significant, were less than those present in 1995, following the mid-term election of November 1994 where Republicans undertook a significant majority, and were also offset by some continuity in terms of the expansion of congressional staff dealing with foreign policy and the increased access of foreign policy interest groups.[87]

Nonetheless, in such an environment of moderately low state capacity, U.S. policymakers understood that, though they may have had fewer constraints than there were during the post-Vietnam period and were in

[86] Lawrence R. Jacobs and Robert Y. Shapiro, "Debunking the Pandering Politician Myth," *The Public Perspective*, April/May 1997, pp. 3–5. According to one authoritative study on the subject, opinion/policy agreement, which had initially increased from 54% in the 1960s to 75% in the 1970s, dropped to 67% in the mid-1980s to 40% during the Bush administration and 37% during the Clinton administration. These statistics were backed up by interviews with more than 100 staff members in both the executive and legislative branches during Clinton's first term. See, for instance, the findings in: Steven Kull and Clay Ramsay, "U.S. Public Attitudes on U.N. Peacekeeping: Part I, Funding," Program on International Policy Attitudes, March 7, 1994, pp. 25–26. For a broader discussion of both points of view, see: Kenneth Jost, "Foreign Policy and Public Opinion: Have Americans Grown Tired of World Affairs?" CQ Researcher, pp. 601–624. For a deeper exploration of this, see: Helene Dieck, *The Influence of Public Opinion on Post-Cold War U.S. Military Interventions* (New York: Palgrave, 2015); and Matthew A. Baum, "How Public Opinion Constrains the Use of Force: The Case of Operation Restore Hope," *Presidential Studies Quarterly*, Vol. 34, No. 2 (June 2004), pp. 187–226.

[87] For a broader context around these trends, see: James M. McCormick, "Interest Groups and the Media in Post-Cold War U.S. Foreign Policy," as seen in: James M. Scott (ed.), *After the End: U.S. Foreign Policy in the Post-Cold War World* (Durham, NC: Duke University Press, 1998); Eugene R. Wittkopf and James M. McCormick, "Congress, the President, and the End of the Cold War: Has Anything Changed?" *The Journal of Conflict Resolution*, Vol. 42, No. 4 (August 1998), pp. 440–466. For a review of an earlier period, see: Barbara Sinclair, *41: Inside the Presidency of George H. W. Bush* (New York: Cornell University Press, 2014), Chapter 6. For a review of the Clinton administration, see: James P. Pfiffner, "President Clinton and the 103rd Congress: Winning Battles and Losing Wars," in: James A. Thurber (ed.), *Rivals for Power: Presidential-Congressional Relations* (Washington, DC: CQ Press, 1996), pp. 170–190.

a context where U.S. relative power had increased, they would still need to tie U.S. foreign policy concerns more directly to American domestic policy interests to attract and sustain interests. As the Clinton administration's first National Security Strategy put it, "the separation between international problems and domestic ones is evaporating; and...the line between domestic and foreign policy is eroding." As they proceeded to do so, this no doubt affected both the level and balance of U.S. commitment to Southeast Asia in the post-Cold War period.

In terms of level, it manifested most clearly in terms of U.S. alliances and partnerships and military deployments. On the former, it meant that U.S. policymakers had an uphill climb just to sustain relationships and prevent contraction, let alone advance new ideas for expanding collaboration. Indonesia was a case in point, with increasing Congressional pressure following rights concerns in East Timor, read by some to be inadequately checked by the Clinton administration, eventually leading to strained ties and even Jakarta pulling out of the IMET program in recognition of the changing domestic environment. Similarly, though normalization with Vietnam was eventually achieved, it had to be sold domestically with a careful focus on factors such as the POW/MIA issue rather than the wider geopolitical and geoeconomics drivers that actually undergirded the move in the first place. "It came down to how much we wanted what and what we wanted to fight on," one former official recalled to the author in an interview.[88]

On the latter, policymakers were well aware that, quite apart from the lowered threat level, low state capacity would also be a challenge to contend with that would affect military deployments. As early as 1990, the Pentagon under George H. W. Bush, then headed by Defense Secretary Dick Cheney, forecasted declining state capacity and baked that into its calculations about the emerging security environment. "Clearly, important U.S. domestic considerations also must be taken into account," the report read. "Significant reductions in the defense budget, generated by domestic perceptions of a diminished Soviet threat as well as by fiscal pressures, are probable."[89] The report then went out to sketch out various pathways to contend with this, including options for restructuring

---

[88] Author conversation with former U.S. official, Washington, DC, April 2021.

[89] Report to Congress, "A Strategic Framework for the Asian Pacific Rim: Looking Toward the 21st Century," April 1990.

U.S. military presence and then noting that it would be "appropriate" for Washington to expect its "prosperous Asian allies," Japan and South Korea, to assume more responsibility for their own defense and contributing more directly to regional stability.

In terms of commitment balance, this was most clearly visible with respect to means and ends and economic engagement. On means and ends, the Clinton administration in particular often ran into criticism that its ambitious ends around mutually reinforcing goals of prosperity, stability and democracy were not properly calibrated in accordance with and adequately supported by the limited means it had. The administration repeatedly struggled to mobilize the necessary support for its objectives, be it additional assistance for allies such as the Philippines or pushing back against Congressional pressure on individual Southeast Asian nations such as Indonesia or Malaysia. Frustrated Southeast Asian governments, which were often the victim of a see-sawing in U.S. policy, were attentive to this, and the reflections of Singapore's former premier Goh Chok Tong about U.S. Southeast Asia policy in the post-Cold War period are worth quoting at length:

> With the end of the Cold War, however, the national priorities of the U.S. and its allies have changed. It seems that greater attention is now accorded to domestic interests. Demands and pressures of domestic lobbies and specific interest groups are growing. Human rights, the environment and humanitarian interests are now active players in the U.S. foreign policy process. These have complicated U.S. interests with some countries in Asia, and distracted the U.S. from its longer-term strategic interests in engaging Asia.[90]

State capacity also influenced the emphasis placed on economics over security in the post-Cold War period.[91] Robert Zoellick has candidly

[90] Goh Chok Tong, "ASEAN-U.S. Relations: Challenges," Speech at the Asia Society, New York, September 7, 2000. See also: Donald K. Emmerson, "US Policy Themes in Southeast Asia in the 1990s," in: David Wurfel and Bruce Burton (eds.), *Southeast Asia in the New World Order: The Political Economy of a Dynamic Region* (New York: St. Martin's Press Inc , 1996), pp. 103–128.

[91] This was a perception shared not just within the U.S. government. For an example of non-government thinking on this point, see, for example: Richard Fisher, "A Jobs Strategy for America: Expanding Free Trade with Asia," Heritage Foundation, April 29, 1993.

noted that the George H.W. Bush administration chose to intentionally up its focus on economic engagement in Asia in part because it recognized that it faced challenges in mobilizing resources and needed to overcome them through messaging. Zoellick in particular notes that the administration felt it needed to show the American public the economic opportunities that Washington got from investing in the region along with the fact that it wanted to counter potential resurgence of U.S. economic nationalism at home and gain support for security ties by making clear that those ties were benefiting U.S. economic interests. Under Clinton, who campaigned with the famous slogan "It's the economy, stupid," this link was made even clearer. Multiple documents and statements directly tied the international economic focus on Asia to U.S. domestic economic growth, and some roles within the government were given added economic responsibilities in this quest to make that link even clearer.[92]

From the aforementioned exploration into the reasons behind the shape of U.S. commitment during the post-Cold War period, it is clear that, as balance of commitment predicted, we did indeed witness a case where a major increase in U.S. relative capabilities, mediated by a low threat level perceived by the American foreign policy elite as well as moderately low state capacity, accounted for a minor decrease in commitment level and major decrease in commitment balance during this period. Table 3 summarizes the findings with respect to the independent variable and intervening variables.

4   EVALUATING U.S. COMMITMENT DURING THE POST-COLD WAR PERIOD

The post-Cold War period offers confirming evidence of the balance of commitment explanation in the U.S. commitment to Southeast Asia

---

[92] For a window into Zoellick's thinking, see: Robert B. Zoellick, "America and APEC's Shared History, and Future," *Wall Street Journal*, May 15, 2014. The 1995 Economic Report directly tied boosting U.S. exports to Clinton regional initiatives. "Export and investment opportunities to emerging markets in Latin America and Asia will be a key engine of growth for the U.S. economy over the next decade." Claude Barfield, "The United States and East Asian Regionalism: Competing Paths to Integration," *International Journal of Korean Studies*, Vol. 16, No. 2, pp. 157–178.

Table 3 Summary of Findings on Balance of Commitment in the Post-Cold War Period

Variable	Type	Finding	Predicted?
Relative power	Independent	Major increase	Yes
Threat level	Intervening	Low	Yes
State capacity	Intervening	Moderately low	Higher than predicted
Overall commitment level and distribution	Dependent	Minor decrease; Major decrease	Balance lower than predicted

Source Generated by Author

under both the Bush and Clinton administrations. While changes in relative power certainly shaped the general level and distribution of U.S. commitment, as balance of power theory would suggest, threat perceptions and state capacity accounted for the specific manifestations of components and categories of that commitment and explain why policymakers ended up adopting the course they did as opposed to others that they may have preferred or considered.

In terms of the dependent variable, which is commitment level and distribution during the post-Cold War period, it is clear that the U.S. role during the period fits with the general expectation of the balance of commitment model. Notably, however, a couple of unexpected results were also observed. Within commitment level, the economic engagement component was higher than anticipated. Additionally, overall commitment balance was lower than expected, with all five components experiencing imbalance for the second case in a row after the post-Vietnam period.

Turning to the independent and intervening variables, there was no clear transmission belt observed directly between the relative distribution of capabilities and commitment level and imbalance, which would have been the case if balance of power theory were correct. Instead, the contours of debates that U.S. policymakers had during the post-Cold War period, whether it be the degree to which they would promote U.S. ideals in Southeast Asia or to what extent they ought to rely on multilateral institutions, were largely around the intervening variables of threat perceptions and state capacity emphasized in balance of commitment. And at times, even though actual capabilities of regional competitors like China did change and Southeast Asian policymakers made that clear to

Washington, U.S. policymakers did not deviate from their approach either because of the "stickiness" of threat perceptions or the stubborn realities of state capacity, which proved to actually be higher than anticipated.

Given all this, balance of commitment can be said to have passed the second of the four case study tests examined here in the context of U.S.-Southeast Asia relations, and one that is significant, difficult and rich. Now that this is clear, we can move on to the next case that occurs in the post-9/11 environment and the George W. Bush administration in the early 2000s.

CHAPTER 6

The Post-September 11 Period

The impression in and out of government after 9/11 was that the next front would be in Southeast Asia. The fight did not start well, and the outcome was hardly certain.
—Michael Green, NSC Asia Director under George W. Bush, 2017[1]

After 9/11 Southeast Asia was seen through the prism of the war on terrorism.
—Singapore Ambassador to U.S. Chan Heng Chee, 2005[2]

1 INTRODUCTION

Following the post-Cold War period, the next most dramatic change to U.S. commitment to Southeast Asia occurred following the September 11 terrorist attacks. The 9/11 attacks led to the region being labeled as the "second front" in the so-called Global War on Terror (GWOT), and a more significant part of the George W. Bush administration's ongoing efforts to shape a "balance of power in favor of freedom" by thwarting terrorists and rogue regimes, harmonizing relations among great powers

[1] Michael Green, *By More Than Providence: Grand Strategy and American Power in the Asia–Pacific Since 1783* (New York: Columbia University Press, 2017), p. 501.

[2] Chan Heng Chee, "George W. Bush in Asia: Retrospect and Prospect," in: Robert M. Hathaway and Wilson Lee (eds.), *George W. Bush and East Asia: A First Term Assessment* (Washington, DC, 2005), pp. 93–99.

© The Author(s), under exclusive license to Springer Nature Singapore Pte Ltd. 2022
P. Parameswaran, *Elusive Balances*,
https://doi.org/10.1007/978-981-16-6612-4_6

and promoting prosperity and democracy across the world.[3] In what one might term the post-9/11 period—which begun following the carrying out of the September 11, 2001 attacks during the George W. Bush presidency and continued on through the end of his first term in office, we saw a moderate increase in commitment level and a moderate decrease in commitment balance.[4]

What accounted for this shift, which took place under a president who came into office with few indications of prioritizing foreign policy in general and Southeast Asia in particular? This chapter will argue that balance of commitment model offers a plausible explanation, and one that is more complete than the next best explanation which is balance of power theory.

To preview the argument, as the balance of commitment model would predict, a minor increase in U.S. relative capabilities, mediated by a moderately high threat level perceived by the American foreign policy elite as well as a medium level of state capacity, accounted for the moderate increase in commitment level and moderate decrease in commitment balance during this period. More specifically, U.S. policymakers felt that an increase in U.S. relative power in previous years had reinforced American primacy in a unipolar world, giving them greater freedom of action to shape their environment to create what the Bush administration had termed a "balance of power in favor of freedom." This, combined with the high threat environment U.S. policymakers perceived following the September 11 attacks, along with the reality that the domestic climate made it easier to mobilize and extract the resources that they needed, eventually led to a moderately increased commitment level and moderately decreased commitment balance. The argument is visually illustrated below in Fig. 1.

If this case does fit with this more complex picture of balance of commitment model, as opposed to a simpler one forecasted by balance of

---

[3] Robin Wright, "Powell Begins Push on War's "Second Front," *Los Angeles Times*, July 30, 2002; The White House, *National Security Strategy of the United States of America*, September 2002; Condoleezza Rice, "A Balance of Power That Favors Freedom," The Manhattan Institute's Wriston Lecture, October 1, 2002; Melvyn P. Leffler, "Think Again: Bush's Foreign Policy," *Foreign Policy*, October 23, 2009.

[4] The period was selected with several considerations in mind, including the significant differences between Bush's first term and second term and needing to space out the current period from the post-Financial Crisis period detailed in the next chapter as well.

Independent Variable   Intervening Variables   Dependent Variable

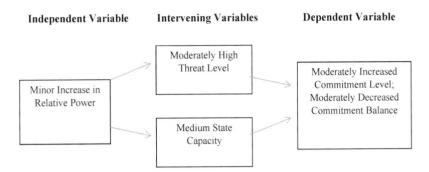

Fig. 1   Balance of Commitment in the Post-9/11 Period (*Source* Generated by Author)

power theory with a stronger, more direct relationship (or "clear transmission belt") between changes in the relative distribution of capabilities and changes in the level and balance of U.S. commitment to the region as balance of power theory would suggest, this would be significant for the purposes of this book for three reasons.

First, the case itself is a rather significant one in terms of post-WWII U.S. commitment to Southeast Asia. As other commentators have observed, at the time, the post-9/11 period constituted the most dramatic increase in U.S. commitment to Southeast Asia since the end of the Vietnam War, and a surprising one since the Bush administration had evinced little interest in the region when it first came to office.[5] The post-9/11 period also till today is pointed to by some as the demonstrative case of the perils of imbalance in U.S. commitment to the region, largely due to the overwhelming focus on counterterrorism.[6] Probing the extent to

[5] Diane K. Mauzy and Brian L. Job, "US Policy in Southeast Asia: Limited Reengagement After Years of Benign Neglect," *Asian Survey*, Vol. 47, No. 4, pp. 622–641; Angel M. Rabasa, "Southeast Asia After 9/11: Regional Trends and U.S. Interests," Testimony Presented to Subcommittee on East Asia and the Pacific House of Representatives Committee on International Relations, December 12, 2001. Charmaine G. Misalucha, "Southeast Asia-US Relations: Hegemony or Hierarchy?," *Contemporary Southeast Asia*, Vol. 33, No. 2 (2011), pp. 209–228.

[6] Catharin A. Dalpino, "US Policy in Southeast Asia: Fortifying the Foundation," A Report and Recommendations From the Southeast Asia in the Twenty-First Century: Issues and Options for US Policy Initiative, The Stanley Foundation, 2005; Amitav Acharya and Arabinda Acharya, "The Myth of the Second Front: Localizing the 'War

which this is true and the factors that led to that will thus be crucial in proving the arguments made in this study.

Second, the post-9/11 period constitutes an important test for balance of commitment because of the intensity and pace of shifts witnessed in the case. Unlike the other cases where there were a significant number of years (and at times even several presidents) for changes in variables to be recorded, the post-9/11 period saw a much more sudden shift in power, perceptions and resources employed. Exploring the ways in which this level of intensity and pace affects both balance of commitment and balance of power will be an important exercise in discerning the value and explanatory power of both arguments in this case.

Third and finally, in terms of sourcing, though much of the period still lacks the extensive declassified documentation that the post-Vietnam period had, this post-9/11 period case study has been buttressed with interviews with some key policymakers with firsthand accounts of what occurred at the time. If enough individuals familiar with U.S. decision-making at the time are able to confirm some of the dynamics at play that balance of commitment would predict and their accounts can be adequately corroborated with other forms of evidence, it would constitute an even clearer confirmation of the theory's validity.

An elucidation of this argument and analyzing its implications for the broader study requires three major tasks. First, it must provide evidence that U.S. commitment to Southeast Asia actually changed, and, more specifically, that there was a moderate increase in commitment level and a moderate decrease in commitment balance. Second, it must verify that the balance of commitment framework provides an explanation for this, and a superior one relative to balance of power theory. And third, it must then reflect on what this means for the broader study and the balance of commitment model, including previous predictions derived from the theory mentioned earlier in the book.

Accordingly, this chapter proceeds in three sections. The first section explores the shape of U.S. commitment to Southeast Asia during the post-9/11 period, delving into the specific indicators and metrics set out in the introduction. The second section then explores the explanations for this level and distribution of U.S. commitment, arguing that balance of

on Terror' in Southeast Asia," *The Washington Quarterly*, Vol. 30, No. 4, pp. 75–90; The Wilson Center, "The Second Front: Fighting Terrorism in Southeast Asia," Washington, DC, April 23, 2003.

commitment offers a good explanation and a better one than balance of power theory. The third and final section then evaluates the findings from the chapter and sieves out key insights that were gained.

2 THE SHAPE OF U.S. COMMITMENT DURING THE POST-9/11 PERIOD

As the United States sought to reshape its role in Southeast Asia, its commitment level and distribution in Southeast Asia both unsurprisingly underwent significant changes during the post-9/11 period. In particular, we saw a moderate increase in commitment level and a moderate decrease in commitment balance.

The 9/11 attacks enhanced the importance of Southeast Asia within U.S. policy and accounted for the Bush administration's initial effort to increase its commitment to the region. On the one hand, that counterterrorism lens did result in somewhat of a narrowing of U.S. focus that affected both the level and distribution of commitment to Southeast Asia. But on the other hand, Washington's focus on the "second front" also helped provide openings for engagement in other domains as well and raised the profile of Southeast Asia in the administration's broader effort to help shape a "balance of power in favor of freedom" by thwarting terrorists and rogue regimes, harmonizing relations among great powers and promoting prosperity and democracy across the world.[7]

The shape of U.S. commitment to Southeast Asia during the post-9/11 period suggests that the notion that Washington saw the region from a purely counterterrorism lens is overly simplistic. A closer analysis of the specific metrics clearly indicates that there were some deeper tendencies with respect to the level and distribution of American commitment to Southeast Asia during this period. Specifically, the U.S. commitment level actually saw a moderate increase while commitment level did experience a moderate decrease.

---

[7] Rice, "A Balance of Power that Favors Freedom," The Manhattan Institute's Wriston Lecture, October 1, 2002; Melvyn P. Leffler, "Think Again: Bush's Foreign Policy," *Foreign Policy*, October 23, 2009.

2.1   Moderate Increase in Commitment Level

Overall, U.S. commitment to Southeast Asia saw a moderate increase during the post-9/11 period: the product of a number of significant expansions amid some contraction. This was evidenced in expansions with respect to military deployments, alliances and partnerships, and economic engagement, even though there was some contraction with respect to diplomatic engagement.

2.1.1   Military Deployments

There was a modest increase in the overall level of U.S. military deployments in Southeast Asia during the post-9/11 period. While U.S. policymakers continued to examine plans to restructure the way American personnel and bases were deployed and organized in the Asia–Pacific more generally, the story in Southeast Asia was one where American policymakers sought to make gradual boosts to U.S. military posture either as part of an ongoing response to terrorism or in recognition of other challenges and their centrality to U.S. interests.

During the post-9/11 period, U.S. policymakers continued to examine plans to restructure the way American personnel and bases were deployed and organized in the Asia–Pacific as they had done in the 1990s. While this general line of thinking was expressed in a series of documents including the 2001 Quadrennial Defense Review (QDR), the best example of this was the Global Defense Posture Review (GDPR) that began in 2001 and was finally issued in 2004.[8] The GDPR aimed to restructure U.S. military posture in the region amid a series of developments—such as the U.S. domestic post-Cold War military transformation and changing strategic circumstances—through various ways including by

---

[8] Thomas B. Fargo, "Regarding US Pacific Command Posture," Testimony of Commander US Pacific Command Before the House Armed Services Committee, United States House of Representatives, March 31, 2004; Statement of Douglas J. Feith, Under Secretary of Defense for Policy before the house Armed Services Committee, Regarding US Global Defense Posture Review, June 23, 2004. For broader context, see: Carnes Lord (ed.), *Reposturing the Force: US Overseas Presence in the Twenty-First Century*, Newport Paper 26 (Newport, Rhode Island; Naval War College Press, February 2006); and Douglas Feith, "Transforming the U.S. Global Defense Posture," Presentation at CSIS, Washington, DC, December 3, 2003.

complementing existing operating bases and power projection hubs with forward operation sites and cooperative security locations.[9]

But the GDPR had varying effects in Northeast Asia and Southeast Asia. In Northeast Asia, there was a clear aggregate reduction in U.S. military personnel in addition to various other aspects of restructuring, with the subregion accounting for most of the 20,000 troops proposed in 2004 to be withdrawn from the Asia–Pacific over a decade (out of a total of 70,000 troops proposed).[10] By contrast, Southeast Asia would be viewed as a place where the United States looked to strengthen its military presence through a series of arrangements, and there were various public and quieter manifestations of this which suggested that this process was underway.[11]

The clearest example of this was in the Philippines, where, building off of the revitalization of the alliance that had begun in the late 1990s that had seen a signing of a Visiting Forces Agreement (VFA) in 1999, the United States kickstarted rotational military deployments and limited use of Philippine bases following the September 11 attacks. A notable development came in late January 2002, the Bush administration deployed around 1,000 soldiers to the southern Philippines in late January 2002 for a period of six months to train, advise and provide logistical assistance to Philippine forces combating the Abu Sayyaf.[12] That made Manila the only Southeast Asian state to welcome U.S. military troops on its territory since the 9/11 attacks, which constituted a reassertion of American influence in Southeast Asia.[13]

[9] Kurt M. Campbell and Celeste Johnson Ward, "New Battle Stations?" *Foreign Affairs*, Vol. 82 (September/October 2003), pp. 95–103; Carnes Lord and Andrew S. Erickson, "Bases for America's Asia–Pacific Rebalance," *The Diplomat*, May 2, 2014.

[10] Ralph A. Cossa, "Global Posture Review: Is Washington Marching Out?," Pacific Forum CSIS, October 6, 2004.

[11] Evan Medeiros, "The US Global Defense Posture Review and the Implications for the Security Architecture in the Asia–Pacific Region," Presentation at *Stiftung Wissenschaft und Politik* (SWP), Berlin, December 2004.

[12] Richard F. Grimmett, "Instances of Use of United States Armed Forces Abroad, 1798–2009," Congressional Research Service, January 27, 2010.

[13] Rommel C. Banlaoi, "The Role of Philippine-American Relations in the Global Campaign Against Terrorism: Implications for Regional Security," *Contemporary Southeast Asia*, Vol. 24, No. 2 (August 2002), pp. 294–312.

There were also some gains with respect to U.S. military presence following arrangements with key Southeast Asian states.[14] For instance, the inking of a July 2005 Strategic Framework for a Closer Cooperation Partnership in Defense and Security not only recognized Singapore's importance as a strategic and defense partner, but also formally facilitated an earlier agreement regarding the U.S. deployment of littoral combat ships to Changi Navy base, making Washington the first foreign navy to be given access to the facility that had opened in 2000.[15] The case was far from an exception. Indeed, during the post-9/11 period, Southeast Asia became an outlet through which the United States was able to up its presence in Southeast Asian states in a limited way through a variety of means. This included, among other things, intelligence sharing, joint surveillance and police training with Indonesia, Malaysia, Singapore and Thailand, at times with the quiet involvement of U.S. security personnel in these countries as well.

2.1.2   Alliances and Partnerships

The post-9/11 period also saw the United States move toward investing more in both its traditional alliances and emerging partnerships in the face of new realities in the region as well as domestically. Though the additional investments by Washington in more complex and comprehensive alliances and partnerships manifested itself in several ways, overall, the picture was one of expansion.

With respect to Washington's two Southeast Asian treaty alliances in Thailand and the Philippines, both of these relationships saw boosts during the period. On the Philippines, as noted earlier, the alliance saw a significant revitalization relative to a low point in the mid-1990s after the closing of U.S. bases, initially under the banner of counterterrorism but then expanding into other areas too, including Washington's support for Philippine defense reforms and even Manila's initial though ultimately

---

[14] Erik Martinez Kuhonta, "US Foreign Policy in Southeast Asia: The Imperative of Institutions," *Harvard Asia Quarterly* (Fall 2004).

[15] Singapore Ministry of Defense, "Factsheet—The Strategic Framework Agreement," MINDEF, July 12, 2005.

short-lived support for the U.S. invasion of Iraq.[16] The Philippines was eventually conferred the status of major non-NATO ally.

Thailand was a somewhat similar story. The post-9/11 period saw U.S.-Thai collaboration under the initial banner of counterterrorism but also broadened into other areas as well, with Washington looking to make inroads on a free trade agreement with Bangkok and expanding some of the regional diplomatic efforts based out of the U.S. Embassy in Thailand, and Thailand being open to providing U.S. access to facilities for operations and offering initial support for U.S. efforts in Afghanistan and Iraq.[17] A high point was Bush's state visit to Bangkok in 2003, where he designated Thailand a major non-NATO ally.

The United States also moved to increase relations with emerging partners as well. Perhaps the clearest example in this respect was with Indonesia. Ties got off to a quick start in the post-9/11 environment with then-president Megawati Sukarnoputri's meeting with Bush on September 19, 2001, and subsequent attacks in Indonesia, including the October 2002 bombing of a tourist area in Bali catalyzed counterterrorism cooperation in spite of lingering concerns that Jakarta had.[18] But the agenda widened to include other areas as well, with joint statements highlighting areas such as economic reform, democratic development and education.[19] The 2004 election of Susilo Bambang Yudhoyono, a retired general and a graduate of the IMET program, further boosted ties, with Washington moving to remove restrictions starting in 2005 that had been

[16] George W. Bush, "The President's News Conference with President Gloria Macapagal-Arroyo of the Philippines," May 19, 2003; Renato Cruz de Castro, "The Revitalized Philippine-US Security Relations: A Ghost from the Cold War or an Alliance for the 21st Century," *Asian Survey*, Vol. 43, No.6, p. 980. For broader context, also see: Larry Niksch, *Philippine-US Security Relations* (Washington, DC: Congressional Research Service, 2000).

[17] Pongphisoot Busbarat, "Thai-US Relations in the Post-Cold War Era: Untying the Special Relationship," *Asian Security*, Vol. 13, No. 3, pp. 256–274; Walter Lohman, "Reinvigorating the US-Thailand Alliance," The Heritage Foundation, September 28, 2011.

[18] Dana Dillon, "The Shape of Anti-Terrorist Coalitions in Southeast Asia," The Heritage Foundation, January 17, 2003.

[19] Joint Statement Between the United States of America and the Republic of Indonesia, Government Publishing Office, Administration of George W. Bush, 2001, September 19, 2001. Ann Marie Murphy, "US Rapprochement with Indonesia: From Problem State to Partner," *Contemporary Southeast Asia*, Vol. 32, No. 3 (2010), pp. 362–387.

in place on military assistance programs since the 1990s due to human rights record of the Indonesian military.[20]

Other key examples in this respect included Singapore and Vietnam. In Vietnam, the administration moved forward with normalization in spite of the challenges it posed, stepping up high-level visits at the political level, advancing a bilateral trade agreement (BTA) on the economic side and expanding the agenda on the defense aspect of ties.[21] With respect to Singapore, the Bush administration moved to solidify both the economic and security pillars of ties, concluding a high-quality free trade agreement, which was the first of its kind in Asia, and inking a Strategic Framework Agreement that strengthened the foundations of a formalized security partnership to a level that one assessment summarized as "a treaty alliance between the two sides in everything but name."[22]

2.1.3   Diplomatic Initiatives

The post-9/11 period saw no expansion, and in some cases a contraction in terms of U.S. diplomatic initiatives in Southeast Asia. In contrast to other aspects of commitment such as military engagement and alliances and partnerships, amid the focus on needs of the moment, there was a relative lack of attention to advancing new diplomatic initiatives and engaging Southeast Asian institutions in this respect.

The most obvious data point is on multilateralism, where the Bush administration's record saw a contraction relative to the Clinton years in Southeast Asia. With respect to existing institutions, the administration showed a lack of attention to their importance within its approach to Southeast Asia, even when it came to basic indicators such as the attendance of high-level officials to regional meetings, a point acknowledged even by those who worked within the administration on Asia policy.[23] While it is certainly true that this ambivalence was due to a

---

[20] Scott Morrissey, "US Lifts Indonesia Arms Embargo," Arms Control Association, January 1, 2006.

[21] For a detailed examination of this episode, see: Mark E. Manyin, "The Vietnam-US Normalization Process," CRS Issue Brief for Congress, June 17, 2005.

[22] CSIS Southeast Asia Initiative, "Out of the Shadows: US Alliances and Emerging Partnerships in Southeast Asia," Center for Strategic and International Studies, Washington, DC, July 2009, p. 35.

[23] Victor Cha, "The Obama Administration's Policy Toward East Asia," *The Korean Journal of Defense Analysis*, Vol. 22, No. 1 (March 2010), pp. 1–14. For a reaction that

series of factors—including the need to focus on the Middle East and the difficulties of engaging ASEAN as a whole due to human rights concerns associated with Myanmar—it is also true that some administration officials saw little reason to invest in what they viewed as unwieldy, underperforming institutions for U.S interests.[24]

The Bush administration also mulled but ultimately did not take action on initiatives that would have boosted U.S. involvement in multilateral institutions in Southeast Asia. A case in point was the decision not to pursue the ratification of the Treaty of Amity and Cooperation (TAC), which continued to leave the United States as being the only country to not sign the TAC and left it out of the East Asia Summit (EAS). The move was debated but ultimately deemed to be potentially too constraining, with pledges to resolve disputes without force potentially limiting the scope for U.S. military power in Asia.[25] Though these were not unfounded concerns, they were also derivative of an approach that placed more of a focus on the advancement of U.S. interests with like-minded states rather than a broad-tent approach.

To be sure, this is not to suggest that the United States did not engage in diplomatic efforts at all in the region in the post-9/11 period.[26] For instance, during the Bush administration, U.S. officials announced a few ASEAN-centered programs—from the ASEAN Cooperation Plan (ACP) in 2003 to the 2005 ASEAN-U.S. Enhanced Partnership—designed to help promote regional integration, strengthen the capacity of the ASEAN Secretariat and promote cooperation to address transnational challenges.

typifies regional perceptions, see: Darren Schuettler, "Interview: Bush No-Show Sends Wrong Signal to SE Asia," *Reuters*, July 20, 2007.

[24] Richard Armitage characterized the ARF as "so flabby and disparate as to [be] unworkable." Peter Hartcher, "Who Will Keep the Peace in Asia When the U.S. Leaves," *Australian Financial Review*, September 11, 1999.

[25] Mark E. Manyin, Michael John Garcia, and Wayne M. Morrison, "US Accession to the Association of Southeast Asian Nations' Treaty of Amity and Cooperation," *Congressional Research Service*, July 13, 2009; Bruce Vaughn, "East Asian Summit: Issues for Congress," Congressional Research Service Reports for Congress, Library of Congress, Washington, DC (December 9, 2005).

[26] It is worth mentioning here that while Bush administration did not evince much interest in Southeast Asian regionalism during the period covered here (2001–2005), it did try to make some inroads in advancing diplomatic ties with ASEAN during the end of the second term that are at times missed when assessing its overall record, including naming a U.S. Ambassador to ASEAN—making Washington the first non-ASEAN country to do so.

In addition to this, the United States also continued to play a key role during periods of crisis that affected Southeast Asian states. Though these were responses to individual events rather than a predetermined, strategic effort, Washington's contributions in this respect, be it coordinating disaster response following the outbreak of the Indian Ocean tsunami among key regional states and accelerating efforts at coming up with common responses to address avian influenza as well, nonetheless did not go unnoticed.[27]

Yet notwithstanding these contributions made by the United States, all in all, the post-9/11 period represented a period of contraction of the extent of U.S. diplomatic commitment to Southeast Asia. During this period, the United States at times failed to meet even the basic requirements of engagement on this score, and U.S. officials remained largely disinterested with respect to the future evolution of multilateral institutions in the region.

2.1.4   Economic Engagement

The post-9/11 period also witnessed an increase in economic engagement as part of the wider expansion of the level of U.S. commitment to Southeast Asia. During this period, U.S. policymakers advanced economic initiatives in the subregion and the level of economic activity between the United States and Southeast Asia clearly increased as well accordingly.

In aggregate terms, data corroborated from multiple sources clearly illustrate that U.S. trade and investment numbers in Southeast Asia continued on an upward trend during the initial years of the post-9/11 period following the downturn following the Asian Financial Crisis and right before the global financial crisis that hit during the 2007–2008 period.[28] Indicators such as the amount of U.S. exports to ASEAN countries as well as the amount of foreign direct investment going into Southeast Asian states both recorded increase during this period, reflecting this expansion.

---

[27] For a more detailed look into this dimension, see: East Asian Strategic Review 2006, "Indian Ocean Tsunami and International Cooperation," The National Institute of Defense Studies, Tokyo, 2006.

[28] Data based on evidence presented in: GAO, "Southeast Asia: Trends in US and Chinese Economic Engagement," August 2015; Peter A. Petri and Michael G. Plummer, "ASEAN Centrality and the ASEAN-US Economic Relationship," East–West Center, Washington, D.C., 2014; US-ASEAN Business Council, "Why ASEAN Matters: Trade and Investment," Updated 2017.

The numbers were reflective of the efforts by U.S. officials to expand economic engagement with Southeast Asia during this period. Early on in the post-9/11 period, the Bush administration revealed its vision for this called the Enterprise for ASEAN Initiative (EAI), which provided a roadmap to get to bilateral free trade agreements (FTAs) with Southeast Asian states following the successful securing of Trade Promotion Authority (TPA) in 2002.[29] While there were some hits and misses on this score—the agreement with Singapore concluded in 2003 was a landmark agreement as it was the first such FTA with an Asian country, but ones with Malaysia and Thailand were ultimately less successful—this was complemented by other measures as well on this so-called roadmap, such as the reaching of Trade and Investment Framework Agreements (TIFAs) with key ASEAN countries, notably Indonesia and Vietnam.

Beyond just expanding engagement with individual countries, the post-9/11 period also saw the United States trying to knit these interactions together as part of a more coherent approach. For instance, U.S. officials clearly noted on multiple occasions that the eventual goal of these bilateral trade pacts with Southeast Asian states was to get to an institutionalized economic relationship with ASEAN of some sort, such as an ASEAN-wide TIFA with the eventual goal of getting to a U.S.-ASEAN FTA as the final destination.[30]

Last and certainly not least, with Singapore's strong support and following the inking of the U.S.-Singapore FTA, the United States also began exploring entering into negotiations with Singapore, Chile, New Zealand, and Brunei—known as the "P4" group of countries—following their conclusion of a Trans-Pacific Strategic Economic Partnership based on U.S. FTAs with Singapore and Chile.[31] This would become the precursor to the Trans-Pacific Partnership (TPP) agreement that would itself be another landmark development within U.S. trade policy.

[29] Fact Sheet, "Enterprise for ASEAN Initiative," White House, Washington, DC, October 26, 2002.

[30] For an example of an articulation of this strategic approach, see: Karan Bhatia, Remarks to US-ASEAN Business Council, July 11, 2006. In those remarks, Bhatia said, "We are looking to support ASEAN integration and to institutionalize our relationship with ASEAN through a trade and investment agreement with ASEAN as an institution."

[31] Susan C. Schwab, "The President's Trade Policy Agenda," United States Trade Representative, March 1, 2008.

Table 1   Summary of Findings on Commitment Level in the Post-9/11 Period

Category	Choices	Finding
Military deployments	Expanded or reduced?	Limited expansion
Alliances and partnerships	Strengthened or weakened?	Selective strengthening
Diplomatic initiatives	Active, reactive, or inactive?	Inactive
Economic engagement	Increased or decreased?	Increased
Overall level	Increase or decrease?	Moderate increase

Source Generated by Author

The sum of these components contribute to an overall sense of a moderate increase in the U.S. commitment level to Southeast Asia during the post-9/11 period. The findings discussed in this section are summarized in Table 1.

2.2   Moderate Decrease in Commitment Balance

The moderate increase in commitment level was accompanied by a moderate decrease in commitment balance with respect to Southeast Asia during the post-9/11 period as well. Specifically, four of the five of the areas set out in the balance of commitment framework witnessed imbalances within them.

2.2.1   Means/Ends

There was no significant and sustained imbalance observed in U.S. commitment to Southeast Asia with respect to means and ends during the post-9/11 period. Though U.S. policymakers did have some ambitious ends during this period, it was also the case that the means available to them were not only not significantly restricted beyond usual pressures, but in some cases and specific areas, those pressures were actually much lower than had been seen in previous periods as well.

U.S. foreign policy ends during the post-9/11 era under the Bush administration have been characterized by some commentators as overly ambitious and misaligned with the means needed to accomplish them. And indeed, in regions such as the Middle East, the effort to promote a so-called "balance of power in favor of freedom" through a three-pillared strategy of thwarting terrorists and rogue regimes, harmonizing relations among great powers and nurturing prosperity and democracy across the globe, did indeed prove a bridge too far, especially in cases like Iraq.[32] "Bush's foreign policy is vulnerable to criticism not because it departs radically from previous administrations, but because it cannot succeed," the historian Melvyn Leffler has argued. "The goals are unachievable because the means and ends are out of sync".[33]

But in Southeast Asia, the post-9/11 period witnessed a trend where there was no significant or sustained imbalance observed between ambitious U.S. ends and more readily available U.S. means in U.S. policy. On key U.S. ends such as waging the war on terrorism in Southeast Asia and competing with China in the region, while the Bush administration was by no means immune to the pressures associated with getting the resources necessary to accomplish its goals, it was largely able to manage them relatively well in large part in order to calibrate means and ends in its approach to the region.

This was most clearly demonstrated with respect to the security side. Given the importance and urgency of the terrorism threat and its centrality within U.S. Southeast Asia policy, the United States did not find it difficult to secure means for its ends. Bronson Percival, an experienced diplomat who also served as counterterrorism coordinator at the East Asia and Pacific bureau at the U.S. State Department, observed in his reflection on the George W. Bush years that the means the Bush administration was able to draw on for its ends was especially impressive given how little resources there were devoted to terrorism in Southeast Asia to begin with. "I did not realize the resources that the United States could and would bring to bear on figuring this out…figuring out what was happening, who was connected, and why," Percival noted. "It was quite extraordinary."[34]

---

[32] The White House, *National Security Strategy of the United States of America*, September 2002. Condoleezza Rice, "A Balance of Power that Favors Freedom," The Manhattan Institute's Wriston Lecture, October 1, 2002; Hal Brands and Peter Feaver, "The Case for Bush Revisionism: Reevaluating the Legacy of America's 43rd President," *Journal of Strategic Studies* (28 July 2017), pp. 234–274.

[33] Melvyn P. Leffler, "Think Again: Bush's Foreign Policy," *Foreign Policy*, October 23, 2009.

[34] Bronson Percival, "Post-9/11 Policy in East and Southeast Asia," Center for Presidential History Collective Memory Project.

On the economic and diplomatic side, while the administration did encounter some of the same obstacles that others before it did in Southeast Asia, in some notable cases it was nonetheless able to secure the means it needed for its ends. This was due to a range of factors, including the relatively greater consensus in U.S. domestic politics about key foreign policy goals being advanced in Southeast Asia as well as the administration's better management of domestic pressures as well. Examples of this included resources that were mobilized for ASEAN capacity-building programs as well as Congressional support for trade agreements such as the U.S.-Singapore free trade agreement and the advancing of the idea of a U.S. ambassador to ASEAN, which was initially accomplished in Bush's second term despite being credited to the Obama administration which took this a step further with a permanent resident envoy in Jakarta.[35]

This is not to say that there were absolutely no imbalances observed or perceived between means and ends with respect to U.S. Southeast Asia policy in the post-9/11 era. On counterterrorism, critics rightly noted that while the administration was able to secure select means for the narrow ends it was advancing in Southeast Asia, it resulted in a rather "one-dimensional" approach that focused on the security aspects at the expense of diplomatic and people-to-people considerations.[36] And with respect to competing with China in Southeast Asia, while the administration was able to obtain some resources for this end, some observers noted that the investments made still paled in comparison to those made by Beijing and thus amounted to a "mismatch of desired objectives and resources".[37] Nonetheless, for the most part, there were no significant imbalances between means and ends observed with respect to U.S. commitment in Southeast Asia during this period.

---

[35] U.S. Government Publishing Office, "S. 2697 (IS) – United States Ambassador for ASEAN Act," 109th Congress, 2nd Section, May 2, 2006; The Nation, "America Strengthens Southeast Asia Ties," April 18, 2008.

[36] Robert M. Hathaway, "George Bush's Unfinished Asian Agenda," *American Diplomacy*, 2012. http://www.unc.edu/depts/diplomat/item/2005/0406/hath/hathaway_asia.html.

[37] The quote comes from Richard Cronin, "The Second Bush Administration and Southeast Asia," Draft Paper, 17 July 2007. Separately, see also: Carin Zissis, "Crafting a US Policy on Asia," Council on Foreign Relations, April 10, 2007.

2.2.2   Interests/Ideals

There were clear imbalances witnessed between ideals and interests during the post-9/11 period. Though the extent of the imbalance may not have been as significant as witnessed during the Clinton years and there were of course variations by case and country concerned, the broad trend was that the United States placed a greater emphasis on ideals over interests in its approach to Southeast Asia during the period in question.

The Bush administration's increased focus on ideals was evident in its wider foreign policy, which was captured as the pursuit of a "balance of power in favor of freedom" as noted earlier, with democracy promotion as an objective. While the actual advancement of this objective was hardly consistent, as was seen in previous U.S. administrations as well, it is also true that Asia in general, and Southeast Asia in particular, were not exempt from this enhanced focus on ideals. For instance, in one notable example, the Bush administration committed to joining other free nations across the region, including Southeast Asia, to establish a new Asia–Pacific Democracy Partnership. In a speech in Bangkok, Bush hailed the organization as "the region's only organization whose sole focus is promoting democratic values and institutions in Asia."[38]

Beyond this general orientation, the greater emphasis on ideals over interests also manifested itself in specific countries. A case in point was Myanmar. Throughout the post-9/11 period, the administration continued to take a tough line on Myanmar and human rights abuses committed under the junta, in spite of the fact that this stood in the way of Washington's ability to engage ASEAN as a whole given that it was one of its ten member states. This stance continued for much of the period, despite the fact that ASEAN officials would continue to urge Washington not to continue to "hold ASEAN hostage to Myanmar."[39]

Myanmar was admittedly a unique case for the administration, especially considering the circumstances in the country and other factors including the personal interest of Bush's wife, Laura Bush, in the issue, known to those familiar with the period. But even apart from Myanmar,

---

[38] Office of the Press Secretary, "Remarks by President George W. Bush in Bangkok, Thailand," White House, August 7, 2008.

[39] Chan Heng Chee, "George W. Bush in Asia: Retrospect and Prospect," in: Robert M. Hathaway and Wilson Lee (eds.), *George W. Bush and East Asia: A First Term Assessment* (Washington, DC, 2005), p. 97.

there was also scrutiny and pressure placed on other countries, particularly those countries in mainland Southeast Asia such as Cambodia, Laos and Vietnam. As Catharin Dalpino has noted, while some of these efforts focused both on general issues such as democracy seen in previous administrations, it was also the case that there were also more specific aspects to a greater degree than witnessed before such as religious freedom, with particular attention given to the treatment of Christians in these countries.[40]

To be sure, as with previous periods in U.S. history, as was mentioned earlier as well, the post-9/11 period did not see the United States adopt a consistent approach across the board, and there were clear instances where interests were placed over ideals. For instance, in recognition of the rising importance of the U.S.-Indonesia relationship to American priorities such as counterterrorism in a post-9/11 period, the Bush administration moved to gradually lift restrictions on U.S. security ties with Jakarta.[41] Nonetheless, in sum, there clearly was an imbalance tilted in favor of ideals over interests with respect to U.S. commitment to Southeast Asia during the post-9/11 period.

2.2.3   Cooperative/Confrontational

Another clear imbalance in U.S. commitment to Southeast Asia post-9/11 period was the one favoring cooperative over confrontational approach to American adversaries. During this time, the U.S. emphasis on a confrontational approach toward a range of U.S. adversaries and competitors as opposed to a more cooperative one, be it in terms terrorist groups, rogue regimes or other rival major powers, manifested itself in Washington's approach to Southeast Asia as well.[42]

The imbalance in favor of confrontational over cooperative approaches to U.S. adversaries was clearly witnessed with respect to counterterrorism

[40] Catharin Dalpino, "Bush in Southeast Asia: Widening Gyres," in "George W. Bush in Asia: Retrospect and Prospect," in: Robert M. Hathaway and Wilson Lee (eds.), *George W. Bush and East Asia: A First Term Assessment* (Washington, DC, 2005), p. 177.

[41] Matthew P. Daley, "U.S. Interests and Policy Priorities in Southeast Asia," Testimony before the House International Relations Committee, Subcommittee on East Asia and the Pacific, Washington, DC, March 26, 2003.

[42] The U.S. record on this front was read by some as evidence of tendencies seen in earlier periods too, rather than an aberration. See, for instance: Mark Beeson, "U.S. Hegemony in Southeast Asia: The Impact of, And Limit to, U.S. Power and Influence," *Critical Asian Studies*, Vol. 36, No. 3 (2004), pp. 445–462.

during the post-9//11 period. In line with its overall approach to rooting out terrorism, the Bush administration in Southeast Asia not only placed a significant focus on the use of military force to root out terrorist groups and sympathizer states, but also seemed to be framing the role of allies and partners in binary terms with some formulations that attracted public attention such as the "with us or against us" slogan. To many observers of Southeast Asian affairs, irrespective of whatever other merits this approach had, this seemed to favor a confrontational rather than a cooperative approach: it relied more on the promotion of U.S. military power rather than genuine consultation, collaboration and coalition-building which would take more time; it overrode some sensitivities perceived among some of the region's mainstream Muslims; and it demonstrated little sensitivity to the domestic constraints on Southeast Asian governments of the region in terms of how they chose to tackle perceived U.S. adversaries and align themselves with Washington.[43]

The imbalance favoring confrontational over cooperative approaches to U.S. adversaries also manifested itself with respect to U.S. policy toward Myanmar, which fit into the administration's category of rogue, undemocratic regimes. Here, Washington pursued a range of coercive measures in the economic domain designed to pressure and isolate the regime in Myanmar during the post-9/11 period, including financial sanctions and visa bans on select officials.[44] It largely persisted with this approach despite repeated calls by its Southeast Asian partners to adopt a softer

---

[43] For broader explorations of this point, see: Robert M. Hathaway, "George Bush's Unfinished Asian Agenda," *American Diplomacy*, 2012; Diane K Mauzy and Brian L. Job, "US Policy in Southeast Asia: Limited Reengagement After Years of Benign Neglect," *Asian Survey*, Vol. 47, No. 4, pp. 622–641; and Catharin A. Dalpino, "US Policy in Southeast Asia: Fortifying the Foundation," A Report and Recommendations From the Southeast Asia in the Twenty-First Century: Issues and Options for US Policy Initiative, The Stanley Foundation, 2005, especially pp. 7–13.

[44] For more general surveys of U.S.-Myanmar policy during the Bush years, see: Asia Society Task Force Report, "Current Realities and Future Possibilities in Burma/Myanmar: Options for U.S. Policy," March 2010; Catharin Dalpino, "Second Chance: Prospects for US-Myanmar Relations," in The National Bureau of Asian Research, "Myanmar's Growing Regional Role," NBR Special Report #45, March 2014, pp. 23–37. Andrew Selth, "United States Relations with Burma: From Hostility to Hope," Regional Outlook Paper, No. 36, 2012.

approach given wider considerations at play as well as the growing recognition among some in the United States about the need for a more balanced policy.[45]

The imbalance favoring confrontational over cooperative approaches on Washington's part was admittedly less clearly evident with respect to China in Southeast Asia, particularly during the post-9/11 period where the administration found more areas to work with Beijing. Even here, however, U.S. officials nonetheless repeatedly portrayed China as being a growing strategic competitor against the United States in Southeast Asia geopolitically and ideationally with respect to democracy and human rights and subsequently positioned their approach to the region from this perspective rather than one that was purely cooperative of collaborative.[46]

2.2.4   Bilateralism/Multilateralism

The third imbalance evident in U.S. commitment to Southeast Asia during the post-9/11 period was one in favor of bilateralism—and, in some cases, unilateralism—over multilateralism. Though the United States still maintained a procedural commitment to multilateralism, Washington during this period had a clear skepticism about multilateral organizations and regimes and treaties more generally that resulted in a tilt toward bilateral approaches.

During the post-9/11 period, U.S. officials were largely skeptical from the outset about the effectiveness of multilateral organizations. The Bush administration's approach to advancing U.S. interests lay primarily in knitting together minilateral coalitions of like-minded states, rather than large, unwieldy multilateral organizations—what was often characterized by observers as "coalitions of the willing."[47] To the extent that the United States invested in multilateralism, U.S. officials made clear that this would

---

[45] For an expansion on this point, see: Michael Green and Derek Mitchell, "Asia's Forgotten Crisis: A New Approach to Burma," *Foreign Affairs*, November/December 2007, pp. 147–158.

[46] For particularly notable examples of this, see: James A. Kelly, "U.S. Trade and Commercial Policy Toward Southeast Asia," Testimony before the House International Relations Committee, Washington, DC, June 25, 2003; and Donald Rumsfeld, "Remarks at the 2005 Shangri-La Dialogue in Singapore," June 4, 2005.

[47] Ralf Emmers, "Security Cooperation in the Asia–Pacific: Evolution of Concepts and Practices," in: See Seng Tan and Amitav Acharya (eds.), *Asia–Pacific Security Cooperation: National Interests and Regional Order* (M.E. Sharpe, 2004), pp. 3–19.

be done selectively, or what Richard Haass, the director of policy planning at the State Department, termed "a la carte multilateralism."[48]

This approach clearly played out in Southeast Asia as well. During the post-9/11 period, U.S. officials devoted significant attention to the construction of bilateral relationships in Southeast Asia that could help serve U.S. interests such as counterterrorism—be it allies like Thailand and the Philippines or partners like Singapore and Indonesia. Yet, at the same time, little attention was paid to the importance of multilateral groupings in Southeast Asia, even when it came to basic indicators such as the attendance of high-level officials to regional meetings.[49] While there were a series of reasons why this was the case, administration officials also clearly saw little reason to invest in unwieldy, underperforming institutions that were seen to matter little when it came to the promotion of short-term, direct U.S interests, finding more value instead in minilateral "coalitions of the willing," be it in terms of alignments such as the quadrilateral formed between the United States, India, Japan, and Australia or initiatives such as the Proliferation Security Initiative.[50]

Of course, Washington did not entirely neglect multilateral institutions and institution-building more generally during this period. Consistent with Haass's characterization of "a la carte multilateralism," U.S. officials did invest selectively in ASEAN-led institutions when it was deemed to be in its interests and continued some routine forms of support. And there is also some truth to the suggestion that some administration officials did genuinely see a convergence between bilateral networks and some gradual multilateralization further down the line, as was the case on trade where a bilateral network of FTAs was seen to eventually lead to an ASEAN-wise agreement of some sort. Nonetheless, for the most part, there was a clear privileging of bilateralism over multilateralism in the advancement of U.S. ends in Southeast Asia.

[48] Tom Shanker, "White House Says US Is Not a Loner, Just Choosy," *New York Times*, July 31, 2001.

[49] Victor Cha, "The Obama Administration's Policy Toward East Asia," *The Korean Journal of Defense Analysis*, Vol. 22, No. 1 (March 2010), pp. 1–14. For a reaction that typifies regional perceptions, see: Darren Schuettler, "Interview: Bush No-Show Sends Wrong Signal to SE Asia," *Reuters*, July 20, 2007.

[50] Richard Armitage once characterized the ARF as "so flabby and disparate as to [be] unworkable." Peter Hartcher, "Who Will Keep the Peace in Asia When the U.S. Leaves," *Australian Financial Review*, September 11, 1999.

2.2.5   Security/Economics

The post-9/11 period also saw a greater imbalance in favor of security over economic considerations in terms of the U.S. commitment to Southeast Asia. During this time, even though the United States did continue to seek to strengthen economic ties with Southeast Asian states, this was clearly overshadowed by Washington's security considerations given the overwhelming focus on counterterrorism.

The prevalence of security relative to economic considerations was most clearly demonstrated in terms of the focus on terrorism in the post-9/11 period. Victor Cha, who served as a key Asia policy adviser in the White House during the Bush administration, has himself admitted that there was a "singular focus" on terrorism by U.S. policymakers with respect to their priorities regarding Southeast Asian states, even if that emphasis may have been justified in terms of Washington's interest in foiling future terrorist plots.[51] Michael Green, who also was at the White House during the Bush years, has also admitted that the lack of an initial comprehensive strategic focus on Southeast Asia, combined with the 9/11 attacks, contributed to the region being seen principally from the security lens of counterterrorism.[52]

Furthermore, the relatively greater focus placed on the security side of the administration's counterterrorism agenda relative to other aspects such as the diplomatic, economic, people-to-people aspects, also further exacerbated the imbalance during this period. The emphasis on aspects such as military deployments, intelligence cooperation and security assistance, rather than economic development and governance support designed to address the underlying root causes behind terrorism and extremism in countries such as Indonesia and the Philippines, contributed to a sense of a "one-dimensional" approach to countering the challenge as noted before.[53] The security-economics imbalance was also intensified by the contrast between the overly securitized U.S. approach to the more broad-based and economics-heavy ones adopted by other Southeast Asian

---

[51] Victor Cha, "The Obama Administration's Policy Toward East Asia," *The Korean Journal of Defense Analysis*, Vol. 22, No. 1 (March 2010), pp. 1–14.

[52] Michael Green, *By More Than Providence: Grand Strategy and American Power in the Asia–Pacific Since 1783* (New York: Columbia University Press, 2017), especially p. 502.

[53] Robert M. Hathaway, "George Bush's Unfinished Asian Agenda," *American Diplomacy*, 2012.

partners such as China, irrespective of how misguided such comparisons may have been.[54]

The imbalance was further illustrated by the securitization of certain aspects of economic policy as well. The most notable example in this respect was the Bush administration's securitization of the agenda at the Asia–Pacific Economic Cooperation (APEC) summit, which was met by concern among some Southeast Asian states. While the administration clearly saw this as an effort to make progress on counterterrorism as a key U.S. priority, it catalyzed regional fears that the long shadow of terrorism had so militarized U.S. foreign policy such that a trade body was at the risk of being securitized under the weight of American pressure.

To be sure, one should not overstate the extent of the imbalance between security and economics that existed in U.S. Southeast Asia policy during the post-9/11 period. To their credit, Asia officials in the George W. Bush administration did continue to see a link between the opening of markets and the promotion of greater freedom, tolerance and moderation that was central to managing threats such as terrorism, and they repeatedly said so in their public statements.[55] Furthermore, partly because they themselves were aware of an overly narrow U.S. approach to the region, top U.S. Asia officials did continue to frame the importance of Southeast Asia not exclusively in terms of security but also in economic terms, with metrics such as growing trade and investment as well as the integration of the subregion into wider U.S. economic goals such as the quest for new FTAs.[56] Nonetheless, overall, one can clearly perceive an imbalance in favor of security over economics with respect to U.S. commitment to Southeast Asia during this period.

[54] For a deeper exploration of this, see: Joseph Liow. *Ambivalent Engagement: The United States and Regional Security in Southeast Asia After the Cold War* (Washington, DC: Brookings Institution Press, 2017), especially pp. 124–137.

[55] Conversation with former U.S. official, Washington, DC, May 2021. For an example of this, see, for instance: Jon M. Huntsman, Jr., "U.S.-Asia Trade After September 11," Remarks at Washington International Trade Association, December 6, 2001.

[56] See, for example: James A. Kelley, "US Trade and Commercial Policy Toward Southeast Asia," Testimony Before the House International Relations Committee, June 25, 2003.

Table 2 Summary of Findings on Balance of Commitment for the Post-9/11 Period

Category	Choices	Finding
Means/ends	Are resources commensurate with goals and objectives?	No imbalance
Interests/ideals	Is attention on ideals or more narrowly on core interests?	Imbalance (ideals)
Cooperative/confrontational	Is approach to adversaries and competitors cooperative or confrontational?	Imbalance (confrontational)
Bilateralism/multilateralism	Is bilateral & unilateral or multilateral approach favored?	Imbalance (bilateral)
Security/economics	Is there a greater attention on security or economics?	Imbalance (security)
Overall balance	Increase or decrease?	Moderate decrease

Source Generated by Author

All told, the post-9/11 period witnessed a moderate decrease in commitment balance, with greater imbalances located in all but one category. The summary of the various categories, choices and findings are summarized in Table 2.

3   EXPLAINING U.S. COMMITMENT DURING THE POST-9/11 PERIOD

3.1   Minor Increase in Relative Power

The distribution of military and economic power between the United States and its competitors both globally and regionally certainly played into Washington's commitment to Southeast Asia during the post-9/11 period, as neorealism would predict. In the minds of key U.S. policymakers, in an environment where Washington experienced a minor increase in relative power, the United States' continued status as a unipolar power, along with its reinforcement of its relative capabilities that followed the September 11 attacks, created a context where despite any challenges that it might confront, Washington would have an increased ability and enhanced willingness to sustain U.S. primary while also shaping a more contested order in Asia in general and Southeast Asia in particular.

During the post-9/11 period, the United States continued to maintain its status as having a preponderance of power in a unipolar world. Despite some arguments about a move to a more multipolar world in the late 1990s and the costs imposed on the United States during the September 11 attacks, U.S. unipolarity continued to persist as illustrated by its actual material capabilities into the post-9/11 period.[57] As Stephen G. Brooks and William C. Wohlforth have argued, U.S. dominance was made clear in terms of its unrivaled position in the standard components of military and economic power across the board—in 2003, for instance, it was set to spend more on defense than the next 15–20 biggest spenders combined, while its economy still remained twice as large as Japan's.[58] Furthermore, Washington's quick demonstration of its ability to project power in several places across the globe after the 9/11 attacks and the fact that it was also able to quickly increase defense spending to further expand its capabilities, only served to reinforce the notion of the preponderance of American power in a unipolar world.[59]

Key administration officials also clearly believed that the relative distribution of capabilities was such that it was reinforcing the preponderance of American power in a unipolar world. As James Mann observed, several of them already come into office with a firm belief rooted in an "extraordinarily optimistic assessment of American capabilities"—they believed that Washington had vastly more power in reserve than usually realized; understood that U.S. power needed to be sustained in the face of growing challengers; and dismissed obstacles that could get in the way of accomplishing U.S. goals, such as the lack of troops or staying

---

[57] Bryan W. Roberts, "The Macroeconomic Impacts of the 9/11 Attack: Evidence from Real-Time Forecasting," Department of Homeland Security, Office of Immigration Statistics Policy Directorate, August 2009.

[58] Stephen G. Brooks and William C. Wohlforth, "American Primacy in Perspective," *Foreign Affairs*, July/August 2002, pp. 22–23.

[59] Evelyn Goh, "Hegemonic Constraints: The Implications of 9/11 for American Power," S. Rajaratnam School of International Studies, Working Paper No. 34, October 2002, especially pp. 2–3.

142   P. PARAMESWARAN

power.[60] The post-9/11 period quickly saw them put into place a worldview that rested on the firm belief in U.S. preponderance of power and
their quest to preserve it. As noted earlier, the administration's National
Security Strategy launched in September 2002 articulated an ambitious
vision seeking to promote a "balance of power in favor of freedom"
by thwarting terrorists and rogue regimes, harmonizing relations among
great powers and promoting prosperity and democracy across the world
with a focus on preemption, hegemony and unilateral tendencies.[61]

Asia in general and Southeast Asia in particular were not immune
from this worldview. Indeed, from the outset, Bush and his key advisers,
most notably four who had deep experience on Asia—Richard Armitage,
Paul Wolfowitz, Bob Zoellick and Richard Cheney—saw Asia as being
central to preserving U.S. preponderance of power globally.[62] Whether it
be immediate threats, such as terrorism in Southeast Asia which gained
salience following the 9/11 attacks, or longer-term challenges to the
United States such as China which was on the administration's mind
long before that, the region was recognized as being key to any effort
to promote a balance of power in favor of freedom.

The way relative capabilities were perceived and employed in turn
affected both the level of U.S. commitment as well as its distribution
in Southeast Asia. With respect to its level, this meant that there would
be increases in the overall level of U.S. commitment in some areas as
Washington, in view of its significant and increasing relative capabilities,
sought to shape the emerging order in Southeast Asia by confronting
a range of security threats and preserving its position of primacy in the
Asia–Pacific. While the primary and immediate threat U.S. policymakers
perceived in Southeast Asia was terrorism, a secondary threat was also
sensed with respect to China and its role in the region even as the Bush

[60] James Mann, *Rise of the Vulcans: The History of Bush's War Cabinet* (New York: Penguin, 2004), pp. 362–363.

[61] The White House, National Security Strategy of the United States of America, September 2002. Condoleezza Rice, "A Balance of Power that Favors Freedom," The Manhattan Institute's Wriston Lecture, October 1, 2002; Melvyn P. Leffler, "Think Again: Bush's Foreign Policy," *Foreign Policy*, October 23, 2009; Brad Roberts, "American Primacy and Major Power Concert: A Critique of the 2002 National Security Strategy," Institute for Defense Analyses, December 2002.

[62] Author conversation with former senior U.S. official, Washington, DC, October 2019.

administration attempted to manage the broader relationship with Beijing as well.

This was most clearly evident on the security side. Here, U.S. policymakers moved quickly to cement a series of new security arrangements with Southeast Asian states to counter the terrorism threat, which included rotational deployments for assets and personnel. Beyond that, as U.S. policy documents released during the post-9/11 era have shown and U.S. policymakers privately indicated—including the Defense Strategy Review, the Quadrennial Defense Review and the Global Posture Review—the Bush administration also quietly used the renewed momentum with respect to its allies and partners to further boost defense ties with a view to dissuade China from challenging the U.S. position in the Asia–Pacific.[63]

With respect to the distribution of commitment, it also meant that there would be imbalances in some areas, since the mindset of unipolarity and U.S. primacy tended to lead to the prioritization of certain realms and perspectives over others as well.[64] The imbalance in favor of bilateral and unilateral approaches rather than multilateral ones is a case in point. While there were certainly other factors at play, it is also true that some personalities within the Bush administration saw multilateral institutions as being overly constraining on Washington and offering few benefits in return at a time when there were other arrangements the United States could use with the freedom of action it had in a unipolar world.[65] To take just one example, a major reason why the Bush administration did not pursue TAC ratification, which would have gotten the United States into the EAS, was because it was perceived to be too constraining, with

[63] John Gershman, "Is Southeast Asia the Second Front?" *Foreign Affairs*, Vol. 81, No. 4 (July/August 2002), pp. 60–74; Aaron Friedberg, "11 September and the Future of Sino-American Relations," *Survival*, Vol. 44, No. 1 (Spring 2002), pp. 40–42; Nina Silove, "The Pivot Before the Pivot: U.S. Strategy to Preserve the Power Balance in Asia," *International Security*, Vol. 40, No. 4 (Spring 2016), pp. 45–88.

[64] The interpretation was just part of a wider debate about the implications of a unipolar world order on U.S. actions. For one broader conception of the debate, see: G. John Ikenberry, "Power and Liberal Order: America's Postwar World Order in Transition," *International Relations of the Asia–Pacific*, Vol. 5 (2005), pp. 133–152.

[65] Author conversation with former senior U.S. diplomat, Washington, DC, March 2020.

pledges to resolve disputes without force potentially limiting the scope for U.S. military power in Asia.[66]

But although the relative distribution of capabilities does give us a sense of the broad thinking behind and general contours of U.S. commitment to Southeast Asia in the post-9/11 era as balance of power theory would expect, it tells us much less about the specifics of the level and distribution of that commitment based on the metrics laid out in the preceding section. For a better sense of how U.S. policymakers reacted to opportunities and challenges they faced domestically, regionally and globally during this period as well as how they managed the limited military, economic, political and diplomatic resources at their disposal, we need to delve into their calculations about power and threats (threat perceptions) as well as their ability to mobilize resources (state power)—the two intervening variables that are key to the balance of commitment framework.

3.2   Moderately High Threat Level

While the relative distribution of capabilities no doubt played a role in shaping U.S. commitment to Southeast Asia during the post-9/11 period, this was also filtered through the lens of elite calculations about power and threats, or, put more simply, threat perceptions. Specifically, during this period, we witnessed a moderately high threat level among the U.S. foreign policy elite with respect to Southeast Asia. This trend of heightened threat perceptions continued on through most of period in question, even amid concerns among some in Southeast Asia and even in the U.S. foreign policy community about growing threats in the subregion.

During the post-9/11 period, the Bush administration operated under moderately high threat perceptions. Memoirs from key decisionmakers and other sources reveal the high level of stress that persisted in the administration in the months and years that followed the attacks,

---

[66] For more detailed examinations of this point, see: Mark E. Manyin, Michael John Garcia, and Wayne M. Morrison, "US Accession to the Association of Southeast Asian Nations' Treaty of Amity and Cooperation," *Congressional Research Service*, July 13, 2009; Bruce Vaughn, "East Asian Summit: Issues for Congress," Congressional Research Service Reports for Congress, Library of Congress, Washington, DC (December 9, 2005).

including about preventing future attacks as well.[67] "9/11 crystallized our vulnerability," Rice explained succinctly when she unveiled the administration's 2002 National Security Strategy a year after the attacks.[68] "In the case of the Bush administration, the evidence we now have suggests the salience of threat perception," the historian Melvyn Leffler has argued. "Fear has shaped policy."[69]

The sense of heightened threat perceptions in turn affected the conduct of U.S. foreign policy in the post 9/11 environment. Most notably, following the September 11 attacks, the environment that we had seen during the post-Cold War period, where there were a range of smaller or longer-term threats to U.S. interests but no clear single, imminent threat, gave way to an environment where countering terrorism, rogue regimes and proliferators of weapons of mass destruction was viewed as the main immediate threat.[70] The post-9/11 environment also saw a greater sense of urgency injected into U.S. foreign policymaking in terms of achieving U.S. ends, further empowering voices that had been calling for more unilateral, hegemonic and preemptive approaches to countering threats.

This in turn had implications for Asia in general and Southeast Asia as well. Most notably, the 9/11 attacks elevated Southeast Asia's immediate importance to U.S. interests within Asia policy in a way that had not been the case at the administration's outset. Whatever the administration's initial focus areas, the reality was that rooting out the terrorism threat in Asia would be an effort focused on Southeast Asia because that was where the challenge lay.[71] Hence, while administration officials would continue

---

[67] For an elaboration of this point, see: Hal Brands and Peter Feaver, "The Case for Bush Revisionism: Reevaluating the Legacy of America's 43rd President," *Journal of Strategic Studies* (July 28, 2017). For examples from policymakers, see, in particular: George W. Bush, *Decision Points* (New York: Broadway Books, 2011), especially Chapter 5; and Dick Cheney, *In My Time: A Personal and Political Memoir* (New York: Threshold, 2011), especially pp. 329–364.

[68] Condoleezza Rice, "A Balance of Power that Favors Freedom," The Manhattan Institute's Wriston Lecture, October 1, 2002.

[69] Melvyn P. Leffler, "9/11 and the Past and Future of American Foreign Policy," *International Affairs*, Vol. 79, No. 5 (October 2003), pp. 1045–1063.

[70] Colin L. Powell, "The Administration's Position With Respect to Iraq," House Committee on International Relations, September 19, 2002.

[71] Author conversation with former senior White House official, Washington, DC, March 2020.

to be attentive to other issues, including the growing challenge that China represented to the United States, the heightened threat level with respect to terrorism represented more of a marked shift relatively speaking. "The impression in and out of government after 9/11 was that the next front would be in Southeast Asia," Mike Green, who served in the White House under Bush, reflected on the level of threat after leaving his position. "The fight did not start well, and the outcome was hardly certain."[72]

Heightened threat perceptions affected both the level and distribution of U.S. commitment to Southeast Asia during the post-9/11 period. With respect to the level of U.S. commitment, various U.S. policy documents, speeches and writings during the post-9/11 period clearly illustrate the notion of Southeast Asia emerging as the second front of the war on terror, which subsequently focused Washington's efforts at eradicating an al-Qaeda-linked terrorist network in maritime Southeast Asia intent on targeting Western interests.[73] Writing in 2007, Bronson Percival, who worked on Southeast Asian affairs during the Bush years, reflected that as a consequence of the heightened threat level, "more high-level attention, albeit exclusively in the context of counterterrorism, has been devoted to Southeast Asia in the past few years than since the American withdrawal in Vietnam in 1973."[74]

With respect to the balance of commitment, an increase in threat perceptions led to imbalances of commitment across several realms when it came to Washington's role in Southeast Asia. For instance, on the shift from multilateralism to more unilateral and bilateral approaches, the increase of threat level heightened the perceived urgency by which policymakers had to act and also reduced the tolerance for the slower work of consensus-building. As Kumar Ramakrishna observed in his evaluation of post-9/11 perceptions in U.S. policy, this in turn contributed to the rise of thinking, including with respect to U.S. policy in Southeast Asia,

---

[72] Michael Green, *By More Than Providence: Grand Strategy and American Power in the Asia–Pacific Since 1783* (New York: Columbia University Press, 2017), p. 501.

[73] Diane K Mauzy and Brian L. Job, "US Policy in Southeast Asia: Limited Reengagement After Years of Benign Neglect," *Asian Survey*, Volume 47, Issue 4, pp. 622–641.

[74] Bronson Percival, *The Dragon Looks South: China and Southeast Asia in the New Century* (Westport: Praeger, 2007), p. 129.

that the United States either had to go it alone or had to assemble quick "coalitions of the willing" rather than slow multilateral institutions.[75] Another manifestation of commitment imbalance was in the greater emphasis on ideals over interests seen during the post-9/11 period. James Moriarty, who served in the Bush White House and worked in South Asia, noted in his reflections about the administration that heightened threat perceptions played an important role in swinging things in the direction of ideals over interests. In Moriarty's telling, the attacks constituted a wakeup call for the United States along the lines of Pearl Harbor and reinforced upon the Bush administration the need to "do what's necessary" to confront terrorists and rogue regimes capable of harming the country.[76] For Leffler, it is this heightened threat perception and elevation of ideals over interests that reinforced the administration's promotion of a "balance of power in favor of freedom."[77] Though this approach was applied unevenly in Southeast Asia, it accounted for various aspects of the administration's approach, whether it be with respect to the fervor with which the GWOT was waged or the continued isolation of Myanmar as part of a worldview that was suspicious of rogue regimes.[78]

The imbalance in favor of confrontational over cooperative approaches is yet another area where threat perceptions had an influence. This was especially the case with respect to terrorism, where the heightened sense of threat led to a Manichean, zero-sum worldview captured by the phrase advanced of countries either being "with us or against us" in the GWOT.[79] As Karl Jackson notes, in Southeast Asia, the heightened focus on the terrorism threat fueled an aggressive "for us or against us" mindset in the region that tended to paint things in black and white terms and showed little regard for the domestic constraints that leaders faced

[75] Kumar Ramakrishna, "Nine Months After 9/11: American Perceptions of the War on Terror at Home and Abroad, Including Southeast Asia," RSIS Commentary, August 1, 2002. For general insights into this line of thinking, see: Jeffrey Legro, *Rethinking the World: Great Power Strategies and International Order* (Ithaca: Cornell University, 2005), pp. 168–169.

[76] James Moriarty, "Interview: Post 9/11 Policy in East and Southeast Asia," Center for Presidential History: Collective Memory Project.

[77] Melvyn P. Leffler, "9/11 and the Past and Future of American Foreign Policy," *International Affairs*, Vol. 79, No. 5 (October 2003), pp. 1045–1063; Melvyn P. Leffler, "Think Again: Bush's Foreign Policy," *Foreign Policy*, October 23, 2009.

[78] Conversation with former U.S. defense official, Washington, DC, July 2019.

[79] CNN, "You Are Either with Us or Against Us," CNN.com, November 6, 2001.

in countries such as Indonesia or Malaysia.[80] Significantly, this approach would also affect Southeast Asian populations' perceptions of the United States as well for years to come.[81]

3.3   Medium State Capacity

The other filter in the balance of commitment framework, in addition to threat perceptions, is state capacity. During the post-9/11 period, we witnessed a period of medium state capacity, where U.S. policymakers found it relatively easy to mobilize resources for intended goals. Though there were certainly the usual pressures from sources including Congress and the wider public, the George W. Bush administration was largely able to get the commensurate capability and willingness to maintain commitments and at times even pursue new ones.

State capacity in the post-9/11 environment was at a medium level, with an overall increase in the wherewithal of the state that partly translated to Southeast Asia as well. Following the 9/11 attacks, the Bush administration operated within a context where there was overwhelming focus within U.S. government agencies, broad bipartisan support within U.S. government institutions, as well as wider public support for the advancement of its foreign policy goals on that score, which allowed it to mobilize resources relatively more quickly for the advancement of its priorities at home and abroad.[82] While there were several manifestations of this, the clearest demonstration of this was the swift approval of legislation authorizing the use of force by the U.S Congress—passed unanimously within the Senate and almost unanimously in the House of Representatives in 2002 (420-1) with a greater margin than the resolutions authorizing the Persian Gulf War in 2001.[83]

---

[80] For a broader exposition of this point, see: Karl Jackson, "Southeast Asia: Off the Radar Screen?" SAISPHERE, Johns Hopkins University, 2004. See also the background to the issue, pp. 19–20.

[81] Author conversation with former senior U.S. defense official, November 2019, Washington, DC.

[82] Derek Chollet and James Goldgeier, *America Between the Wars: From 11/9 to 9/11* (New York: Public Affairs, 2008), especially p. 316. For a broader evaluation of this, see: Hal Brands and Peter Feaver, "The Case for Bush Revisionism: Reevaluating the Legacy of America's 43rd President," *Journal of Strategic Studies* (July 28, 2017), pp. 234–274.

[83] For a broader comparative perspective, see: Richard Haass, *War of Necessity, War of Choice: A Memoir of Two Iraq Wars* (New York: Simon and Schuster, 2010).

This post-9/11 context had significant implications for how U.S. commitment played out in Asia in general and Southeast Asia in particular relative to previous periods in U.S. foreign policy. In particular, as Robert Sutter has previously observed, in marked contrast to the post-Cold War period, where divisions had repeatedly undermined the quest for consensus and affected aspects of U.S. Asia policy, the September 11 attacks both reduced the extent of those divisions among the public, between key U.S. institutions, and among government agencies, and also further energized support for a more assertive U.S. foreign policy that had been building since the late 1990s among some segments.[84] That in turn meant that it would be relatively easier to focus attention, mobilize resources and extract commitments in various aspects of U.S. commitment, even though the effects would not be equally felt across all realms.

The medium level of state capacity partly reflects the fact that the post-9/11 context did not guarantee that there would be a direct mobilization of resources for Southeast Asia more specifically, relative to other regions such as the Middle East or South Asia. To take just one example to illustrate this point, at times, as indicated in the previous section, the Bush administration's preoccupation with the Middle East, including its wars in Iraq and Afghanistan, distracted it from advancing priorities in Asia and diverted resources that could have been used there as well. Writing in 2008, Michael Green reflected that while many of the arguments about Iraq's impact on U.S. policy in Asia during the Bush administration had been overblown by critics, the notion that it took necessary attention, time and resources away from the U.S. government to focus on Asia—the very idea that would motivate the Obama administration's pivot or rebalance to Asia in subsequent years—certainly had some merit. According to Green:

Yet the Iraq war had one important pernicious impact on U.S. interests in Asia: it consumed U.S. attention in a way that has limited the ability of the administration and Congress to reinforce positive developments in the region and to build on partnerships and institutions that will be critical over the course of this century. This problem has been a gradual and

---

[84] Stanley R. Sloan, Robert G. Sutter, and Casimir A. Yost, "The Use of U.S. Power: Implications for U.S. Interests," Georgetown University, 2004, p. 83.

indirect result of the war. It is not irreparable but will require attention and recalibration.[85]

More specifically, with respect to the arguments here, the environment of medium state capacity affected both the level and distribution of U.S. commitment to Southeast Asia. With respect to its level, it created a more permissive environment where the United States was able to attain resources for the pursuit of its goals. This was especially the case on military deployments, given the military focus of the counterterrorism priority. As Sutter has rightly observed, during the initial years of the Bush administration, "there was little opposition in the United States to the increased U.S. military and other counterterrorism cooperation with Southeast Asian governments after September 11, 2001, terrorist attack on America."[86] While that opposition would intensify in subsequent years, the initial stages certainly saw a process where high state power facilitated U.S. military advancements in Southeast Asia.

Resource mobilization also helped power increased American commitment toward U.S. alliances and partnerships in Southeast Asia during the post-9/11 period. In line with Michael Green's observation from his time in the Bush White House that "the most immediate and far-reaching impact of 9/11 in Asia was on U.S. alliances," the September 11 attacks created a favorable situation that saw the United States able to take on greater commitments with respect to its Southeast Asian allies and partners—most notably its treaty allies Thailand and the Philippines—in the name of their increased support for counterterrorism.[87] For instance, in exchange for increased access for its personnel and assets or support for the wars in Iraq and Afghanistan from both Bangkok and Manila, U.S. policymakers were better able to marshal commitments that they would otherwise have found more difficult to draw on such as support for new military assistance and even the coveted non-NATO ally designations.[88]

---

[85] Michael Green, "The Iraq War and Asia: Assessing the Legacy," *The Washington Quarterly*, Vol. 31, No. 2 (Spring 2008), pp. 181–200.

[86] Robert Sutter, *The United States in Asia* (Lanham, MD: Rowman & Littlefield, 2009), p. 107.

[87] Michael Green, *By More Than Providence: Grand Strategy and American Power in the Asia–Pacific Since 1783* (New York: Columbia University Press, 2017), p. 501.

[88] Author conversation with former senior White House official, March 2020, Washington, DC.

Medium state capacity also played a role in commitment imbalances in Southeast Asia during the post 9/11 period as well. This was evident most clearly with respect to the imbalance in favor of security over economics, which stemmed from the relative ease with which resources could be mobilized in each of these two realms. U.S. policymakers found it easier to extract resources on the security side for the advancement of counterterrorism goals given the greater focus on them, and multiple U.S. officials during the Bush administration noted that beyond some smaller tussles, securing security-related assistance was a relatively easier task to accomplish.[89] By contrast, the economic side saw the administration encounter similar—and in some cases even greater—domestic constraints with respect to mobilizing resources to advance economic priorities, be it in crafting free trade agreements or be it growing skepticism among the American public on the benefits of free trade; the fraying of a bipartisan coalition for free trade in Congress; and growing partisanship more generally.[90]

From the aforementioned exploration into the reasons behind the shape of U.S. commitment during the post-9/11 period, it is clear that, as the balance of commitment model predicted, we witnessed a case where a minor increase in relative power, mediated by a moderately high threat level and medium state capacity, accounted for a moderate increase in commitment level and moderate decrease in commitment balance. Table 3 summarizes the findings.

4   EVALUATING U.S. COMMITMENT DURING THE POST-9/11 PERIOD

The post-9/11 period offers confirming evidence of the balance of commitment explanation in the U.S. commitment to Southeast Asia during the first years of the Bush administration. While changes in the strategic environment certainly shaped the general level and distribution of U.S. commitment, as balance of power theory would suggest, threat

---

[89] Randy Schriver, Interview: Post 9/11 Policy in East and Southeast Asia," Center for Presidential History: Collective Memory Project.

[90] A good exploration of this is found in: Amy Searight, "The United States and Asian Economic Regionalism: On the Outside Looking In?," in *A Pacific Nation: Perspectives on the US Role in an East Asia Community* (Tokyo: Japan Center for International Exchange, 2011), pp. 43–75.

Table 3   Summary of Findings on Balance of Commitment in Post-9/11 Period

Variable	Type	Finding	Predicted?
Relative power	Independent	Minor increase	Yes
Threat level	Intervening	Moderately high	Yes
State capacity	Intervening	Medium	Yes
Overall commitment level and distribution	Dependent	Moderate increase; Moderate decrease	Yes

Source Generated by Author

perceptions and state power accounted for the specific manifestations of components and categories of that commitment and explain why policy-makers ended up adopting the course they did as opposed to others that they may have preferred or considered.

In terms of the dependent variable, which is commitment level and distribution during the post-9/11 period, it is clear that the U.S. role during the period did largely align with expectations of the balance of commitment model. Notably, a couple of difference were also observed. Most notably, the level of expansion seen on military deployments and alliances and partnerships were more modest than anticipated, and commitment balance actually came up higher than had been predicted going into the study.

Turning to the independent and intervening variables, there was no clear transmission belt observed directly between the relative distribution of capabilities and commitment level and balance, which would have been the case if balance of power theory were correct. Instead, the contours of debates that U.S. policymakers had during the post-9/11 period, whether it be the best pathways to accomplish security objectives or to advance U.S. ideals, were largely around the intervening variables of threat perceptions and state power emphasized in the balance of commitment model.

Given all this, the balance of commitment framework can be said to have passed the third of the four case study tests examined here in the context of U.S.-Southeast Asia relations, and one that is a significant, complex and rich case. Now that this is clear, we can move on to the next case that occurs in the post-Global Financial Crisis (GFC) period under the administration of U.S. President Barack Obama.

CHAPTER 7

The Post-Global Financial Crisis Period

The Obama administration has devoted more attention to building ties with Southeast Asia than any administration since the Vietnam War.
—Tom Donilon, former National Security Adviser under Barack Obama, 2014[1]

Not least, I underscored how it was important to avoid the impression of a unidimensional U.S. presence in the region through a focus on the deployment of military assets, to the detriment of the "soft power" capacities it possessed, and the need to avoid the suggestion that U.S. engagement in the region was focused on managing the rise of China.
—Marty Natalegawa, former foreign minister of Indonesia, 2018[2]

1 INTRODUCTION

The first years under U.S. President Barack Obama witnessed the most significant increase in U.S. commitment to Southeast Asia since the end of the Vietnam War. Coming into office amid a financial crisis and two wars, the Obama administration pursued a foreign policy that prioritized

---

[1] Tom Donilon, "Obama in China: Preserving the Rebalance," Brookings Institution, Washington, DC, November 5, 2014.

[2] Marty Natalegawa, *Does ASEAN Matter? A View From Within* (Singapore: ISEAS, 2018), p. 97.

restoring America's image, emphasizing multilateralism, engaging with authoritarian regimes and perceived adversaries, and confronting common transnational threats.[3] As part of that, it orchestrated a fundamental refocusing of U.S. foreign policy that included a greater focus on Asia in general and Southeast Asia in particular—the so-called "pivot" or "rebalance" and the "rebalance within the rebalance"—where Washington was perceived to be underinvested.[4]

As a consequence of this, in what one might term the post-global financial crisis (GFC) period—which began after the fallout from the collapse of Lehman Brothers in September 2008 and lasted through mid-2014[5]—we saw a moderately increased commitment level and a moderately increased commitment balance from the United States with respect to Southeast Asia. What accounted for this moderate expansion and greater balancing of U.S. commitment to Southeast Asia that continued on for several years, in spite of the relative decline in power

---

[3] For a survey of assessments of Obama's foreign policy, see: Daniel W. Drezner, "Does Obama Have a Grand Strategy? Why We Need Doctrines in Uncertain Times," *Foreign Affairs*, July/August 2011; Derek Chollet, *The Long Game: How Obama Defied Washington and Redefined America's Role in the World* (New York: Public Affairs, 2016); Ben Rhodes, *The World as It Is: A Memoir of the Obama White House* (New York: Random House, 2018); James Mann, *Obamians: The Struggle Inside the White House to Redefine American Power* (New York: Penguin, 2013); and David E. Sanger, *The Inheritance: The World Obama Confronts and the Challenges to American Power* (New York: Harmony Books, 2009); and Hal Brands, "Barack Obama and the Dilemmas of American Grand Strategy," *The Washington Quarterly*, Vol. 39, No. 4, pp. 101–125.

[4] Obama was the first U.S. president to declare Asia as the highest priority region within U.S. foreign policy. Though the public unveiling of the policy was in a *Foreign Policy* article that Hillary Clinton authored in October 2011, administration officials have said it had been brewing since Obama first took office. See: Michael Green, *By More Than Providence: Grand Strategy and American Power in the Asia–Pacific Since 1783* (New York: Columbia University Press, 2017), pp. 518–524. The administration's focus on Southeast Asia within Asia policy was often termed the "rebalance within the rebalance." See: Susan Rice, "Explaining President Obama's Rebalance Strategy," Medium.com, September 5, 2016.

[5] The periodization chosen here is approximate—2008 is chosen because it was following the Lehman crash in 2007, even though the official timeline for the recession was from December 2007 to June 2009. 2014 is chosen because it is tied to the mid-2014 point when the U.S. economy recovered all jobs lost from the recession, even though economic indicators such as jobs growth and stock market value began turning upward and recovering to pre-recession levels between late 2012 up to May 2014 when that job recovery point was reached. Jim Puzzanghera, "Economy Has Recovered 8.7 Million Jobs Lost in Great Recession," *Los Angeles Times*, June 6, 2014.

and domestic constraints that the United States was encountering after the GFC? This chapter will argue that the balance of commitment model offers a plausible explanation, and one that is more complete than the next best explanation which is balance of power theory.

To preview the argument, as balance of commitment would predict, a moderate decrease in U.S. relative capabilities, mediated by a moderately high threat level perceived by the American foreign policy elite and moderately low state capacity, accounted for a moderate increase in commitment level and minor increase in commitment balance during this period. More specifically, U.S. policymakers felt that a decrease in U.S. relative power in previous years had eroded American capabilities, constraining Washington in what it could do with respect to its commitments abroad. This, combined with a moderately high threat level that U.S. policymakers perceived from China's rising capabilities, along with the reality that the domestic climate made it more difficult to mobilize and extract the resources that they needed, eventually led to a moderate increase in commitment level and a minor increase in commitment balance in the region. The argument is visually illustrated in Fig. 1.

If this case does fit with this more complex picture of the balance of commitment model, as opposed to a simpler one forecasted by balance of power theory with a stronger, more direct relationship (or "clear transmission belt") between changes in the relative power and changes in the level and distribution of U.S. commitment to the region as balance of

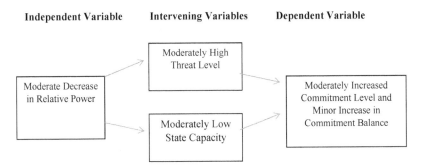

Fig. 1 The Balance of Commitment Model in the Post-GFC Period (*Source* Generated by Author)

power theory would suggest, this would be significant for the purposes of this book for three reasons.

First, the case itself is of significance since it represents the greatest increase in U.S. commitment to Southeast Asia since the end of the Vietnam War. While the so-called "pivot" or "rebalance" to Asia—which included a "rebalance within the rebalance" with the focus on Southeast Asia as some officials had termed it—has been the subject of commentary, far fewer accounts have subjected it to the immense scrutiny required to understand how the administration's rhetoric actually translated to reality, and, relatedly, how it managed to refocus its attention, time and resources to Southeast Asia even as it was tackling a long list of domestic challenges at home.[6] Probing these questions and the factors that played into them will thus be crucial in proving the arguments made in this study as well as its wider policy relevance.

Second, the post-GFC period constitutes an important test for balance of commitment because of the unique features and complexities associated with the case. For instance, since this is the only case of the four in this book where an administration specifically sought to make Southeast Asia in particular a focus of its foreign policy irrespective of what else was occurring around the world, studying it can help uncover one of the key considerations mulled at the beginning of this study: the relationship between the regional and the global levels. There are other complexities as well in this case that can unveil some additional insights into how to measure intervening variables and take this theory even further, whether it be significant divergences in threat perceptions between the president himself and his key advisers, and heated debates about the extent to which the resource constraints the administration faced were related to capacity or will.[7]

---

[6] For a range of assessments of Obama's pivot to Asia, see: Robert Sutter et al., "Balancing Acts: The U.S. Rebalance and Asia–Pacific Stability," Paper for the Sigur Center for Asian Studies Rising Power Initiative, August 2013; Michael J. Green, "The Legacy of Obama's 'Pivot' to Asia," *Foreign Policy*, September 3, 2016; David Shambaugh, "President Obama's Asia Scorecard," *Wilson Quarterly* (Winter 2016).

[7] For a survey of some of these considerations, see, for instance: Nicholas D. Anderson and Victor D. Cha, "The Case of the Pivot to Asia: System Effects and the Origins of Strategy," *Political Science Quarterly*, Vol. 132, No. 4 (Winter 2017–2018), pp. 595–617; Phillip C. Saunders, "China's Rising Power, the U.S. Rebalance to Asia, and Implications for U.S.-China Relations," *National Defense University, Issues & Studies*, Vol. 50, No. 3 (September 2014), pp. 19–55; and East Asian Strategic Review 2013, "Chapter 8:

Third, in terms of sourcing, though much of the period still lacks the extensive declassified documentation that the post-Vietnam period had, this post-GFC period case study has been buttressed with conversations with key policymakers who had firsthand accounts of what occurred at the time, along with the author's own familiarity with some decision points based on interactions with U.S. and Southeast Asian officials throughout the administration. If there is enough congruence between the U.S. decision-making process and the dynamics that balance of commitment would predict, and these accounts can be adequately corroborated with other forms of evidence, it would constitute an even clearer confirmation of the model's validity.

An elucidation of this argument and analyzing its implications for the broader study requires three major tasks. First, this examination must provide evidence that U.S. commitment to Southeast Asia actually changed, and, more specifically, that U.S. commitment level and balance both experienced a moderate increase and minor increase respectively. Second, it must verify that balance of commitment provides an explanation for this, and a superior one relative to balance of power theory. And third, it must then reflect on what this means for the broader study and balance of commitment, including previous predictions derived from the framework.

Accordingly, this chapter proceeds in three sections. The first section explores the shape of U.S. commitment to Southeast Asia during the post-GFC period, delving into the specific indicators and metrics set out in the introductory chapter. The second section then explores the explanations for this level and distribution of U.S. commitment, arguing that balance of commitment offers a good explanation and a better one than balance of power theory. The third and final section then evaluates the findings from the chapter and sieves out key insights that were gained.

2   THE SHAPE OF U.S. COMMITMENT DURING THE POST-GFC PERIOD

As the United States sought to reshape its role in Southeast Asia, its commitment level and distribution in Southeast Asia both unsurprisingly

The United States: Challenges for the Obama Administration's Second Term," National Institute for Defense Studies, Tokyo.

underwent significant changes during the post-GFC period. In particular, there was a moderate increase in both commitment level and commitment balance.

The Obama administration's quest to increase the commitment to Southeast Asia even as the United States recovered from the global financial crisis and underwent a fundamental rebalancing of its foreign policy yielded mixed effects. On the one hand, U.S. commitment was certainly boosted in the most comprehensive fashion seen in all four cases in this book and advanced in clear ways in line with the administration's intended approach. But on the other hand, as a result of the balancing acts required in balancing contending priorities, there still were areas where commitment increases were not as high, and aspects where commitment imbalances were clearly reflected in reality despite the administration's rhetoric.

The shape of U.S. commitment to Southeast Asia during the post-GFC period indicates that suggestions that the Obama administration saw an enhanced attention and focus on the region across the board are overly simplistic. A closer analysis of the specific metrics clearly indicates that there were some deeper tendencies with respect to the level and distribution of American commitment to Southeast Asia during this period. Specifically, there was a moderately increased commitment level and a minor increase in commitment balance.

2.1   Moderately Increased Commitment Level

Overall, U.S. commitment to Southeast Asia experienced a moderate increase during the post-GFC era: the product of a number of significant expansions across all four indicators. This was evidenced in expansions with respect to military deployments, alliances and partnerships, diplomatic engagement and economic engagement.

2.1.1   Military Deployments

There was a limited increase in the overall level of U.S. military deployments in Southeast Asia during the post-GFC period. As U.S. policymakers continued to examine plans to restructure the way American personnel and bases were deployed and organized in the Asia–Pacific more generally, the story in Southeast Asia was one where American policymakers sought to make some adjustments in terms of military deployments that amounted to a slight overall increase.

The post-GFC period witnessed the United States attempting to restructure its military deployments in the Asia–Pacific amid constraints as well as ongoing changes in prioritization.[8] The Obama administration moved to do so through a variety of steps in line with its broader adjustments to its global structure. While some regions saw drastic cuts to U.S. military presence, in Asia there were efforts made at initial reinforcements of the over 320,000 U.S. troops in the Pacific region with additional forces such as marines in Darwin; expanding U.S. military exercises; and increasing percentage of ships deployed in the Pacific from 50 to 60%.[9]

Southeast Asia was not immune from these wider trends at play, and there was no doubt some modest overall increase in terms of deployment of U.S. personnel and assets in the region. This biggest case in point was the conclusion of the Enhanced Defense Cooperation Agreement (EDCA) with the Philippines in 2014. The agreement was significant from a security perspective because it allowed for the rotational deployment of U.S. troops in personnel in select facilities predetermined by both sides.[10]

There were also other manifestations of this where Washington did secure some incremental gains in terms of the deployment of U.S. personnel and assets in Southeast Asia.[11] A case in point was Washington's securing of the ability to rotationally deploy up to four littoral combat ships (LCS) out of Singapore, which cemented the Southeast Asian state as a hub for U.S. military presence in Southeast Asia. U.S. services also secure additional sites from Southeast Asian states in a

[8] The Obama administration made clear that even as defense spending may be cut in some areas, the Asia–Pacific would remain a theater of focus. The main articulation of this was in the 2012 Strategic Guidance, where it is emphasized that "we will of necessity rebalance toward the Asia–Pacific region." Department of Defense, "Sustaining U.S. Global Leadership: Priorities for 21st Century Defense," January 2012, p. 2.

[9] Figures drawn from: Mark E. Manyin et al., "Pivot to the Pacific? The Obama Administration's 'Rebalancing' Toward Asia," March 28, 2012. Congressional Research Service; Janine Davidson and Lauren Dickey, "Fact: America's Rebalance to Asia Has Some Serious Military Muscle," *The National Interest*, April 16, 2015. Elisabeth Bumiller, "Words and Deeds Show Focus of the American Military on Asia," *New York Times*, November 10, 2012.

[10] Agreement Between the Government of the Republic of the Philippines and the Government of the United States of America on Enhanced Defense Cooperation, Author copy, April 2014.

[11] Sheldon Simon, "The US Rebalance and Southeast Asia: A Work in Progress," *Asian Survey*, Vol. 55, No. 3, pp. 572–595.

quieter fashion albeit in much more modest ways, whether it be Malaysia for surveillance-related activities or Vietnam for the prepositioning of equipment.[12]

As significant as these expansions were, it is also important to stress that there were limitations to them as well. For instance, while the administration was keen to point out EDCA constituted a formalized agreement that would pave the way for increased U.S. military deployments, in actual fact, since it progressed quite slowly and was only legally upheld on the Philippine side in 2016, there was no actual increase in deployments during this period in question and there continued to be disagreements about cost sharing as it got underway. The sorts of capability upgrades offered to the Philippines and brought to bear by the alliance also did little to affect the overall correlation of forces with respect to issues where U.S. interests were at stake, such as in the South China Sea. Some other areas of expansion were slowed as well, either due to serious challenges of implementation or budgeting.[13] A case in point in Southeast Asia was the slowing of the schedule for the deployment of the LCS vessels in Singapore.

2.1.2   Alliances and Partnerships

The post-GFC period also saw the United States move toward expanding its traditional alliances as well as investing in emerging partnerships in the face of new realities. While the effects were mixed and at times there was a mixture of expansion and some limited contraction depending on areas concerned, overall, the picture was one of expansion.

With respect to Washington's two treaty alliances, the U.S.-Philippine relationship offered the clearest case of expansion. During this period, the alliance saw significant revitalization across the economic, security and people-to-people realms, with some of the notable moves including the conclusion of a new defense agreement, the expansion of trade and

---

[12] *The Straits Times*, "Four US Warships to Operate Out of Singapore by 2018," February 18, 2015. Josh Rogin, "Malaysia and US in Talks to Ramp Up China Spying," *Bloomberg*, September 3, 2015. Dzirhan Mahadzir, "Base for the P-8? The View from Malaysia," CIMSEC, September 17, 2014; National Security News, "US to Preposition War Material, Gear in Asia and Europe in Preparation for Rising Threats," March 23, 2016.

[13] For a report that lays out some of these challenges, see: Michael J. Green et al., "Asia–Pacific Rebalance 2025: Capabilities, Presence, and Partnerships," CSIS Report, January 19, 2016.

investment and the establishment of the new U.S.-Philippines Society in Washington, D.C..[14] Both sides also invested in upgrading the diplomatic architecture of the relationship, with the incorporation of a bilateral security dialogue and a "2 plus 2" meeting between their top diplomats and defense chiefs as well.

Turning to partnerships, there were some notable efforts at creative expansion during the post-GFC period. Particularly significant was the inking of a series of new strategic and comprehensive partnerships with key Southeast Asian states—Indonesia, Malaysia, Singapore and Vietnam—which administration officials intentionally furthered in order to institutionalize and lock in the attention to and gains made in these relationships across a comprehensive set of security, economic and people-to-people realms as well as collaboration across regional and international issues.[15]

Among these, particularly notable were those with respect to Malaysia and Vietnam, since these represented new formal, institutionalized partnerships with these countries as opposed to upgrading of previous ones. In Vietnam, while this represented the advancement of normalization of ties over several administrations, the comprehensive partnership framework nonetheless helped structure various areas of collaboration and also birthed a new political and diplomatic mechanism at the ministerial level to oversee ongoing progress.[16] And on Malaysia, the comprehensive partnership capped a quick expansion of ties that had gotten underway early on in the Obama administration, with then then-U.S. Assistant Secretary of State for East Asian and Pacific Affairs Kurt Campbell at the end of 2010 already describing U.S.-Malaysia relations as the most improved in U.S. ties with Southeast Asian states.

To be sure, expansion was by no means uniform across the board and over the entire period. Thailand, for instance, was a more complex story, in part because some of the efforts to boost the alliance were partly offset by some contraction following the military coup in May 2014, which saw a period of cooling in ties as well as the imposition of some

---

[14] Prashanth Parameswaran, "Recalibrating US-Philippine Alliance Under Duterte," *Rappler*, October 1, 2016.

[15] Prashanth Parameswaran, "Explaining US Strategic Partnerships in the Asia Pacific," *Contemporary Southeast Asia*, Vol. 36, No. 2 (August 2014), pp. 262–289.

[16] Carlyle Thayer, "The US-Vietnam Comprehensive Partnership: What's in a Name?," *The Strategist*, July 31, 2013.

restrictions by Washington on the security side. Nonetheless, efforts at expansion were evident here too, whether it be in the inking of a new joint vision statement for the alliance in November 2012 that charted out some common areas for alliance collaboration or efforts to further boost trade and investment ties as well.[17]

2.1.3   Diplomatic Initiatives

The post-GFC period also saw the United States invest significantly in diplomacy in Southeast Asia as well. During this time, the Obama administration not only upgraded U.S. participation in multilateral institutions, but also invested significant time and resources in advancing diplomatic breakthroughs on tough issues that had previously bedeviled U.S. relations with Southeast Asia, be it Myanmar or the South China Sea.

The clearest manifestation of U.S. increased investment in diplomatic initiatives during the post-GFC period was evident in the approach to multilateral institutions. In contrast to the Bush administration, the Obama administration quickly undertook a series of landmark steps in this respect, including: ratifying the Treaty of Amity and Cooperation (TAC); becoming the first non-ASEAN country to appoint a resident ambassador to ASEAN; joining the East Asia Summit (EAS); institutionalizing annual U.S.-ASEAN summits, inking a strategic partnership with ASEAN; and even holding the first-ever U.S.-ASEAN summit on U.S. soil at Sunnylands. Obama himself maintained a fairly regular record of attending ASEAN summits—a powerful testament of U.S. commitment to diplomacy given the fact one of the most valuable markers of American commitment is the president's time.[18] Taken together, this investment in multilateralism was particularly notable for a U.S. Asia bureaucracy that had long been largely dominated by Northeast Asian concerns.[19]

---

[17] Catharin Dalpino, "Obama in Thailand: Charting a New Course for the Alliance," *Asia–Pacific Bulletin*, No. 188 (December 4, 2012); White House, "Remarks by President Obama and Prime Minister Shinawatra in a Joint Press Conference," November 18, 2012.

[18] Indeed, if it were not for the cancelation of his visit to the October 2013 East Asia Summit in Brunei, Obama would have been the first sitting U.S. president to visit all ten ASEAN countries. U.S. Secretary of State Hillary Clinton did become the first secretary of state to visit all ten ASEAN countries. See: Catherine Putz and Shannon Tiezzi, "Did Hillary Clinton's Pivot to Asia Work?," *FiveThirtyEight*, April 14, 2016.

[19] Prashanth Parameswaran, "Why the US-ASEAN Sunnylands Summit Matters," *The Diplomat*, February 11, 2016.

Another important manifestation of this increased focus on diplomatic initiatives during the post-GFC period was Myanmar. During this period, the Obama administration expanded significant energy in normalizing ties with Naypyidaw following decades of isolation under a policy approach that was termed "action for action," with consistently high-level attention from Obama's top advisers throughout the process.[20] The process itself unveiled over the process of several years, including lifting some economic restrictions and upgrading and building out diplomatic relations as the country initially moved toward a path of reform.[21]

The focus on diplomatic initiatives was evident even on risky issues where success was much less assured such as the South China Sea, where the post-GFC period also saw the United States try to help claimant states reach some sort of settlement to manage their differences. The most high-profile instance of this was in 2012, when Washington attempted—unsuccessfully—to broker a deal between China and the Philippines by asking both countries to pull out their ships following a months-long standoff in Scarborough Shoal (ultimately, only the Chinese did).[22] More generally, the United States also publicly floated a proposal for a South China Sea freeze in 2014 between China and other ASEAN claimant states, including a moratorium on land reclamation efforts.[23] While this initiative also did not gain much traction, it was nonetheless reflective of an administration that clearly wanted to invest heavily in this aspect of its commitment to the region even on tough issues.

2.1.4   Economic Engagement

With respect to economic engagement, U.S. commitment to Southeast Asia saw some modest, limited expansion. Though the Obama administration attempted to expand economic opportunities with Southeast Asian states as well as with ASEAN as a whole as well through various means,

---

[20] Ben Rhodes, "Remarks on Burma Policy," Center for a New American Security, May 17, 2016.

[21] Jurgen Haacke, "The United States and Myanmar: From Antagonists to Security Partners?," *Journal of Current Southeast Asian Affairs*, Vol. 32, No. 2, pp. 55–83.

[22] Manuel Mogato, "Philippines' Aquino Says China Breaks Deal on South China Sea Outcrop," *Reuters*, May 26, 2016.

[23] Paul Mooney and Lesley Wroughton, "US Call for South China Sea 'Freeze' Gets Cool Response from China," *Reuters*, August 9, 2014.

these also suffered from some significant constraints and limitations during the period in question.

In aggregate terms, available U.S. government data clearly illustrate that despite some ups and downs, in general, U.S. trade and investment numbers in Southeast Asia continued on a generally, modest upward trend during the initial years of the post-GFC period. Indicators such as the amount of U.S. exports to ASEAN countries as well as the amount of foreign direct investment going into Southeast Asian states both recorded some increase during this period relative to previous years, reflecting this expansion.[24]

Those numbers alone, however, do not tell the full story of a more general pattern of modest, limited expansion of U.S. commitment in the economic engagement aspect with the region as a whole and with individual countries. Regionwide, a notable example of this was the U.S.-ASEAN Connect Initiative, which had a range of old and new activities around its four pillars—business, energy, policy and innovation—which the administration then attempted to operationalize in consultation with the U.S. government agencies as well as with Southeast Asian countries.[25]

The regionwide approach was paired with more targeted ones focused on individual countries and particular groups of states. With respect to groupings of states, an important initiative was the Lower Mekong Initiative (LMI), a subregional program designed to promote cooperation and capacity building with the lesser developed states of Southeast Asia in fields such as education, health, environment and connectivity.[26] Beyond the value of the initiative itself, the LMI had additional significance because it illustrated the administration's commitment to bridging the significant gaps between the lesser developed ASEAN states and the

[24] Figures drawn from: GAO, "Southeast Asia: Trends in US and Chinese Economic Engagement," August 2015. Also see: Peter A. Petri and Michael G. Plummer, "ASEAN Centrality and the ASEAN-US Economic Relationship," East–West Center, Washington, DC, 2014; and US-ASEAN Business Council, "Why ASEAN Matters: Trade and Investment," Updated 2017.

[25] Ziad Haider, "Operationalizing U.S.-ASEAN Connect: A Framework for Shared Prosperity," November 18, 2016.

[26] State Department, "Fact Sheet: Lower Mekong Initiative," Office of the Spokesperson, Washington, DC, July 13, 2012; Prashanth Parameswaran and Ernest Z. Bower, "US Moves to Strengthen ASEAN by Boosting the Lower Mekong Initiative," CSIS Commentary, July 24, 2012.

Table 1 Summary of Findings on Commitment Level in the Post-GFC Period

Category	Choices	Finding
Military deployments	Expanded or reduced?	Limited expansion
Alliances and partnerships	Strengthened or weakened?	Strengthened
Diplomatic initiatives	Active, reactive, or inactive?	Active
Economic engagement	Increased or decreased?	Limited increase
Overall level	Increase or decrease?	Moderate increase

Source Generated by Author

more developed ones, which was also a focus of ASEAN as an institution itself.

Finally, while not a solely Southeast Asia-based initiative, the Trans-Pacific Partnership (TPP) ought to feature in any evaluation of economic engagement during this period because it was comprised of four ASEAN countries—Brunei, Malaysia, Singapore and Vietnam. With several other Southeast Asian countries that had initially considered joining as well, such as the Philippines, Thailand and Indonesia, the TPP was pitched by the administration as representative of the kind of rules that Southeast Asian states should aspire to.

While these initiatives were demonstrative of efforts to expand U.S. economic engagement during the post-GFC period, it is also important to emphasize that they suffered from various limitations and constraints. The most notable example in this respect is TPP, which ultimately was left unratified and thus did not constitute a concrete expansion of U.S. economic engagement. Some other initiatives also ultimately did not constitute the expanded economic engagement that they had promised. The LMI faced immense resourcing difficulties throughout the Obama administration that undermined its effectiveness, while the U.S.-ASEAN Connect Initiative was quite slow to come together, such that it was announced years after it was originally conceived in government circles[27] (Table 1).

---

[27] Ziad Haider, "Operationalizing U.S.-ASEAN Connect: A Framework for Shared Prosperity," November 18, 2016.

2.2   Minor Increase in Commitment Balance

The moderate increase in the level of U.S. commitment in Southeast Asia was accompanied by a minor increase in commitment balance during the post-GFC period as well. Specifically, three of the five areas set out in the balance of commitment framework witnessed imbalances within them to some degree during the period in question.

2.2.1   Means/Ends

The first imbalance seen in U.S. commitment to Southeast Asia during the post-GFC period was with respect to means and ends, albeit in a more limited sense. During this period, even though Obama administration officials did factor constraints into their views and attempted to use less available means to serve more limited ends, they nonetheless found that the means were not quite available even for the more limited ends that they sought, creating an imbalance that was difficult to address.

Throughout the post-GFC, U.S. policymakers grappled with this imbalance between available means and intended ends. This manifested itself in several forms. The clearest of these were restrictions related to money, resources and political will regarding aspects of U.S. policy affecting Southeast Asia. Regarding money, several of the programs that the administration had announced with respect to Southeast Asia, such as the U.S.-ASEAN Connect Initiative, suffered from budget issues because occasional, modest increases in certain aspects still left levels far below those necessary to actually boost U.S. commitment along the lines of what the administration had expected to accomplish.[28]

Resourcing and staffing more generally was an issue as well, including with respect to the diplomatic aspects of the administration's approach. According to a report released by the Senate Foreign Relations Committee in April 2014 on diplomatic resourcing with respect to the rebalance strategy, resources for diplomatic engagement in key U.S. agencies, such as the State Department's Bureau of East Asian and Pacific Affairs or the U.S. Department of Commerce, did not see a substantial increase even though these were central to the accomplishment of the ends spelled out in the Obama administration's rebalance strategy.[29]

---

[28] Author conversation with former senior U.S. diplomat, Washington, DC, May 2021.

[29] U.S. Government Printing Office, "Re-balancing the Rebalance: Resourcing U.S. Diplomatic Strategy in the Asia–Pacific Region," April 17, 2014.

At times, the lack of political will also contribute to the gap between means and ends as well. A case in point in this respect was the TPP. The Obama administration issued repeated statements reinforcing the importance of reaching a deal on TPP in terms of its wider ends, not just because of the economic benefits therein but also because it could help catalyze a "race to the top" among Southeast Asian states via the provision of common, high-level standards.[30] But even those within the administration admit that there was not nearly enough political capital spent soon enough to overcome the obstacles necessary to see the agreement through.[31] While U.S. Trade Representative Ron Kirk notified Congress that Obama planned to enter negotiations back in 2009, Obama remained hesitant to push for Trade Promotion Authority (TPA) in cognizance of other legislative priorities until toward the end of 2014, despite repeated calls to do so.

To be sure, some of the gaps between means and ends were narrowed by the administration in creative ways, be it protecting certain line items in the defense budget dedicated to the Asia–Pacific or bringing together resources from other outside partners or Southeast Asian states themselves. Administration officials also repeatedly affirmed that the U.S. commitment to Asia in general and Southeast Asia in particular would continue in spite of these challenges.[32] Nonetheless, that did not change the overall reality that there were imbalances between means and ends during the post-GFC period.

2.2.2   Interests/Ideals

The second imbalance was witnessed with respect to interests and ideals. During the post-GFC period, the balance was repeatedly tilted in favor of interests over ideals in several key cases in U.S.-Southeast Asia relations under the Obama administration.

---

[30] For a wider discussion of rules-based arguments and rule-making in the TPP, see: Ben Dolven et al., *The Trans-Pacific Partnership: Strategic Implications* (Congressional Research Service, February 3, 2016); and Todd Allee and Andrew Lugg, "Who Wrote the Rules for the Trans-Pacific Partnership?," *Research and Politics* (July–September 2016), pp. 1–9.

[31] Author conversation with former senior White House official, November 2019.

[32] Tom Donilon, "Obama in China: Preserving the Rebalance," Brookings Institution, Washington, DC, November 5, 2014.

While the exact calibration varied across cases, in general, the post-GFC period saw the privileging of interests over ideals. The Obama administration, eager to depart from the lecturing of Southeast Asian states seen in the past including during the Clinton and Bush years, not only did not present a coherent policy for balancing interests and values, but also, when it came to several key cases involving countries, tended to prioritize the advancement of U.S. interests instead of U.S. ideals.[33] As Clinton herself noted in her *Foreign Policy* article unveiling the administration's pivot to Asia, while democracy and human rights would be on the agenda with countries such as Vietnam and Myanmar, this would not deter the administration from plans to "deepen engagement with partners with whom we disagree."[34]

The most striking example that illustrated this was the U.S. approach to Myanmar. Here, despite persistent democracy and human rights concerns and criticism from certain rights groups and opponents at home, the Obama administration continued its historic step-by-step effort to normalize ties with Myanmar in recognition of the country's centrality to U.S. interests as well as an ongoing reform process underway there. While administration did not publicly admit at the time that they were putting interests over ideals and repeatedly emphasized that they were also reacting to changes in Myanmar itself, the articulation of U.S. policy toward Myanmar, which was flagged as a policy legacy item during Obama's time in office in spite of some disappointments in the reform process that played out, certainly made that clear, and key officials involved in the process privately acknowledged that necessary trade-offs were made along the way in recognition of the need for greater risk tolerance to advance creative diplomatic initiatives.[35]

While Myanmar was the notable case with respect to interests and ideals in U.S.-Southeast Asia relations during the post-GFC period, there were other cases as well. For example, despite the deterioration of rights issues in Malaysia, including a high-profile corruption scandal

---

[33] For an example of this line of criticism, see: Joshua Kurlantzick, *The Pivot in Southeast Asia: Balancing Interests and Values*, The Council on Foreign Relations Report, Washington, DC, January 8, 2015.

[34] Hillary Clinton, "America's Pacific Century," *Foreign Policy*, October 11, 2011.

[35] Author conversation with former senior U.S. official, Washington, DC, May 2021. Ben Rhodes, "Remarks on Burma Policy," Center for a New American Security, May 17, 2016.

surrounding the country's premier, U.S. officials continued to advance ties with Malaysia given its centrality to American interests.[36] A similar case was witnessed in Vietnam where, despite lingering issues regarding democracy and human rights that opponents continued to flag, U.S. policymakers not only did not allow it to harm ties but also moved forward on items that had been advanced nonetheless such as the historic lifting of a U.S. arms embargo.[37]

Of course, this is not to say that the Obama administration was not committed to the advancement of U.S. ideals at all. The administration attempted to indirectly advance democracy and human rights through attempts to address rule of law challenges in Southeast Asian states, through such efforts as the Open Government Partnership to promote good governance and transparency, and democracy programs in individual Southeast Asian states such as the Philippines.[38] And it invested in the young people of Southeast Asia through initiatives such as the Young Southeast Asian leaders Initiative (YSEALI) launched in 2013, partly out of the belief that investing in the youth was a way to win the long game of promoting more progress. That said, on balance, it was clear that there was an imbalance in favor of interests over ideals.

2.2.3   Cooperative/Confrontational

Another clear imbalance in U.S. commitment to Southeast Asia post-GFC period was the one favoring cooperative over confrontational approaches. During this time, the U.S. emphasis on a cooperative approach toward a range of U.S. adversaries and competitors, as opposed to a more confrontational one, be it in terms of rogue regimes or other rival major powers, manifested itself in Washington's approach to Southeast Asia.

The clearest case of this, as noted before, was with respect to U.S. policy toward Myanmar. As a product of a broader approach focused on normalizing U.S. ties with what the Bush administration had considered rogue regimes—from Iran to Cuba—the Obama administration pursued

[36] Josh Lederman, "In Asia, Obama Takes Softer Tone on Human Rights, Corruption," *The Associated Press*, November 22, 2015; Nurul Izzah Anwar, "What Obama Must Do in Malaysia," US News and World Report, November 17, 2015.

[37] Krishnadev Calamur, "Why Obama Is Overlooking Human Rights Worries in Vietnam," *The Atlantic*, May 24, 2016.

[38] The White House, "Face Sheet: The Open Government Partnership". September 20, 2011.

a clear and consistent approach designed to normalize relations with the government in Naypyidaw and persisted with that approach even as realities changed over time and amid criticism from some of its opponents and other actors.

The imbalance favoring confrontational over cooperative approaches on Washington's part was also evident in terms of how it viewed its position relative to China in Southeast Asia. While the extent of this varied during the post-GFC period, in general, U.S. officials remained wedded to an approach to cultivate China as a cooperative partner rather than a competitor or adversary—which was initially dubbed "strategic reassurance".[39] For most of the first part of the administration which is what this study covers, the administration remained wedded to this approach even as China showed few signs of acquiescing to U.S. requests for areas of joint cooperation and appeared increasingly confident and at times assertive Beijing, including with respect to its behavior in the South China Sea, in part due to a perceived fear that this may undermine cooperation in other areas.[40]

---

[39] The essence of "strategic reassurance," was rooted in a focus on helping ease Beijing's insecurities, building trust, and broadening out areas of collaboration on regional and global issues, including climate change and Iran, while managing any differences between the two countries. For an elaboration of this concept and its evolution, see: James B. Steinberg, "Obama Administration's Vision of the U.S.-China Relationship," Keynote Address at the Center for a New American Security, Washington, DC, September 24, 2009; and James Steinberg and Michael O'Hanlon, *Strategic Reassurance and Resolve: US-China Relations in the Twenty-First Century* (Princeton, NJ: Princeton University Press, 2014). For a critical perspective, see: Kelley Currie, "The Doctrine of 'Strategic Reassurance'," *The Wall Street Journal*, October 22, 2009.

[40] Jeff Bader, who served on the NSC under Obama, summarized the logic of this approach when he said that the first principle of the administration's China approach was that "China should not be considered an inevitable adversary, but rather a potential partner in resolving critical global issues." The approach, Bader went on to note, stemmed from a recognition that cooperative elements "could and should outweigh" the competitive elements in the relationship, as well as the realization that U.S. allies and partners wanted a stable U.S.-China relationship as well. For a critiques of the Obama administration's China approach on this count, see: Victor Cha, "The Unfinished Legacy of Obama's Pivot to Asia," *Foreign Policy*, September 6, 2016. For a wider account, see David Sanger, *Confront and Conceal: Obama's Secret Wars and Surprising Use of American Power* (New York: Broadway Books, 2012), Part V. See also, Josh Rogin, *Chaos Under Heaven: Trump, Xi and the Battle for the 21st Century* (Boston: Houghton Mifflin Harcourt, 2021); and Ryan Hass, *Stronger: Adapting America's China Strategy in an Age of Competitive Independence* (New Haven and London: Yale University Press; 2021).

To be sure, this is not to say that the post-GFC period saw the United States take an *exclusively* cooperative approach as opposed to a confrontational one. For instance, the Obama administration remained resolute in its efforts in combating terrorism and violent extremism, though it did so the partnership with other states more so than was witnessed during the Bush years. The administration was also more calibrated than it is often portrayed to be, and it did harden its approach to Beijing over time, as evidenced by Obama's clear message to Chinese President Xi Jinping about the U.S. red line with respect to reclamation activities around Scarborough Shoal, which Xi then subsequently violated. Nonetheless, the imbalance in favor of cooperative rather than a confrontational approach was clear.

2.2.4   *Bilateralism/Multilateralism*

There was no discernable imbalance detected with respect to U.S. commitment to Southeast Asia during the post-GFC period. Instead, the Obama administration invested in a range of bilateral, multilateral and minilateral mechanisms, viewing them as part of a growing network of countries that could forge joint cooperation and collective action to tackle a range of complex challenges.

As a product of a broader approach of engaging emerging powers and regional institutions to address a range of complex problems and preserve the post-WWII U.S.-led international order, the Obama administration invested in a range of bilateral, multilateral and minilateral institutions during the post-GFC period. Southeast Asia was among the priority regions for this approach.[41] From the outset, the administration made clear that the basis for its approach to engagement with Southeast Asia and ASEAN was that it saw a greater investment in emerging powers and multilateral institutions as being a vital part of preserving what it had referred to as the rules-based international order.[42]

---

[41] As one Obama administration official reflected, Southeast Asia and ASEAN served as a good example of the sort of the region that it wanted to invest more in: for all its limitations, and in contrast to other parts of the world, had emerged as peaceful and prosperous since ASEAN's founding in 1967 despite its tremendous diversity. Author conversation with former senior U.S. defense official, Washington, DC, March 2020.

[42] Office of the President of the United States, *National Security Strategy*, May 27, 2010; Barack Obama, "Remarks by President Obama at Opening Session of the US-ASEAN Summit," February 15, 2016; Kurt Campbell, *The Pivot: The Future of American Statecraft in Asia* (New York: Twelve, 2016), especially pp. 11–32; Ben Rhodes, "Remarks

In Southeast Asia, this approach saw the administration invest in a wide range of mechanisms. Bilaterally, this meant not just strengthening existing alliances and partnerships, but forging new institutionalized ones as well with countries that previously got little sustained U.S. attention, such as Laos or Myanmar. And multilaterally, it meant investing in multilateral institutions through a variety of steps as noted earlier, such as joining the East Asia Summit and inking a historic strategic partnership agreement with ASEAN as an organization, in recognition that ASEAN, in the words of Hillary Clinton, was a "fulcrum" of the region's emerging architecture.[43]

The administration's keenness to invest comprehensively and in a balanced way across a wide range of mechanisms was also evident in the linkages that officials consistently made between them. A case in point was the approach by the administration regarding the lesser developed countries of the Mekong region. The approach combined engaging partners such as Singapore bilaterally to boost combined assistance to third countries; contributing to the advancement of ASEAN initiatives on connectivity and integration directed at narrowing gaps between mainland and maritime Southeast Asian states; and advancing new minilateral, subregional U.S.-led initiatives such as the Lower Mekong Initiative (LMI).[44] The minilateral institutions were viewed comprehensively as creating "bridging options" to link states with bilateral partners and multilateral groupings.

2.2.5   Security/Economics

No significant U.S. commitment imbalances in Southeast Asia were detected between security and economic realms in the post-GFC period. Rather than a significant tilt toward militarization or one in the direction of a greater focus on economic development at the expense of security

on U.S. Policy in Southeast Asia," Center for New American Security, Washington, DC, May 17, 2016.

[43] Hillary Rodham Clinton, "America's Engagement in the Asia–Pacific," Speech at the East–West Center, Honolulu, Hawaii, October 28, 2010. https://2009-2017.state.gov/secretary/20092013clinton/rm/2010/10/150141.htm.

[44] Joshua Kurlantzick, *The Pivot in Southeast Asia: Balancing Interests and Values*, The Council on Foreign Relations Report, Washington, DC, January 8, 2015; Phuong Nguyen, "Washington Needs a New Approach to the Lower Mekong—'The Next South China Sea'," CSIS Commentary, Washington, DC, April 17, 2014; John F. Kerry, "From a Swift Boat to a Sustainable Mekong," *Foreign Policy*, February 2, 2015.

ends, U.S. policymakers sought to invest in both areas simultaneously in a balanced way within the constraints they had, while also being actively conscious of potential imbalances as well.

U.S. policymakers in the post-GFC period sought to invest in both security and economic realms in Southeast Asia in a balanced way within the constraints they were operating under. The attention to and quest for balance in this area derived from a worldview held by several top officials in the administration as well as Obama himself that apart from the increasing interconnection between economics and security more generally, there also needed to be a correction in the overly frequent use of U.S. military power at the expense of other components of American capabilities.[45] For instance, during her tenure as secretary of state, Clinton would repeatedly delve into defense issues in line with her approach to what she termed "comprehensive engagement," which balanced what she termed the 3 Ds of foreign policy for short—defense, diplomacy and development.[46]

This approach was seen with respect to Southeast Asia as well during the post-GFC period. On the one hand, the Obama administration did not shy away from boosting security relationships with partners such as the Philippines and Vietnam to address a wide range of traditional and non-traditional security threats. But on the other hand, this was paired with an attention to the need to boost economic and people-to-people ties with these countries as well to ensure that these relationships were broad-based and comprehensive. The interconnectedness of these realms was also repeatedly emphasized by officials to make this point: whether it be on individual initiatives, such as the TPP that was sold as not just an economic commitment, but a security one as well, or the administration's public messaging on Southeast Asia's importance, which combined its economic potential with its strategic significance.

Of course, this is not to say that the lack of a significant imbalance between economics and security was a universally accepted notion. For instance, despite its best efforts, along with the reality that it actually reduced the U.S. global military footprint, there were still some voices in

---

[45] For a broader reflection of this point, see Robert M. Gates, *Duty: Memoirs of a Secretary of State at War* (New York: Knopf, 2015), Chapter 15, pp. 566–597.

[46] Hillary Rodham Clinton, "Secretary Clinton's Speech on Regional Engagement in Asia," U.S. Mission to ASEAN, October 28, 2010.

Table 2 Summary of Findings on Commitment Balance for the Post-GFC Period

Category	Choices	Finding
Means/ends	Are resources commensurate with goals and objectives?	Limited imbalance (ends)
Interests/ideals	Is attention on ideals or more narrowly on core interests?	Limited imbalance (interests)
Cooperative/confrontational	Is approach to adversaries and competitors cooperative or confrontational?	Imbalance (cooperative)
Bilateralism/multilateralism	Is bilateral and unilateral or multilateral approach favored?	No imbalance
Security/economics	Is there a greater attention on security or economics?	No imbalance
Overall balance	Increase or decrease?	Minor increase

Source Generated by Author

the United States and in the region that criticized the Obama administration for its overmilitarized commitment to Asia in general and Southeast Asia in particular. Yet this was largely the product of issues related to resourcing and sequencing rather than the administration's approach per se.

In sum, U.S. commitment to Southeast Asia during the post-Vietnam period saw a minor increase in commitment balance—the only recorded increase of all the four case studies in this book—with three of the five categories moving toward greater balance. This is reflected in Table 2 which summarizes the findings on commitment balance in the post-GFC period.

3   EXPLAINING U.S. COMMITMENT DURING THE POST-GFC PERIOD

Having detailed the shape of U.S. commitment during the post-GFC period, which was found to have experienced a moderate increase in commitment level and a minor increase in commitment balance, we can now move to explaining how and why this occurred. This section argues that, as the balance of commitment model would predict, we witnessed a case where a moderate decrease in U.S. relative power, mediated by a moderately high threat level perceived by the American foreign policy elite as well as moderately low state capacity, accounted for a moderately high commitment level and a minor increase in commitment balance during this period.

3.1   Moderate Decrease in Relative Power

The distribution of military and economic power between the United States and its competitors both globally and regionally certainly played into Washington's commitment to Southeast Asia during the post-GFC period, as neorealism would predict. U.S. policymakers recognized that in the wake of the constraints placed on U.S. military and economic capabilities due to the wars in Iraq and Afghanistan and the global financial crisis, Washington needed to be more cautious about the application of its own power to sustain its longer-term primacy while at the same time stabilizing the evolution to a broader multipolar order in Asia in general and Southeast Asia in particular.

There was a moderate decrease in relative U.S. power during the post-GFC period. That was hardly surprising considering Obama's heritage. At home, the United States faced deep financial issues, with significant job losses and marked declines in the stock market. Abroad, the United States was engaged in two wars with unsustainable budgets and a military force stretched to the breaking point, powers were rising in significant regions such as Asia, and the U.S. standing in the world was greatly diminished by policies that undermined its ideals, such as torture, or ones that isolated itself, such as on climate change.[47] "By nearly every measure," writes Derek Chollet who served in multiple positions during the Obama administration, "the US in 2008 was a declining power."[48]

Addressing this state of relative decline required a fundamental rebalancing in U.S. foreign policy general—with a greater focus on rebuilding the foundations of American leadership at home and a more comprehensive and calibrated approach to deploying U.S. power abroad beyond just military power and in regions that mattered for long-term American

---

[47] For accounts that sketch these general contours, see: Ben Rhodes, *The World as It Is: A Memoir of the Obama White House* (New York: Random House, 2018); James Mann, *Obamians: The Struggle Inside the White House to Redefine American Power* (New York: Penguin, 2013); and David E. Sanger, *The Inheritance: The World Obama Confronts and the Challenges to American Power* (New York: Harmony Books, 2009).

[48] Derek Chollet, *The Long Game: How Obama Defied Washington and Redefined America's Role in the World* (New York: Public Affairs, 2016), pp. 46–47.

interests.[49] As Obama's former National Security Adviser Tom Donilon has noted, the pivot or rebalance to Asia was rooted in an idea *that applied globally* tied to an assessment of U.S. capabilities where the United States, in recognition of the limits of its power and resource constraints, needed to recalibrate its engagement by scaling down in areas it had *overinvested* in, such as the Middle East, and focus more on areas it was *underinvested* in, such as Asia, to include Southeast Asia.[50]

Asia in general and Southeast Asia in particular were not immune from this worldview. Indeed, with the administration having recognized Asia as a key region for the United States to invest in, a priority from the outset was reassuring U.S. allies, partners and friends that despite a decade of war and economic woes at home, the United States was not going to disengage from the region where several countries had grown increasingly nervous about China's rise.[51] Hal Brands summarized the Obama administration's foreign policy thinking on this score recognizing both opportunities and challenges as: "The Asia–Pacific region is likely to be the cockpit of global security competition and economic growth in the twenty-first century, and the rise of China in particular presents the greatest long-term challenge for American foreign policy."[52]

Southeast Asia in particular seemed a logical place of focus given not just its strategic import and economic weight, but also the presence of emerging middle powers such as Indonesia and Vietnam.[53] Yet, at the same time, as the Obama administration attempted to rebalance its focus

[49] Ben Rhodes, one of Obama's closest advisers who remained with him throughout his time in office, summarized in one sentence Obama's foreign policy vision that was clear even before he came to office, "After eight years of George W. Bush, we had to wind down the wars, reinvigorate diplomacy, and restore America's standing in the world. Ben Rhodes, *The World as It Is: A Memoir of the Obama White House* (New York: Random House, 2018), p. 22.

[50] Tom Donilon, "Obama in China: Preserving the Rebalance," Brookings Institution, Washington, DC, November 5, 2014.

[51] Robert Sutter et al., "Balancing Acts: The U.S. Rebalance and Asia–Pacific Stability," Paper for the Sigur Center for Asian Studies Rising Power Initiative, August 2013, pp. 1–2.

[52] Hal Brands, "Breaking Down Obama's Grand Strategy," *The National Interest*, June 23, 2014.

[53] Obama himself in an interview directly contrasted Southeast Asia favorably with the Middle East, noting that in the former case, young people there were thinking about getting ahead rather than killing Americans. See: Jeffrey Goldberg, "The Obama Doctrine," *The Atlantic*, April 2016.

to Southeast Asia abroad while contending with resource constraints at home, it all but ensured that there would be some impact on how U.S. commitment manifested itself in reality as compared to the rhetoric.[54]

That in turn affected both the level of U.S. commitment as well as its distribution. With respect to its level, it was clear that even as the United States rebalanced to the Asia–Pacific in general and Southeast Asia in particular, while Washington would seek to "lock in a substantially increased investment" in the region, as Clinton had declared, there would not be as significant of a rise in the level of U.S. commitment across all realms.[55] Even as U.S. policymakers recognized that Southeast Asia was a priority region for the United States, the perceived state of decline in U.S. capabilities, along with a focus on domestic priorities and a caution with respect to foreign entanglements, that stemmed from that, meant it continued to be a struggle to actually marshal resources to advance commitments. That partly accounts for why, for instance, both the military deployments and economic engagement aspects of U.S. commitment saw only limited increases in terms of their level.

With respect to distribution, it was also clear that this could shape U.S. commitment balances in Southeast Asia during the post-GFC period as well. One example is the lack of an imbalance recorded on bilateral and multilateral approaches. That lack of imbalance occurred in part as a product of the administration's assessment of a decline in U.S. relative capabilities, which subsequently led to a greater comfort with both burden-sharing on a bilateral basis and more of a commitment to regional institutions in ASEAN on a multilateral basis in paving the way for a more multilateral order. Kurt Campbell, who served as assistant secretary of state during the Obama administration and was a key architect of the pivot, was fond of noting that given the state of U.S. relative power, Washington should move beyond just shaping a balance of power in Asia but also create a "shared agreement" to build up Asia's operating system—a more multipolar conception that rested in a hybrid of bilateral, minilateral and multilateral mechanisms.[56]

---

[54] Conversation with former U.S. State Department official, Washington, DC, January 2020.

[55] Hillary Clinton, "America's Pacific Century," *Foreign Policy*, October 11, 2011.

[56] Campbell defines Asia's operating system, roughly, as a complex arrangement of institutions, norms and values that would help realize opportunities and confront challenges

But although the relative distribution of capabilities does give us a sense of the broad thinking behind and general contours of U.S. commitment to Southeast Asia as balance of power theory would expect, it tells us much less about the specifics of the level and distribution of that commitment based on the metrics laid out in the preceding section. For a better sense of how U.S. policymakers reacted to opportunities and challenges they faced domestically, regionally and globally during this period as well as how they managed the limited military, economic, political and diplomatic resources at their disposal, we need to delve into their calculations about power and threats (threat perceptions) as well as their ability to mobilize resources (state power)—the two intervening variables that are key to balance of commitment.

3.2   Moderately High Threat Level

While the relative distribution of capabilities no doubt played a role in shaping U.S. commitment to Southeast Asia during this post-GFC period, this was also filtered through the lens of elite calculations about power and threats, or, put more simply, threat perceptions. Specifically, during this period, we witnessed a moderately high threat level among the U.S. foreign policy elite with respect to Southeast Asia, which was derivative of their broader views about the region and the world as well.

The post-GFC period saw U.S. foreign policymakers operate within the context of moderately high threat levels. The overall sense of threat certainly did not manifest the same way as that of the Bush administration following the 9/11 attacks, and the Obama administration recognized that there was a need to have a more restrictive definition of U.S. interests and a more calibrated approach to threat perceptions than its predecessor lest it succumb to overreaction and deal with day-to-day fires without focusing on longer-term challenges.[57] That said, unlike terrorism, where

Kurt Campbell, *The Pivot: The Future of American Statecraft in Asia* (New York: Twelve Books, 2016), p. 135.

[57] The negative version of this has been characterized as "Don't Do Stupid Stuff" following Jeffrey Goldberg's interview with Obama. A more positive formulation focused on the need to focus attention not just on short-term crises, but longer-term challenges in a more sustainable way. Jeffrey Goldberg, "The Obama Doctrine," *The Atlantic*, April 2016; Susan Rice, "Explaining President Obama's Rebalance Strategy," Medium.com, September 5, 2016; Gideon Rose, "What Obama Gets Right: Keep Calm and Carry the Liberal Order On," *Foreign Affairs*, September/October 2015.

Southeast Asia was a second front, the focus on the loss of U.S. competitive advantage with Asia as the center of attention meant that Southeast Asia factored much more directly in the sense of threat perception. As such, the Obama administration also recognized that there was a string of challenges at the global and regional level that would shape its foreign policy.

Globally, threats abounded as Obama entered office. Beyond the fact that the United States was facing the worst economic conditions since the Great Depression and was still engulfed in two wars, the global economic crisis had undermined confidence in globalization and the liberal economic model; electoral democracy seemed to have stalled; longer-term challenges such as climate change had been ignored but were still compounding; European integration was under severe strain; the Middle East was in a state of disarray, and authoritarian powers were on the rise in China and Russia. Robert Gates, Obama's first defense secretary who had also served several other presidents before him, noted that "It is hard to think of a president who entered office facing more challenges of historic magnitude."[58]

While some of these challenges were present in the past, there seemed to be more of them in more places and less of a U.S. ability to respond. "It was a double-sided problem," Chollet would later note. "The international agenda was unforgiving, while the reservoir of American capacity and credibility to project power was in danger of being depleted. This was a daunting inbox, and there was a profound sense of urgency."[59] Brands emphasize the contrast between the 1990s and 2000s and the time when the Obama administration came into office running into the 2010s thusly:

> During the 1990s and 2000s, Washington faced rogue states and jihadist extremism but not intense great power rivalry. America faced conflicts in the Middle East, but East Asia and Europe were comparatively secure. Now, old threats still exist, but the more permissive conditions have vanished. The United States confronts rogue states, lethal jihadist organizations, and great power competition; there are severe challenges in all

---

[58] Robert M. Gates, *Duty: Memoirs of a Secretary of State* (New York: Knopf, 2015), p. 323.

[59] Derek Chollet, *The Long Game: How Obama Defied Washington and Redefined America's Role in the World* (New York: Public Affairs, 2016), p. 51.

three European theaters. The United States thus faces not just more significant but also more numerous challenges to its military dominance than it had for at least a quarter century.[60]

Regionally, too, the situation that was brewing in the Asia–Pacific was no better either. The most significant challenge was the fact that the rise of China was weighing more on U.S. calculations as it suggested that great power competition may intensify in the coming years and that Washington's position of dominance in the Asian theater may be undermined. In no place was that clearer than in Southeast Asia, where China had embarked on a "charm offensive" designed to consolidate its position while Washington had been distracted in the Middle East, which created anxieties among some countries that desired a more balanced state of affairs. "By the end of the Bush presidency," Joseph Liow writes, "the fact that China's relations with Southeast Asia had undergone a fundamental transformation compared with the state of affairs since the end of the Cold War is undeniable."[61]

Though the Obama administration did not single out the China challenge at the outset, there was a clear recognition on its part that Beijing's rise was generating anxiety in regional capitals and cementing the notion that it could pose a longer-term challenge to U.S. presence in the Asia–Pacific.[62] And while some officials did initially place confidence in its ability to foster collaboration with China, the sense of threat only rose after its first year in office as Beijing not only spurned opportunities for U.S.-China cooperation, but also upped its maritime assertiveness in the East and South China Seas involving Japan and Southeast Asian states, leading some of these countries to register their concerns with Washington as well.[63]

[60] Hal Brands and Eric Edelman, "Toward Strategic Solvency: The Crisis of American Military Primacy and the Search for Strategic Solvency," Army War College, 2017, p. 30.

[61] Joseph Liow, *Ambivalent Engagement: The United States and Regional Security in Southeast Asia After the Cold War* (Washington, DC: Brookings Institution Press, 2017), p. 124.

[62] David Sanger, *Confront and Conceal: Obama's Secret Wars and Surprising Use of American Power* (New York: Broadway Books, 2012), Part V; Hal Brands, "Breaking Down Obama's Grand Strategy," *The National Interest*, June 23, 2014.

[63] Nicholas D. Anderson and Victor D. Cha, "The Case of the Pivot to Asia: System Effects and the Origins of Strategy," *Political Science Quarterly*, Vol. 132, No. 4 (Winter 2017–2018), pp. 595–617; For a broader account, see: Jeffrey A. Bader, *Obama and*

That environment of heightened threat perceptions certainly affected U.S. policy in Asia in general and Southeast Asia in particular. The proliferation of challenges at the global level reinforced the administration's perception that discipline needed to be set into U.S. thinking that prioritized certain regions and issues over others. The concerns around the rise of China at the global level meant that there was a growing recognition by Washington about Beijing's inroads into Southeast Asia and its negative impact on regional states, even if U.S. policymakers would do so from the perspective of a longer time horizon that would see them continue to work toward collaboration.[64] By the time of the public launching of the pivot with Clinton's *Foreign Policy* article, the United States had begun taking a series of actions designed to shape a regional order to push back against growing Chinese assertiveness. "The new U.S. policy is also based on a need – widely felt throughout most of the Asia–Pacific region – for strategic reassurance in the face of a rising and increasingly assertive China," one report on the rebalance summarized succinctly.[65]

Threat perceptions affected both the level and the distribution of U.S. commitment to Southeast Asia during the post-GFC period. With respect to the level of commitment, it partly accounted for the gains that Washington recorded in its ties with Southeast Asian states. In the domain of military deployments, for instance, the conclusion of the EDCA agreement with the Philippines was catalyzed by Chinese assertiveness in the South China Sea and Manila's desire for Washington to help it balance against Beijing's actions there. And on economic engagement, though the TPP found favor with Southeast Asian states for other reasons as well— including their need for an external push to catalyze domestic reform and desire not to be left out of something their neighbors would be part of— the idea also had traction in terms of these states wanting to reduce their dependence on China economically as well.

Threat perceptions also affected the distribution of U.S. commitment to Southeast Asia during the post-GFC period as well. A case in point is the imbalance in favor of interests over ideals. Officials have conceded privately that part of the rationale for why the Obama administration

China's Rise: An Insider's Account of America's Asia Strategy (Washington, DC: Brookings Institution Press, 2012).

[64] Interview with former U.S. defense official, Washington, DC, June 2019.

[65] Robert Sutter et al., "Balancing Acts: The U.S. Rebalance and Asia–Pacific Stability," Paper for the Sigur Center for Asian Studies Rising Power Initiative, August 2013, p. 1.

tended to put interests over ideals in several key Southeast Asian cases—notably Myanmar and Vietnam—was that it perceived that there was more to be gained from engaging these countries which had grown more cautious about China's behavior with respect to their foreign policies even through their domestic politics may raise concerns for some in the United States. "The China factor didn't dictate, but it factored highly into our cost–benefit analysis, and also theirs, don't forget" one diplomat who led the Obama administration's effort to engage Myanmar recounted.[66]

3.3   Moderately Low State Capacity

The other filter in the balance of commitment model, in addition to threat perceptions, is low state capacity. During the post-GFC period, we witnessed a period of low state capacity where it was difficult for U.S. policymakers to mobilize resources for their intended goals. Specifically, increased congressional activism and a war-weary public combined to produce an environment of low elite autonomy, which made it difficult for the foreign policy elite to get the commensurate capability and willingness to keep old commitments, let alone pursue new commitments as well.

The post-GFC saw a trend where the power of the executive branch was curtailed by several forces at home following two wars and an economic crisis, most notably public opinion and congressional activism. To take just one example, defense spending decreased by nearly one-fourth from 2010 to 2015—from $768 billion to $595 billion—with defense spending as a percentage of GDP declining from 4.7 to 3.3%.[67] This low state power environment incentivized the Obama administration to develop an approach that would balance the internal constraints it had at home with the external pressures it faced abroad, what Randall Schweller calls "a low-cost model for U.S. global management." As Schweller details:

> The Obama administration tried to reconcile its desire to preserve American hegemony in the face of a rising China, dangerously high national indebtedness, a war-weary public, and dwindling domestic support for

---

[66] Author conversation with former senior U.S. official, Washington, DC, February 2020.

[67] Author calculations from SIPRI database.

anything international—much less foreign entanglements—by developing a low-cost model for US global management. In practice this meant relying on economic sanctions to punish enemies, targeting terrorists with drones, fighting wars with robots and smart computerized weapons, avoiding unilateralism in favor of 'leading from behind', and pivoting to Asia within an overall grand strategy of 'selective engagement' and balancing China.[68]

Asia in general and Southeast Asia in particular were no doubt affected by the environment of moderately low state power that the United States was in. Factors such as bureaucratic politics, budgetary cuts and political gridlock significantly constrained the administration's ability to resource the rebalance to Asia.[69] "The standard policymaking process has been insufficient in bringing about the shift in resources that the rebalance calls for," one Congressional study on the resourcing of the pivot warned ominously.[70] Campbell himself, in his candid assessment of the risks to the success of the rebalance based on his experience working in the administration, argued that four of the eight he outlined related to state power—fracturing foreign policy consensus; deadlock and dysfunction; inadequate defense spending; and retrenchment in the United States.[71]

Moderately low state power contributed to both the level and distribution of the U.S. commitment to Southeast Asia in the post-GFC period. In terms of the level, given a climate where it was difficult to get the

[68] Randall Schweller, "Opposite But Competing Nationalisms: A Neoclassical Realist Approach to the Future of US-China Relations," *The Chinese Journal of International Politics*, Vol. 11, No. 1 (March 1, 2018), pp. 23–48. Alternate conceptions of this include Hal Brands' notion of "selective engagement, selective retrenchment" and Gideon Rose's distinction between Obama's commitment to the "core" as opposed to the "periphery" of the liberal international order. See: Hal Brands, "American Grand Strategy and the Liberal Order: Continuity, Change, and Options for the Future," RAND Corporation, 2016; and Gideon Rose, "What Obama Gets Right: Keep Calm and Carry the Liberal Order On," *Foreign Affairs*, September/October 2015.

[69] For a good survey of these considerations, see: Strategic Review 2013, "Chapter 8: The United States: Challenges for the Obama Administration's Second Term," National Institute for Defense Studies, Tokyo, 2014.

[70] U.S. Government Printing Office, "Re-balancing the Rebalance: Resourcing U.S. Diplomatic Strategy in the Asia–Pacific Region," April 17, 2014, p. 4.

[71] The other four relate to longer term issues with U.S. foreign policymaking and those in other regions—continuing challenges in the Middle East; longer-term planning; developing human capital; and mutual frustrations and decoupling. See: Kurt Campbell, *The Pivot: The Future of American Statecraft in Asia* (New York: Twelve Books, 2016), pp. 294–317.

necessary public approval and legislative authorization for resources, it was no surprise that this resulted in only a limited strengthening of areas involving the commitment of more security and economic resources— specifically the U.S. military deployments and economic engagement components. In the case of economic engagement, for instance, even some of the modest investments the administration made fell victim to the difficulties of low state power. Innovative programs introduced by the administration, such as the Lower Mekong Initiative (LMI), quickly faced budget shortfalls that were never overcome.[72]

Moderately low state capacity also affected the distribution of U.S. commitment in the post-GFC period. The clearest indication of this was the gap between means and ends. Throughout this period, the Obama administration fell prey to criticism that its end of increasing the focus on Southeast Asia was not justified by the means it employed to advance that goal, leading to gulfs between rhetoric and reality and shortfalls in terms of manpower or money. This was particularly troubling on the defense side, especially after the 2011 Budget Control Act, which set into motion across the board automatic reductions (sequestration).[73] As Green notes, the gap between means and ends in this realm was visibly demonstrated by the fact that in the same week that Obama was in Australian parliament delivering a key speech unveiling the pivot, including potential efforts in Southeast Asia as well, U.S. Defense Secretary Leon Panetta told Congress that the U.S. Navy was in danger of shrinking to its smallest size in over a century.[74]

Another example was the imbalance between ideals and interests. As Brands rightly notes, part of the reason why the Obama administration elected to pursue an approach that tended to favor interests over

---

[72] Phuong Nguyen, "Washington Needs a New Approach to the Lower Mekong—'The Next South China Sea'," CSIS Commentary, Washington, DC, April 17, 2014.

[73] For a survey of the defense issues from a general perspective, see: Michele Flournoy and Janine Davidson, "Obama's New Global Posture: The Logic of U.S. Foreign Deployments," *Foreign Affairs*, July/August 2012.

[74] See: Michael Green, *By More Than Providence: Grand Strategy and American Power in the Asia–Pacific Since 1783* (New York: Columbia University Press, 2017), p. 521. The challenge in some senses got even harder as time went by. By 2014, Katrina McFarland, the assistant secretary of defense for acquisition, was reduced to candidly saying, "right now, the pivot is being looked at again, because candidly it can't happen," a statement that she then walked back. Zachary Fryer-Biggs, "DoD Officials: Asia Pivot "Can't Happen' Due to Budgetary Pressures, *DefenseNews*, March 4, 2014.

Table 3 Summary of Findings on the Balance of Commitment Model in the Post-GFC Period

Variable	Type	Finding	Predicted?
Relative power	Independent	Decrease	Yes
Threat level	Intervening	Moderately high	Yes
State capacity	Intervening	Moderately low	Higher than expected state capacity
Overall commitment level and balance	Dependent	Moderate increase; Minor increase	Lower than expected commitment level

Source Generated by Author

ideals—what he terms "selective engagement, selective retrenchment" with respect to the furthering of the international liberal order—was because it was cognizant that the difficulties of mobilizing state power at home necessitated being more "selective, discerning, and prudent" in the short term as part of playing a long game.[75] Administration officials involved in Southeast Asian affairs repeatedly emphasized the fact that the president's personal investment in efforts such as YSEALI and other programs aimed at good governance were part of an incremental effort that sought the promotion of democracy and human rights in its own way.[76]

From the above exploration into the reasons behind the shape of U.S. commitment during the post-GFC period, it is clear that, as balance of commitment predicted, we did indeed witness a case where a moderate decline in U.S. relative capabilities, mediated by a moderately high threat level perceived by the American foreign policy elite as well as moderately low state power, accounted for a moderate increase in commitment level and minor increase in commitment balance during this period. Table 3 summarizes the findings with respect to one independent variable and two intervening variables.

---

[75] Hal Brands, "American Grand Strategy and the Liberal Order: Continuity, Change, and Options for the Future," RAND Corporation, 2016, p. 16.

[76] Author conversation with former senior White House official, Washington, DC, March 2020.

4   Evaluating U.S. Commitment During the Post-GFC Period

The post-GFC period offers confirming evidence of the balance of commitment explanation in the U.S. commitment to Southeast Asia during the first years of the Obama administration. While changes in the strategic environment certainly shaped the general level and distribution of U.S. commitment, as balance of power theory would suggest, threat perceptions and state power accounted for the specific manifestations of components and categories of that commitment and explain why policymakers ended up adopting the course they did as opposed to others that they may have preferred or considered.

In terms of the dependent variable, which is commitment level and distribution during the post-GFC period, it is clear that the U.S. role during the period conformed to expectations. But there were some differences that were also observed. Most notably, commitment balance was lower than anticipated, with only a minor increase in spite of the fact that the Obama administration had initially actively sought to reduce commitment imbalances in some areas as a policy priority. The moderate increase in commitment level was not unexpected but may also appear surprising at first glance to observers given the attention that was attempted to be given to Southeast Asia at the outset.

Turning to the independent and intervening variables, there was no clear transmission belt observed directly between the relative distribution of capabilities and commitment level and imbalance, which would have been the case if balance of power theory were correct. Instead, the contours of debates that U.S. policymakers had during the post-GFC period, whether it be the degree to which they would promote, were largely around the intervening variables of threat perceptions and state power emphasized in balance of commitment. Admittedly, state capacity was actually found to be higher than was initially anticipated, suggesting that there might have been more room for commitment expansion.

Given all this, balance of commitment can be said to have passed the fourth of the four case study tests examined here in the context of U.S.-Southeast Asia relations, and one that is a significant, rich and most recent case. Now that this is clear, we can move on to assessing some of the conclusions we can draw from this study as well as some key implications for policymakers too.

CHAPTER 8

Shaping U.S. Southeast Asia Strategy and Policy

1 Introduction

This book has sought to answer a key question in U.S. strategy and policy toward Southeast Asia: *What accounts for the changes in the level and distribution of the United States' commitment to Southeast Asia over time?* The argument advanced in this book has been that the balance of commitment model, an originally designed foreign policy framework, accounts for these variations in U.S. commitment to Southeast Asia over time more so than neorealism or balance of power theory.

The four cases examined in this study—the post-Vietnam war period; the post-Cold War period; the post-September 11 period; and the post-2007–2008 Financial Crisis period—clearly illustrate that the balance of commitment model offers a better and more complete explanation of variations in U.S. commitment than balance of power theory. More specifically, in all four cases, variations of U.S. commitment to the region have been proven to be *not just* the direct outcomes of power shifts between the United States and its competitors, but a consequence of how American policymakers balance perceiving those shifts and threats with mobilizing and extracting the resources to respond to them. The intervening variables of threat perception and state capacity have important effects here as well beyond relative power.

Having tested balance of power theory against the balance of commitment model in its ability to explain variations in U.S. commitment to

© The Author(s), under exclusive license to Springer Nature
Singapore Pte Ltd. 2022
P. Parameswaran, *Elusive Balances*,
https://doi.org/10.1007/978-981-16-6612-4_8

Southeast Asia with respect to four main case studies, this concluding chapter attempts to analyze the key findings and note some of the implications for U.S. policy and strategy as well as limitations that were observed along with recommendations and suggestions for future research in this area.

It will seek to do so in three separate sections. The first section will evaluate the key findings in this book from the four cases, examining the relationships between independent, intervening and dependent variables as well as additional insights based on cross-case comparisons. The second section will then note some of the limitations of the study and chart out some directions for future research. The third and final section will provide some theoretical and policy implications that might be sieved out from the study.

2   Evaluating Key Findings

This section will seek to evaluate some of the key findings that were uncovered in this book in the four case studies. The section will be divided into the insights for commitment balance and distribution (the dependent variable); neorealism and the balance of power (the competing theory or explanation); and neoclassical realism (balance of commitment, the model advanced in this book).

2.1   Commitment Level and Distribution

With respect to commitment balance and distribution, the dependent variable in this book, the findings confirm the central problem identified at the outset of this book with respect to the ebbs, flows and imbalances evident in U.S. commitment to Southeast Asia. The legacy of underperforming commitment levels and near-persistent commitment imbalance is evident to varying degrees across all four cases studied, and in some cases, this in fact has been even clearer than initially anticipated.

The first case of the post-Vietnam period saw the United States try to reduce and reshape its commitment to Southeast Asia after a period of perceived overcommitment. The case constituted the most extreme case in this respect, and there was a major decrease in both commitment level and commitment imbalance. In addition to the notable intensity witnessed here relative to the other cases, additionally significant was the fact that commitment balance and distribution remained unchanged on these extremes for a particularly long period of around a decade, and across three different Democrat and Republican administrations in Nixon, Ford and Carter.

In the second case of the post-Cold War period, we witnessed a minor decrease in commitment level and a major decrease in commitment balance as the United States sought to reshape its engagement with several regions of the world amid a newfound status of unprecedented preponderance following the fall of the Soviet Union. Here too, it was notable that these levels with respect to the dependent variable were as low as they were given the position that Washington was in terms of relative power, and, additionally, that they lasted across two different Republican and Democrat administrations in George H.W. Bush and Bill Clinton.

The third case of the post-9/11 period saw the George W. Bush administration, in the context of Washington's continued status as a unipolar power and following an attack on the homeland, seek to reinforce its position in Asia amid the threat from terrorism and longer-term competition with China. Apart from the commitment level and commitment balance that resulted—a moderate increase and a moderate decrease, respectively—one of the striking features of this period was how quickly and intensely U.S. commitment was shaped in contrast to the earlier two cases as this occurred in a single administration over a period of just a few years.

The fourth and final case of the post-GFC period witnessed the United States, in the face of a sense of decline of Washington's relative capabilities following wars in the Middle East and a global financial crisis as well as growing concerns about Chinese inroads, attempt to increase its commitment to Southeast Asia. Yet despite U.S. policymakers devoting attention to increasing U.S. commitment to Southeast Asia and being aware of commitment imbalances, the resulting outcome was nonetheless one where there was a moderate increase in commitment level and a minor increase in commitment balance. This was further testament to the enduring nature of the ebbs, flows and imbalances in U.S. commitment to the region.

That said, even though the four cases largely confirmed the findings that balance of commitment expected, there was also some degree of variance in expected observations and what was eventually found. While the predictions made with respect to commitment level and balance were largely correct in all four cases, the cases also showed signs where commitment level and balance also diverged from expectations somewhat.

In terms of commitment level, it is striking that in one case—the post-Vietnam period—the actual commitment level was lower than what was initially predicted. While a single case may not suggest that the issue of underperforming commitment levels may in fact worse than originally thought, it nonetheless speaks to why the post-Vietnam period continues to be pointed to as an extreme case of drop-off on commitment levels in spite of the best efforts of U.S. policymakers.

Furthermore, the actual commitment level range was also from major decrease to moderate increase in all four cases, with an upper bound that did not quite reach major increase. The post-GFC period is particularly illustrative here because despite the Obama administration's efforts to specifically elevate U.S. commitment to Southeast Asia rhetorically, commitment level still did not reach very high levels in practice as noted earlier.

In terms of commitment balance, it was also the case that in one of the four cases—the post-GFC period—the actual level of commitment imbalance was higher than was initially predicted. While a single case may not necessarily suggest that the issue of commitment imbalances may in fact be worse than was originally thought, it does nonetheless point to why there was some unease about aspects of the U.S. pivot to Asia.

Furthermore, the actual commitment imbalance range was also strikingly from major decrease to minor increase, which was more restrictive than the range for commitment level. The fact that even the Obama administration, which actively tried to narrow some commitment balances, was only able to record a minor increase, reinforces the point that imbalance is a vexing issue all administrations have to confront to some degree and it is likely to remain challenging to achieve a level of major increase in commitment balance.

The differences witnessed between expected and actual outcomes for commitment level and commitment imbalance for all four cases are summarized in Table 1.

2.2   Balance of Power

With respect to balance of power theory, which constitutes the competing explanation to the balance of commitment model, the findings in the four cases confirm that it does shape some of the change witnessed in U.S.

Table 1 Expectations vs. Actual Outcomes for Commitment Level and Balance

Case	Commitment level (expected)	Commitment level (actual)	Commitment balance (expected)	Commitment balance (actual)
Post-Vietnam (1969–1978)	Moderate decrease	Major decrease	Major decrease	Major decrease
Post-Cold War (1989–1995)	Minor decrease	Minor decrease	Major decrease	Major decrease
Post-9/11 (2001–2005)	Moderate increase	Moderate increase	Moderate decrease	Moderate decrease
Post-GFC (2009–2014)	Moderate increase	Moderate increase	Moderate increase	Minor increase

Source Generated by Author

commitment to Southeast Asia. In other words, this study confirms that balance of power theory does account to some degree for variations in the level and distribution of U.S. commitment, even though it cannot explain them completely and in a more comprehensive and granular way.

The general form hypothesis for neorealism or balance of power theory set out at the beginning of this book was that changes in relative power between the United States and other competing powers would cause changes in the level and distribution of U.S. regional commitment. It was also suggested that more specific indicators, such as the intensity, urgency and probability of power shifts, could also affect commitment level and balance as well.

In all four cases, changes in the relative distribution of capabilities—be it decreases in U.S. relative power witnessed in the post-Vietnam period and the post-GFC period, or increases as was seen in the post-Cold War and post-9/11 periods—did affect how U.S. policymakers thought about the level and distribution of American commitment to Southeast Asia. But at the same time, it did not reveal much about how exactly this would translate into a particular commitment level or balance or suggest evidence of a direct transmission belt that suggests direct causation.

In the first case of the post-Vietnam era, as described in the case study chapter, the context of decreasing U.S. relative capabilities did indeed suggest that policymakers would have to recalibrate U.S. commitment to areas of the world, including possibly a decreasing commitment level in Southeast Asia given that the U.S. involvement in the Vietnam War was a significant part of that. That context, as well as its intensity, imposed constraints and pressures on U.S. policymakers that affected commitment level and commitment balance as well, including limiting the available resources they could deploy to Southeast Asia and incentivizing them to seek arrangements with allies and adversaries that would reduce burdens on the United States and strengthen its relative power.

Yet balance of power theory did not determine the exact course of U.S. commitment level and balance to Southeast Asia during the post-Vietnam period. Some of the key tendencies U.S. policymakers displayed during this period—including a less anxious attitude toward some Soviet and Chinese gains in the region and a continued aversion to making necessary investments in regional alliances and partnerships that would have advanced administration priorities—were rooted more in their unique calculations about threats and opportunities in the international system as well as the particular difficulties they had in mobilizing resources even for the limited ends that they felt they needed to achieve.

In the second case of the post-Cold War period, the context of increasing U.S. relative capabilities following the fall of the Soviet Union did leave the United States in a state of unprecedented preponderance, thereby giving Washington an increased ability to sustain its primacy while shaping a broader multipolar order in Asia in general and in Southeast Asia in particular. The intensity of the shift in capabilities that resulted also created a more permissive environment for administrations to take a more activist role in Asia as well as adopt a more broad-based conception of U.S. interests that extended beyond narrow economic and security interests and also covered the advancement of democracy and human rights and the promotion of multilateralism.

But relative capabilities did not determine the particular course that the United States adopted in terms of its commitment to Southeast Asia. Some of the main considerations that played into the minds of policymakers during that period, such as the opportunity to shape a more collaborative, multipolar order in the absence of a single, imminent, major threat or the ability to influence public opinion and resist domestic pressure, were a product more of the beliefs that they held about a low threat environment as well as a context where resource mobilization was possible in cases where a strategic case could be made that was tied to domestic interests.

In the third case of the post-9/11 period, the U.S. commitment to Southeast Asia was indeed shaped by Washington's continuing status as a unipolar power, which created a context where despite any challenges it may confront, including in the homeland, it would have the ability and willingness to sustain U.S. primacy and shaping a more contested order in Asia. China's rising capabilities vis-à-vis the United States in Southeast Asia also reinforced the region's role as a locus for long-term competition with Beijing. Additionally, there was also an added sense of urgency in the post-9/11 period for the United States to act on the basis of the position that it held.

However, at the same time, while Washington was responsive to shifts in the regional and global distribution of power, as balance of power theory would expect, the theory was less able to explain the nuances of U.S. commitment levels and commitment balance in Southeast Asia during the post-9/11 period. The more specific contours of Washington's commitment to the subregion during this time, whether it be its prioritization of dangers that ranged from terrorism to China, the lukewarm attitude toward multilateral institutions, or the ease with which it was able to summon the funds for security assistance, were rooted in the combination of an environment of high threat perceptions and high state power.

In the fourth case of the post-GFC period, the U.S. commitment to Southeast Asia was shaped by a combination of both a sense of decline of Washington's relative capabilities following the wars in Iraq and Afghanistan and the Global Financial Crisis, as well as the growing realization that China rising capabilities in the Asia–Pacific required Washington to respond to Beijing's actions. These considerations did influence the Obama administration's decision to prioritize Southeast Asia as among the key areas of selective U.S. commitment while reassuring allies, partners and friends that Washington would readjust but not disengage from the region amid Beijing's rising assertiveness there.

Yet balance of power theory did not dictate the exact course of U.S. commitment level and balance to Southeast Asia during the post-GFC period. Instead, some of the key contours of U.S. commitment during this period, be it gains recorded with allies and partners on the security side or the difficulty in mobilizing resources to give heft to the much-ballyhooed U.S. pivot or rebalance to Asia, were rooted more in policymakers' calculations of threats and the difficulties they faced in mobilizing resources to achieve their intended aims.

2.3   Balance of Commitment

Switching to the balance of commitment model, which is the new and original framework advanced in this book, the model offers a more complete and nuanced explanation for the shifts in the United States' commitment to Southeast Asia than does balance of power theory.

The general form hypothesis for neoclassical realism and the balance of commitment framework set out at the beginning of this book was that changes in relative power, mediated by elite threat perceptions and state capacity, will cause changes in the level and distribution of U.S. regional commitment. Additionally, it was also hypothesized that certain combinations of the two intervening variables would map onto different levels of commitment level and commitment balance as well.

All four cases confirm the general form of the hypothesis. In the first case of the post-Vietnam era, the context of decreasing U.S. relative capabilities did suggest that policymakers would have to recalibrate U.S. commitment to areas of the world, including possibly a decreasing commitment level in Southeast Asia. But what ultimately shaped the nature of U.S. commitment level and balance in Southeast Asia was the reality that policymakers were operating in an environment of low threat perceptions and low state power.

Put more specifically, with U.S. policymakers adopting a more risk-prone attitude toward potential dangers and power vacuums in the international system while also finding resource extraction difficult in an environment of domestic dissensus, they were both less likely to commit resources to Southeast Asia and more likely to be selective about which commitments they made. As a result, it was no surprise that both U.S. commitment level and U.S. commitment balance saw major decreases.

In the second case of the post-Cold War period, the context of an increase in U.S. relative capabilities following the collapse of the USSR did indeed leave Washington in a state of unprecedented preponderance and suggested that it had a greater ability to sustain its primacy in regions of interest such as the Asia–Pacific. But the exact course of U.S. commitment was also shaped more fundamentally and directly by an environment of low threat level and moderately low state power.

In particular, during this period, policymakers saw the lack of a single, imminent, major threat as an opportunity to shape a more collaborative, multipolar regional order, and in some cases, they were able to mobilize the resources to achieve their ends if they expended the necessary effort to align their objectives with the national interest. The result was a minor decrease in commitment level and a major decrease in commitment balance.

In the third case of the post-9/11 period, the context of Washington's continued status as a unipolar power certainly created a context where despite challenges it confronted, including in the homeland, it would have the ability to sustain U.S. primacy, including in the Asia–Pacific given China's rising capabilities there. Yet here again, as with the previous two cases, it was evident that what ultimately shaped the nature of U.S. commitment level and balance in Southeast Asia was the intervening variables of threat perceptions and state power.

Put more specifically, U.S. policymakers felt that a moderately high threat level had heightened the perceived urgency by which they would have to act, and that they were operating in an environment where it would be much easier to extract resources even for the advancement of their most ambitious goals. That environment of moderately high threat perceptions and medium state power ultimately accounted for the shape of U.S. commitment during this period, which was characterized by a moderate increase in commitment level and moderate decrease in commitment balance.

In the fourth and final case of the post-GFC period as well, U.S. commitment to Southeast Asia was in part influenced by considerations of relative power, be it the sense of decline of Washington's own relative capabilities following two wars and a global financial crisis, or the realization of China's rising capabilities in the Asia–Pacific. But here too, it was clear that the intervening variables of threat perceptions and state power ultimately played a greater role in shaping the nature of U.S. commitment during this period.

In particular, during this period, policymakers perceived a range of threats to U.S. interests while simultaneously contending with an environment that proved difficult for resource mobilization, including for specific foreign policy priorities laid out in Southeast Asia. That environment of moderately high threat perceptions and moderately low state power ultimately accounted for the shape of U.S. commitment during this period, which was characterized by a moderate increase in commitment level and minor increase in commitment balance.

A summary of observations found with respect to each of the independent, intervening, and dependent variables and each of the cases is displayed in Table 2.

Table 2 Summary of Observations for All Variables Across Cases

Case	Relative power	Threat level	State capacity	Commitment level and balance
Post-Vietnam	Minor decrease	Low	Low	Major decrease; Major decrease
Post-Cold War	Major increase	Low	Moderately low	Minor decrease; Major decrease
Post-9/11	Minor increase	Moderately high	Medium	Moderate increase; Moderate decrease
Post-GFC	Moderate decrease	Moderately high	Moderately low	Moderate increase; Minor increase

Source Generated by Author

That said, there was also some degree of variance in expected observations and what was eventually found. While the predictions made with respect to threat perceptions and state power were largely correct in all four cases, two of the four cases also showed signs where they also diverged from expectations somewhat.

The two cases were the post- 9/11 period and the post-GFC period. In the case of the post-9/11 period, the level of threat level was actually lower than anticipated—at moderately high rather than high. Also, in the post-GFC period, the level of state capacity was higher than anticipated— at moderately low rather than low. Table 3 shows how the expected outcomes mapped onto the actual outcomes for the intervening variables in question.

2.4   Additional Findings from Cross-Case Comparisons

In addition to the findings that came from within each of the four cases, there were also additional findings that were discerned from across all of them as well via cross-case comparisons. These additional findings are

Table 3   Expected vs. Actual Outcomes for Intervening Variables

Case	Threat level (expected)	Threat level (actual)	State capacity (expected)	State capacity (actual)
Post-Vietnam (1969–1978)	Low	Low	Low	Low
Post-Cold War (1989–1995)	Low	Low	Moderately low	Moderately low
Post-9/11 (2001–2005)	High	Moderately high	Medium	Medium
Post-GFC (2009–2014)	Moderately high	Moderately high	Low	Moderately low

Source Generated by Author

important as they may suggest broader trends or dynamics at play, with implications not only for this book itself, but also for theory and practice as well as future study more generally.

First, while the four case studies illustrate that ebbs, flows and imbalances do certainly continue to be an issue across time for policymakers, it is also interesting that there does seem to be some suggestion of trends over time within these case studies up to this point. More specifically, commitment level has shown a tendency to display some increase over time, while commitment balance has moved away from major decrease seen in the first case.

This is not to suggest that there is some linear trajectory that will endure over time with respect to commitment level and commitment balance. Indeed, the Trump administration's legacy, which saw some contraction in commitment level and intensification of commitment balance issues before some offsetting under the Biden administration, is a reminder that reversals can indeed occur. The more interesting question, however, is whether or not the baseline for commitment level and commitment balance is improving over time irrespective of what path any administration seeks to pursue, and this is something worth monitoring in the coming years.

Second, the ranges of commitment level and commitment imbalance witnessed across cases raise interesting questions about U.S. commitment more generally. With respect to commitment level, the fact that the Obama administration put such a significant focus on commitment to Southeast Asia relative to its predecessors only for commitment level to be recorded as a moderate increase raises the question about the extent to which there may be a limit on U.S. commitment levels to Southeast Asia. Similarly, if the range of commitment balance only ranges from major decrease to minor increase as is evidenced, it might be asked whether this represents some sort of "ceiling" on the level of commitment balance.

Of course, it would seem premature to conclude that based on just the ranges in these four case studies alone, this necessarily means that there is a "commitment level peak" for U.S. commitment level, or a "commitment balance ceiling" for U.S. commitment imbalance. Nonetheless, these cross-case findings do suggest that it is interesting to contemplate what shapes the upper and lower bounds of commitment level and commitment imbalance.

Third, certain individual components of commitment level and balance seem to display variance across cases with respect to their sensitivity to change relative to others. For instance, when it comes to commitment level in the four case studies in this book, alliances and partnerships tend to be a component that is far more enduring than perceived, with multiple cases showing instances where changes were mulled but ultimately deferred or not pursued, while diplomatic engagement has displayed a tendency to be more sensitive to change in accordance with specific initiatives or interactions.

That sensitivity variance is important to note. At the most basic level, it suggests that we should expect some individual components of commitment level and balance to change more readily and frequently than others in particular periods. Further, and equally importantly, it also reinforces the point that the mix of individual components included for commitment level and commitment balance is fundamentally important because it could affect aggregate figures as well.

Fourth, the cases display a clear difference with respect to the kind of capability and power shifts which could play into the shaping of commitment level and commitment balance. For instance, while post-Cold War period saw major shifts in U.S. capabilities tied to the structure of the international system that took place over a longer period of time, the other two cases of the post-9/11 period and the post-GFC period could be characterized as more sudden crises of a more limited duration. These variations in turn affected the sorts of pressures and constraints that were exerted on policymakers.

The variations at play in the four cases and their effects on U.S. commitment reinforce the fact that it is important to not just comprehend power shifts, but classify the different kinds of shifts as well as their different impacts on commitment level. The sub-hypotheses mentioned at the beginning of the study, such as on intensity, urgency, and probability, were an attempt to help do this, and this deserves further examination as well in future study of the subject.

Fifth and finally, and in a similar vein, while attention was paid to the level of threat perceptions in this book as an intervening variable, the four cases examined also illustrate that the type of threat in question during a particular period, the ranking of threats and challenges or the "threat hierarchy," and how policymakers weigh threats against opportunities, also matter as well. In just the last two cases examined, for example, the Bush administration's increased priority devoted to counterterrorism post-9/11, and the Obama administration's insistence on not letting rising notions of a China threat get in the way of opportunities to be advanced, had a significant influence on commitment level and commitment balance.

3 LIMITATIONS AND AREAS FOR FUTURE RESEARCH

The study of these four cases has also pointed to some of the limitations involved in this theoretical framework and the approach undertaken in this study more generally. The first is with respect to sourcing. As was noted at the outset of the book, while interviews and conversations as well the author's personal experiences did help supplement other available primary and secondary source material across cases, there was nonetheless an unevenness observed given the relatively greater availability of archival information in earlier periods.

The second is regarding scope. Though this book has sought to both broaden the conception of commitment and to explore the complexities of different variables in affecting the shape of that commitment, there were aspects that were not included even in that broad scope, both in terms of the dependent variable as well as the forces driving the intervening variables in question.

For instance, in the case intervening variables, in examinations of state power in particular, there was less of a focus on the role of specific, smaller interest groups and communities in driving some of the constraints that later worked their way up to the institutions focused on in the case studies. And in the case of individual components of the dependent variable, though aspects of people-to-people ties were considered as part of U.S. commitment, specific manifestations such as numbers of students were not separated out as their own categories in the interest of parsimony.

A third issue was with respect to endogeneity. During the course of the study, it was challenging to entirely disentangle threat perceptions from regional power shifts in order to prove that they have an independent effect on the dependent variable. This is important because the problem of endogeneity tends to dog more complex explanatory frameworks that seek to examine linkages among different variables, in contrast to more parsimonious explanations.

Efforts were made to disentangle the effects of different variables and to reinforce aspects of this, such as the fact that elite threat perceptions were influenced by but were not exclusively the effect of relative power shifts in the region. Though some inroads were made by approaches such as charting out different possibilities available to policymakers based on structural realities and how they, as agents, then narrowed down their options to get to the eventual outcomes, it was nonetheless challenging to entirely dismiss the possibility of some overlap during the study of these four cases.

The fourth and final issue was regarding measurement. While there has been significant attention given to measuring variables in this book across four cases, at times that measurement process could not fully account for the extent of variation among the cases in question. This is important because it can affect not only how metrics are scored in each case, but how relative comparisons are made across cases.

For instance, with respect to the one component of the dependent variable—military deployments in U.S. commitment level—this framework cannot fully account for the fact that while there were increases or decreases recorded across four periods, the scope of change in fact significantly narrowed in the post-9/11 and post-GFC periods relative to the two previous cases. With respect to threat perceptions, a few interviewees commented that while it may be understandable given the specifics, it was nonetheless a bit surprising at first glance to see that the commitment level in the Obama administration was similar to that of the George W. Bush administration.

While the scope of change had to be measured manually in the study where it saw dramatic shifts, there could be adjustments made in future research, including the introduction of a wider range of change such as a numerical system of 1 to 10 rather than just gradients in between increases and decreases and high, medium and low.

There are also several areas that could be ripe for future research. A first potential area for future research is the inclusion of additional cases to test the balance of commitment model. Though this book has attempted to provide a good range of cases, additional cases during different time periods and administrations would provide more tests for the theory that could help sieve out additional insights.

A second potential area for future research is the application of balance of commitment to other regions of the world beyond Southeast Asia. Applying the theory to another single region such as Latin America, the Middle East or Africa would enhance its generalizability. It would also reveal how differences in regions on various counts relative to Southeast Asia, such as increased geographic proximity or geopolitical importance, can affect the independent, intervening and dependent variables.

In particular, cross-regional comparisons across multiple periods would have the additional benefit of providing insights about how U.S. commitment to various areas of the world can wax and wane during a specific time. This would reveal how changes of focus or emphasis can affect the thoughts and actions of a global superpower, and essentially simulate what can amount to a competition for a finite amount of U.S. commitment between regions of the world and how this evolves.

A third and final potential area for future research is the application of balance of commitment to other countries beyond just the United States. While there are no doubt dynamics that are unique to Washington, at the same time, there is also no reason why there would not be some similar relationships at play between relative power, threat perceptions and state power witnessed in some other countries as well.

Such an application would not only help broaden the applicability of balance of commitment, but also potentially shed light on how relationships between independent, intervening and dependent variables may differ across countries and what factors may be behind the extent of variations that are witnessed. It would also potentially introduce newer and better ways of measuring these variables in different contexts.

4   Theoretical and Policy Implications

Apart from the limitations and areas flagged for future research, there are also a number of theoretical and policy implications that can be gleaned from this study as well that deserve elaboration.

4.1   Theoretical Implications

These findings in this book have several theoretical implications that might be gleaned. These relate to the study of commitment itself, the focus on regions of the world and Southeast Asia in particular, and the advancement of realism in general and neoclassical realism in particular in terms of theories of international relations.

First, the original balance of commitment framework developed in this book and the illustration of its applicability across four cases advances the theoretical grounding with respect to analyzing commitment. In all four cases examined in this study, perceptions of U.S. commitment in Southeast Asia either increasing or decreasing in an aggregate sense betrayed the complexity in the reality of those cases, where specific components of commitment level and commitment balances moved in different directions at the same time.

This suggests the more rigorous and careful attention that is needed to measuring U.S. commitment in general and to Southeast Asia in particular. More generally, there ought to be a greater focus on not just aggregate U.S. foreign policy outcomes, but also the balance or distribution between specific components of foreign policy that might allow for a better detection of subtle policy shifts.

Second, the findings in this book reinforce the case for a greater focus on foreign policy outcomes at the regional level. In all four of the case studies examined, it was notable there were repeated instances where there were inconsistencies or contradictions between how U.S. foreign policy was being shaped and adopted in general and in Asia and how these dynamics played out in Southeast Asia more specifically. Some of these dynamics recurred in different periods, suggesting that there might be deeper, structural reasons for their occurrence.

This strengthens the need to examine why some manifestations of U.S. commitment may influence different regions of the world differently, and why this might be the case. This ties into the growing literature on how the state of particular regional orders can play into broader variables such as the relative distribution of capabilities and threat perceptions.

Third, and more specific to the study of U.S.-Southeast Asia relations, this book also advances the discussion on U.S. commitment to the region and American approaches to Southeast Asia more generally by moving beyond the analytically rich but atheoretical and security-centric accounts of particular periods, with most of them being from the end of the Second World War up to the end of the Vietnam War.

Specifically, the pattern of repeated ebbs, flows and imbalances, along with the trends observed in the case studies, reinforces the need to focus on the reasons behind the recurrence of these patterns and the examination of broader structural dynamics, instead of a focus on a single facet of commitment or one event or administration. It is hoped that other works will also seek to examine this question from a theoretical perspective to further elevate the level of debate.

Fourth, the approach adopted in this book and the analysis that has flowed from it can help advance the ongoing discussion about the utility of various schools of realism, including neorealism and neoclassical realism, in explaining foreign policy outcomes. By setting up a direct test of the two theoretical approaches in each of the four case studies, this study has shed light on some of the complex and nuanced linkages between systemic imperatives and foreign policy choices of nation states and their leaders, as opposed to just focusing on one or the other.

Making direct and specific comparisons between these theories is important to both advancing the debates within the realist school as well as between theories of international relations more generally. The four case studies have also helped reveal both the value as well as the limitations of introducing additional complexity to explanatory frameworks for foreign policy outcomes that will be useful in refining future studies.

Fifth and finally, this book has reinforced the explanatory power of neoclassical realism more specifically and enhanced its applicability as a theory. The fact that all four case studies examined in this study confirm that neoclassical realism can explain variations in U.S. commitment in a key region of the world is itself a significant boost for the theoretical approach.

It is additionally significant that the reinforcement of neoclassical realism's explanatory power and enhanced applicability is occurring with respect to Southeast Asia, a region where it has been less frequently applied to date, and regarding commitment, which is a type of foreign policy outcome that has yet to be tested with this theory. It is hoped that further tests of the theory will follow on both these counts and in other contexts that will shed light on the value and limitations of this approach relative to other competing theories.

4.2   Policy Implications

If the findings in this book and balance of commitment advanced within it can help us understand past episodes of U.S. commitment variation in Southeast Asia and generate some interesting theoretical implications, they also have some potential policy implications as well for contemporary U.S. strategy and policy in Southeast Asia and the future direction of this. In recognition of the reality that the specifics of policy recommendations will vary from administration to administration, there are a few guiding points that can be set out that could be tailored to particular contexts over time.

First and most directly, policymakers should endeavor to raise and sustain the commitment level to Southeast Asia within the constraints they have. To be sure, it is unreasonable to expect that commitment levels will not change over time given what the history of U.S. commitment to Southeast Asia has shown us. Nor is it realistic to assume that Southeast Asia's importance will rise on a linear trajectory and that this will be equally recognized across the U.S. government across multiple administrations, even though this is the outcome that advocates of the region would hope for. A more modest goal would be to create an effective "floor" on U.S. commitment to Southeast Asia to limit any drop-offs in commitment we see during periods of contraction which could well occur in administrations that have a narrower conception of Southeast Asia's significance, and, following from that, thereby minimizing the work that would be needed to recover any loss that could otherwise distract from proactively advancing new initiatives.

This starts with ensuring a consistent appreciation across all administrations of a broad understanding of Southeast Asia's importance for its own sake, as opposed to being defined exclusively or primarily relative to broader priorities such as China. As has been demonstrated in the case studies, though there is a general understanding of the stakes that Washington has in the subregion—which includes its strategic location amid key sea lanes, its rising economic weight and its role as a hub for regional institutions—in practice, policymakers have at times toggled between overly expansive or narrow conceptions of the region's importance.

Ensuring that a broad-based understanding of this is consistently baked into standard administration-wide reviews and is also publicly messaged by Congress and other non-government actors such as think tanks and businesses will be important components of generating an effective whole-of-society effort to sustain U.S. commitment to the region. Building up Congressional attention to Southeast Asia, whether it be via encouraging interest by new or existing Congressmen or advancing efforts put in place such as formal caucuses and working groups, could prove useful on the legislative side. In terms of wider society, efforts such as statistical information or polling undertaken by think tanks in the United States such as CSIS and the East–West Center can help enhance the understanding of Southeast Asia.

Words should be followed by action, especially since Southeast Asian policymakers are well-attuned to the gaps between rhetoric and reality coming from Washington. Though having rough metrics for the minimum levels of military deployments or economic assistance required to advance U.S. objectives in Southeast Asia might be desirable, more attention should also be placed on dedicating certain budget line items to Southeast Asia and then protecting those elements of resourcing across the U.S. government. If this proves challenging to do for Southeast Asia itself, this can also be worked into wider priorities as we have seen with some of the earlier work on the Southeast Asia Maritime Security Initiative which began under the late Senator John McCain. Similarly, on the economic side, while certain periods in U.S. domestic politics might make it difficult to advance wholly new bilateral or multilateral trade agreements, policymakers can take more incremental steps such as sectoral pacts with individual countries or minilateral groupings.

Additional work is also needed to strengthen the U.S. domestic environment to build support for commitment to Southeast Asia. Part of this is ensuring this occurs within the U.S. government, through steps such as ensuring the elevation of more Southeast Asianists to higher levels of Asia policy which has tended to be largely though not exclusively dominated by either China or Japan specialists—a point that has been publicly made by seasoned Asia hands including Kurt Campbell. Beyond this, efforts should also be made to boost commitment in non-governmental realms by exposing more Americans to Southeast Asia. The education sector offers a particularly valuable area in this regard, with even more attention devoted to boosting the study of Southeast Asia and two-way exchanges of students building on already existing efforts such as the Young Southeast Asia Leaders Initiative.

Additionally, policymakers and other interested actors can also try to shape how U.S. commitment is portrayed in the media and in popular opinion in order to bridge the gulf between loose uses of the term in common parlance tied to individual events and more sustained efforts on the part of administrations to make comprehensive gains. Policymakers can themselves be more cautious and specific when they do introduce notions of commitment at the outset of a new administration out of reassurance rather than the reality of policy, which can then in turn lead to imbalances later on. Apart from that, think tankers and scholars can also help to the extent that this is consistent with their own pursuits by popularizing more comprehensive notions of commitment, introducing regular measures of components of this and explaining some of the structural dynamics behind certain persistent imbalances that are witnessed.

Second, attention should be placed on properly managing and moderating commitment imbalances. While some imbalances are to be expected, the emphasis should be on being mindful of the balances that need to be struck and minimizing imbalances across realms to the extent possible to limit any potential challenges to the execution of U.S. commitment to the region.

This can begin even with some basic steps. For instance, on the imbalance between economics and security, though this may prove challenging to fix given the realities of the Pentagon's massive resourcing advantage relative to the State Department, even communicating a recognition of this imbalance would go a long way toward attention in the region to this with the advent of a new administration. Officials can also take nuanced steps to address this as part of their strategic communications. To take just one example, periodically and intentionally restructuring a speech on U.S.-Southeast Asia policy to begin with economics or people-to-people ties when there is more anxiety on these measures rather than the security domain, would be a clear signal of prioritization in a region like Southeast Asia where nuance is appreciated. Some of this may involve recalibrating the sequence of policy rollouts in a new administration and finding regularized opportunities for expounding on non-security policy components in the first half of the year, in a way that the Shangri-La Dialogue in Singapore has served as a venue for U.S. policymakers to elaborate on Washington's defense policy in Asia more broadly.

Of course, this would need to be backed up by actions as well. One low-hanging fruit in this regard is ensuring consistency across administrations regarding high-level attendance at annual Asian summitry led by ASEAN. Instead of creating what can amount to an excessive focus around whether or not a U.S. president is attending every year that can at times get close to the summitry itself, absent a major crisis, administrations should announce this decision as early as possible integrated with a plan for how this drop-off in engagement will be managed. For instance, should the president not be able to attend, the announcement on non-attendance should be accompanied by details on the high-ranking official who will be representing the president as well as creative ways to signal presidential commitment, including standard virtual remarks from him or her. As the late ASEAN Secretary-General Surin Pitsuwan has indicated publicly, Southeast Asian states had been aware of this issue even before they admitted the United States into the East Asia Summit, and the onus remains on Washington to manage its messaging on this front.

An additional consideration is finding ways to advance longstanding U.S. objectives while appreciating short-term changes in regional conditions and individual circumstances. A case in point in this regard is the balance between ideals and interests. While Southeast Asian policymakers have long been aware that a focus on ideals is part of Washington's DNA and that its actual exercise is actually quite inconsistent over time and across countries, U.S. policymakers could hone policy messaging and execution to better customize these objectives for a Southeast Asian audience to achieve better effectiveness. This can include administrations drawing on the experiences of some of the U.S. embassies in Southeast Asia, some of which have exhibited creativity on this score through various ways including promoting more interactive, two-way discussions acknowledging U.S. limitations on certain components of race as well as empowering youth who may share a vision for a more people-centric Southeast Asia with better governance. Policymakers should also not underestimate the power of seemingly symbolic acts to have substantive effects: for instance, the visit of minority cabinet-level officials to Southeast Asia can sometimes say more about U.S. efforts to promote diversity in the region than countless U.S. government statements on this score.

Third, U.S. policymakers should be mindful of managing the implications of changing balances in relative power, given that it is likely to continue to be a key variable in explaining the evolution of U.S. commitment to Southeast Asia in the coming years as it has previously.

In addition to being a reality in international relations, relative power is also tied to a primary U.S. interest of not allowing another hegemon to dominate Southeast Asia following the experiences of Japan during World War II and the Soviet Union along with Vietnam toward the latter part of the Cold War. In the immediate future, the intersection of both rising uncertainties about U.S. relative decline globally as well as China's rise in Asia and Southeast Asia regionally will ensure that relative power will continue to be at the center of U.S. policymakers' minds.

Though the magnitude of these power differentials as well as their distribution across domestic, regional and global realms do not themselves determine what Washington may do, they do need to be managed because they can prompt wider reevaluations of the U.S. position in Asia and the world and can create constraints and pressures that can in turn play into how policymakers shape and calibrate their engagement. For instance, in the first two decades of the twenty-first century alone, developments such as the 9/11 attacks, the Global Financial Crisis and the rise of China have prompted variances in perceptions about how administrations were perceived to be acting in terms of polarity in the international system in the post-Cold War period irrespective of the reality: unipolarity (Bush II) multipolarity (Obama) and bipolarity (Trump). Though Washington is hardly unique in having differences of views on power, perceptions that Washington can keep toggling between interpretations of polarity can deepen doubts about its ability to properly assess capabilities and correspondingly lead to skepticism when power shifts are declared.

U.S. policymakers should also comprehend that their assessments of relative power may look quite different to those of some of their Southeast Asian counterparts. Part of this is due to some ambivalence about the objectives of particular U.S. administrations that can vary beyond the general list of interests in the region—be it sustaining a version of primacy or cultivating a more multipolar order. As one senior Southeast Asian official once put it quite memorably: "Sometimes you can feel the sense that the difference between the United States and us in the region is this: the United States does not want anyone to dominate Southeast Asia except itself; we don't want anyone to dominate the region including the United States."

Additionally, in terms of the distribution of power, the expectations on the changing regional and subregional balance of power are less clear but nonetheless important to monitor. Regionally, though the future of relative power can be narrowly framed as a contest between the United States and China, the broader question is whether Washington and its allies and partners—not just among Southeast Asian states but also including Japan, India and Australia—can shape a more multipolar order that avoids either China's dominance or a bipolar competition between Washington and Beijing that unnecessarily constrains the choices of Southeast Asian states. Subregionally, it would be a mistake to take the balance of power within Southeast Asia for granted. Should dynamics within Southeast Asia change in the coming years in the face of changing realities—be it the rise of some individual countries relative to others, the weight of mainland Southeast Asia relative to the maritime part of the subregion, or ASEAN's declining role in managing tensions between member countries and major powers—this would add yet another facet to an examination of balance of power dynamics.

Fourth, threat levels will need to be carefully calibrated. While there will always be a tendency for Washington's wider threat perceptions to affect how it views Southeast Asia—as we saw with the end of the Cold War or the 9/11 attacks—the key is to manage these changing threat levels so they do not become the sole prism through which Washington views the region and subsequently distorts its own picture of realities and its own position.

Part of that involves calibration with respect to the full hierarchy of threats Washington confronts to ensure proper and measured prioritization. The notion that threats related to Asia should be prioritized in an Asia-first foreign policy given the region's growing weight and rising U.S. stakes there relative to other regions like the Middle East is one that seems fairly easy to appreciate at an abstract level. Yet the true challenge is ensuring that this sense of threat hierarchy is sustained even in the wake of crises in other parts of the world and at home that will continue to demand Washington's attention.

The other aspect of this is ensuring that adequate consensus is built around particular threats and challenges that U.S. policymakers face. To be sure, this is easier said than done, and achieving threat consensus can be challenging in a democratic context like the United States. For instance, despite the focus on aspects of China's behavior in the 2010s, the real question is why it took so long for the United States to actually firmly declare that it was in a strategic competition with China as finally declared during the Trump administration, albeit with its own challenges.

Even as they evaluate threats, policymakers should also do so from the lens of what might term an opportunity-threat balance rather than an exclusively threat-focused one. Particularly in Southeast Asia, policy-makers should not lose sight of the focus that the region itself offers tremendous opportunity relative to other regions of the world given its economic weight, diplomatic relevance, in spite of its manifold challenges. Proper calibration between threats and opportunities can also feed into the shaping of more positive public messaging of U.S. commitment which can sound more appealing than one that seems to be more reactive to what others are doing.

Fifth and lastly, state capacity challenges should be properly managed. Though the difficulties in extracting and mobilizing resources are far from new and hardly unique to the United States, the fact that the range for the state capacity intervening variable was only at medium at its highest with respect to the four cases of U.S. commitment to Southeast Asia examined in the post-Vietnam period should reinforce the point that this is a key point of concern.

Part of managing this challenge will involve policymakers finding the right balance in elite autonomy between insulation from public pressure to make decisions and securing adequate input to sustain U.S. policy decisions as they pertain to Southeast Asia. Engaging advocates—but also potential fence-sitters, skeptics and opponents—from other parts of government and wider society, including legislators, businesses and think tanks, will be important to do early on in any new administration in order to send early signals about coalition-building before crises occur and to build later support that may be needed.

While it is true that aspects of coalition-building can at times vary by administration due to political dynamics—including the extent to which private sector collaboration is promoted or how much civil society groups are engaged—being as broad as possible early on would maximize opportunities later on. It would also acknowledge broader state-society realities, including the growing pressure for more non-government input and diversity of voices from the bottom-up as well as the incremental growth of diasporas from certain Southeast Asian countries in policymaking which affect government-to-government engagement in various ways.

Policymakers can also look to ways in which institutional cohesion can also be boosted. Finding opportunities to generate interagency conversations on aspects of Southeast Asia policy early on in a new administration would be an important avenue to seek input ahead of time rather than just in times of individual crises. This is true even if does not take the form of a time-consuming, full policy review of the subregion afforded to some functional and regional areas of interest.

Apart from this, U.S. policymakers should also do their best to anticipate potential challenges in state capacity and communicate about them candidly to U.S. and Southeast Asian audiences to shape the narrative. While so-called "Lippman gaps" in resourcing, particularly in areas such as the defense budget, may be thought of in parts of Washington as a routine part of a domestic U.S. renegotiation with every new administration, they can very quickly come to dominate regional perceptions about an administration's entire approach. Being clear about the broader realities at play as well as illustrating that an administration is doing all it can to protect parts of the budget that involve Southeast Asia will help at least balance out some of the more sensationalist interpretations of what this means for U.S. commitment.

Of course, in spite of all the above, one can nonetheless reasonably expect the ebbs, flows and imbalances of U.S. commitment to Southeast Asia to be a challenge that continues to endure a certain degree in the near term for policymakers and for this to be an aspect to manage within broader strategy and policy. The standard for every administration should not be attached purely to particular metrics on commitment levels or imbalances, but the extent to which it tried to manage these changes to the best of their capabilities while being mindful of the constraints they face as affected by broader, more enduring factors such as the relative distribution of capabilities, threat perceptions and state power. In that sense, it is that active search for these balances that matters, rather than the fact that they may nonetheless eventually continue to prove elusive as this book has illustrated.

CPSIA information can be obtained
at www.ICGtesting.com
Printed in the USA
LVHW081646280322
714606LV00008B/806

9 789811 666117